ORTHODOX PRAYER LIFE

The Interior Way

ALSO BY MATTHEW THE POOR

The Communion of Love

Orthodox Prayer Life

The Interior Way

by

Father Matta El-Meskeen
(Matthew the Poor)

Translated in the Monastery of St Macarius the Great,
Wadi El-Natroun, Egypt

ST VLADIMIR'S SEMINARY PRESS
CRESTWOOD, NEW YORK 10707

Library of Congress Cataloging-in-Publication Data

Matta al-Miskin, 1920–
   [Hayat al-salah al-Urthudhuksiyah. English]
   Orthodox prayer life: the interior way / by Father Matta El-
   Meskeen (Matthew the Poor).
   p. cm.
   Includes bibliographical references (p.)
   ISBN 0-88141-250-3
   1. Prayer. 2. Coptic Church. I. Title.
BX136.2.M3713 2003
248.3'2—DC21

2003052438

Copyright © 2003

ST VLADIMIR'S SEMINARY PRESS
575 Scarsdale Rd, Crestwood, NY 10707
1-800-204-2665 ◆ www.svspress.com

ISBN 978-0-88141-250-5

PRINTED IN THE UNITED STATES OF AMERICA

Contents

Acknowledgments

The Monastery of St Macarius wishes to thank the group of people who helped in translating and editing this book, namely Dr Nancy Hottel-Burkhart and Ms Edith Dimond of the American University in Cairo, and Mr John Waters and Mr Edward Thomas of the Anglican Church in Egypt.

Preface

T HIS BOOK IS NOT COMPOSED by an intellectual who sat down to write what he had gathered or visualized about prayer. Rather, it is a record of my overflowing experience. At first, prompted by the Spirit of God, I wrote notes and passages as reminders to myself and for my own spiritual benefit. From time to time I would return to this record to gaze at its beauty and delve further into its depths. I had no idea that it would one day become a book to be read by others.

The story began in August 1948. I had just embarked on the solitary life. My longing for such a life could never have materialized had it not been for the direct intervention of God. It is he who had miraculously absolved me of all my responsibilities in the world.

It is said, "Not everything one desires one attains." However, I have attained all that my soul yearns for by winning such a thoroughgoing solitude with God. This is the thing for which I had been praying for four years. What had attracted me to the solitary life and absorbed my mind was the idea that once I had attained it I would turn it all into prayer—and prayer alone.

I would like first to give the reader an idea about the wonderful way in which God met my hopes and expectations.

A few days before my departure for the monastery that God had chosen for me, I was visited by a young engineer[1] who carried with him a gift. It had been given to him by a British pilgrim[2] to Jerusalem who had lived in Russia and mastered the Russian language. In old manuscripts, he had found sayings of the Russian fathers, both ancient and modern, on prayer. He translated them into English together with some other sayings of the Eastern saints. This typed manuscript was only 122 pages. The young engineer handed it to me with his best wishes for success in my new life.

I did not open the manuscript, as I was in a hurry getting ready for my long journey. I only included it in my belongings.

[1]Eng. Yassa Hanna, manager of Marconi Co. at that time.
[2]Archimandrite Lazarus Moore.

No sooner had I settled in my new residence than I realized the great blessing in which I found myself. I stood on my feet to thank God in tears for the mighty hand that brought me out of this world. I marveled at how God had snatched me from its cares in such power and compassion! This was the first spark that ignited my spirit with prayer.

Renunciation of the world and its possessions had been my greatest concern. I thus left the world without keeping the least connection with it. My belongings were nothing more than a Bible, a copy of St Isaac the Syrian, and some empty notebooks. The monastery also exchanged my poverty for its own. There were no books at all of any kind except a single copy of *The Paradise of the Fathers*, which was read aloud during meals in the refectory.

I thus realized at once that what I had asked for had materialized. Prayer was now the only profession of my life—not by way of choice but by way of obligation. Prayer indeed became now my only anchor.

I do not wish now to bother the reader with my affairs. Let it suffice to know that God meant to besiege me with prayer. Whenever physical hunger turned cruel against me, I found my gratification in prayer. Whenever the biting cold of winter was unkind to me, I found my warmth in prayer. Whenever people were harsh to me (and their harshness was severe indeed) I found my comfort in prayer. In short, prayer became my food and my drink, my outfit and my armor whether by night or by day. This was all the more true in my case, for I had no spiritual father or friend. I had neither a colleague nor a comrade for my journey. The voice of God was the only answer for all my needs. It was the voice of father, friend, comrade, and guide. No sooner did I feel the need for his voice than I heard it speaking inside me a thousand times stronger than an ear would ever hear. For what the ear hears, the mind forgets. But what the heart hears, time can never erase.

When I finally opened the manuscript of the English pilgrim and found that it contained sayings on prayer, my heart leapt for joy. A wave of happiness and exhilaration overwhelmed me. How did God bring this treasure into my hand? This was my only inheritance from the world. I did not believe my eyes when I began reading of experiences that most strongly told of my own. They expressed my hope and the joy of my life. So I decided to pray in the words of these sayings. I sat down to read each of them many times until they became impressed on my mind. I would then stand up to turn them into prayer, and then sit down to read again, and then stand up to pray in the words that I had just read, and so on. My spirit thus became aflame as if with fire. I never stopped thanking God, while my soul remained full with the utmost joy.

Thus would I spend the whole night in prayer, reciting one or two passages together with other psalms and praises and making countless prostrations. While reciting the sayings of this or that Father, I would visualize him standing before me. I would then beseech him to clarify further to me the meaning of his words, and God would answer my plea. I would thus emerge every night with a new friendship with the spirits of these saints together with a knowledge and illumination that grew day after day. This knowledge evolved into an awareness of the different stages the spirit of man undergoes in a life of prayer. However, I would seldom record on paper the knowledge I gained. I had not the least idea that this could be published one day. I considered it for my own life only, limited to the purpose of rectifying my journey toward God.

However, I heard God telling me in prayer that what he gave me was not for myself but for others. If I keep such spiritual knowledge exclusively for myself, it would be held back. I thereupon began to translate and edit in Arabic the sayings of those saintly fathers, blending them with my own experience and commentary. I then divided them into chapters and added a prelude to each. If the reader examines my editing and commentary closely and compares it with the words of the Fathers on the relevant topic, he will notice how my spirit has been molded by theirs. It might be difficult for him to discern my language from their own. He will thus realize that the spirit of the Fathers and their thought have been deeply impressed on my own spirit and mind. This is the result of the extreme veneration I had for these saints. I was deeply devoted to their life, sanctity, and savor, which arrested my soul, heart, and mind. I thus lost what is mine to gain what is theirs. It is as if I were a robber—robbing the Spirit and life in the Spirit: "The kingdom of heaven has suffered violence, and men of violence take it by force" (Mt 11.12).

However, I soon found that what was contained in the notes of the British pilgrim was not enough to cover the wide panorama of prayer. I thus began to collect other sayings of the Fathers, both of the East and West, from all the sources that reached my hand. I wished to present to the reader what should suffice for covering the whole course of a prayerful life. But I never resorted to intellectual authorship. Apart from my experience, I never dared to write anything. For I considered writing on prayer as prayer *per se*. This is what I have learned and what God has taught me.

And now the reader may understand the reason why I wrote this preface. The purpose behind the quotes and all that is written on prayer in this book is not for reading but for prayer. The mystery of this book lies in turning the sayings on prayer into prayer. This is why the words "prayer life" are included in the title.

Matthew the Poor
(Matta El-Meskeen)

Introduction to the Second Edition[1]

T HE WORLD NOW THIRSTS to see living faith in the person of Jesus Christ; not simply to hear about it, but to live it. So many books tell about Christ; so many preachers speak about Christ; but so few people live and speak *with* Christ.

The Church cannot live on principles of faith to be studied. Faith in Christ is not a theory. It is a power that changes lives. Everyone in Christ should have this power. One must be able to change one's own life and renew it through the power of Christ.

But our faith in Christ will ever remain powerless until we meet him face to face within ourselves. In all patience, long-suffering, and courage, we must bear the shame that will cover us when our souls are stripped naked before God's pure and searching eyes. It is only then that we will emerge with an authentic spiritual experience and renewal for our souls. We will then gain a true knowledge and awareness of the holiness and kindness of Christ.

Every meeting with Christ is a prayer of renewal. Every prayer is an experience of faith. Every experience of faith is eternal life. But that does not mean that the facts of faith, doctrine, or theology can be shaped or changed according to man's inward experience. The facts of faith are as firmly established as is God himself. However, our experience only intensifies their clarity and throws them into sharper relief, for God is truly revealed in his saints. Thus we know God, and always will know him only in proportion to the experience of his saints, those who fear him throughout the ages.

There is still another fact we cannot ignore. Although the saints' experiences of faith shed its light on the way of knowledge before us, it can by no means supply us with living faith without a special witness springing from the depths of our own experiences and lives. Christ must belong to each of us as he belongs to every saint, since he died for each of us individually.

[1]Written in the Desert of Wadi El-Rayyan in 1968.

Christ has granted us not only to know him and believe in him, but also to live in him. He gave us the Holy Spirit not only to teach us, but also to dwell within us, remold us, and renew our minds. The Holy Spirit takes every day what is Christ's and gives it to us.

Life in Christ then, is action, experience, renewal, and ceaseless growth in the Spirit. But all this growth and action, which supposedly takes place in the individual man, should be identical with the general experience of the whole Church. It must never go beyond the fixed and prescribed boundaries of the Church doctrines.

Christ calls upon us to pray before God. He persists in asking us to pray and not lose heart, to pray with persistence and passion. This call points to the source from which we receive the power for conversion, renewal, and growth. This is how Christ explains the need for prayer. For through prayer we gain something that cannot be gained otherwise. This "thing" that can only be granted by prayer belongs to God: "How much more will the heavenly Father give the Holy Spirit to those who ask him" (Lk 11.13)![2]

Prayer is spiritual contact with God. God's purpose in urging us to pray without growing weary is that prayer progressively brings about an essential day-by-day change in us. Prayer must be made with constant zeal in order that we should be changed into something higher than our nature. This is actually realized in us when we feel that we have become something more than ourselves. And this is what summons us to more pleading and urgency until our prayer is answered. For through prayer, we receive what we do not basically deserve.

For this reason, we have to realize that prayer is an essential action through which conversion, renewal, and the growth of one's soul take place. This is brought about through God while man remains unconscious of the change.

Neither bliss, nor interior peace, nor a feeling that prayer is answered, nor any other feeling is equal to the hidden action of the Holy Spirit in one's soul. Such action qualifies the soul for eternal life.

---

[2]St Antony, the first Christian monk, says that the acquisition of the Spirit of God in one's heart is the ultimate end of a God-loving man. He says addressing his disciples, "I love you with all my heart because of the godhead which is in you; for because you have acquired God within your hearts, you have gained a favorable position in my sight. Therefore, I ask God that the godhead may increase and grow within your hearts in love" (Chitty, *Letters of St Antony the Great* 13, translated from the Arabic version). In the same vein, St Seraphim of Sarov, the nineteenth-century Russian saint, says, "The ultimate aim of the Christian is to acquire the Holy Spirit."

Prayer is the most powerful effective spiritual work and has its own spontaneous reward without the evidence of feelings. Prayer could not have an end or an aim higher than itself. It is the highest aim of the highest work.

Prayer is opening oneself toward the effective, invisible, and imperceptible power of God. Man can never leave the presence of God without being transformed and renewed in his being, for this is what Christ has promised. However, such transformation will not be in the form of a sudden leap. It will take its time and course as an imperceptible but meticulous build-up.

Whoever persists in surrendering himself to God by praying without growing weary receives in the end more than he desired. He even receives more than he deserves. Everyone who lives by prayer in the end gathers and gains for himself an immense trust in God, so powerful and so certain that it can almost be seen and touched. His soul becomes imbued with God through and through, even to its very depths. Man thus perceives God in a most vivid way. He feels as though his soul has become greater and stronger. Neither ignoring his own weakness nor forgetting his shortcomings, he becomes sure of the existence of another being higher than his own temporal one.

This sure feeling of the existence of God and of his power broadens the scope of the soul's perception of divine realities. It also widens its power of discernment and vision. Thus the soul witnesses within itself a new birth, a new horizon, and a new world. This is its beloved world, the world of Jesus. God, not one's own sense or ego, is the source of this world. Man comes to lay hold of this knowledge, not through his own mind, but through the will of the Holy Spirit, without any intervention of human will, effort, or worldly wisdom.

When the soul ascends to the world of true light, which is within its own self, it begins to feel in harmony with God through constant prayer. It then loses all dichotomy as well as doubt and anxiety when truth pervades all its feelings and movements. Its past and present experiences are melted in the fire of divine love. This excludes all prejudice and fears of the self, as well as the flaws of selfishness and doubt. It leaves no feelings in the soul except total awareness of the sovereignty of the Spirit and absolute obedience to his will.

When Christ exhorts us to persevere in prayer to the Father in his name, he unveils to us his peculiar intercession as a mediator. From our union with him in prayer, we receive a power that launches us into the sphere of the spirit, a sphere that transcends our potential, our powers of perception, our senses, and all our capabilities.

Every prayer we offer to the Father in the name of Jesus Christ is a sort of spiritual force that gushes out of the heart of Christ and pours into our own. It bears with it the power of a holy life—invisible and imperceptible. This power pervades us and rests in the innermost recesses of our spirit. It lifts us up above ourselves until it brings us to the home of our Father.

The secret behind the mediation of Christ in every prayer raised to the Father in his name lies in his intercession as a high priest and in his shedding his blood as an atoning sacrifice. This made him "able for all time to save those who draw near to God through him, since he always lives to make intercession for them" (Heb 7.25).

Christ commands us to pray and then guarantees the answer to our prayer. He thus holds us responsible and guilty if we do not pray and persevere until we receive the answer which pleases him. Prayer then becomes one of our most important and powerful activities through which we may enter into direct communion with Christ, so that our pleas are immediately heard by God the Father.

But the thing we should never allow to escape our minds is that, ultimately, prayer has no purpose other than to glorify God. It is also to have a taste of his mercy, his faithfulness, and the wonderful truthfulness of all his promises. When we are praying, we must therefore examine ourselves and see whether the ultimate aim of our prayer is the revelation of God's glory alone.

Under this glorious aim are listed, in the first place, all the prayers of intercession that the Church raises for weary, sick, or lost souls. The church has prescribed these prayers as a general duty for all its members without exception. At every *oushia* (the Coptic word for "collect"), the deacon cries out amidst the church for every one to raise his prayers and supplication for the salvation of every soul. This presumes that the whole church, through the presence of Christ, has become "a kingdom and priests to his God and Father" (Rev 1.6). Every individual is thus obliged to intercede and supplicate for those near and those far off. This is a duty, not an option.

The experience of prayer is not all delight, nor power, nor tangible gain. To reach maturity under God's hand, man has to undergo countless stages of purifying and discipline. God puts to death to bring back to life; he breaks to bind up, wounds to heal, smites to embrace, and banishes to restore to his bosom. To all God's elect, there is no escaping his rod. To all those who love him, there is no alternative to the bitterness of abandonment and the gall of alienation. God's children must suffer from his fatherly anger and rebuke.

He who enters into a covenant of prayer with the Father in the name of Christ has first to consign himself to "Chastisement Kindergarten," then to "Suffering Primary School," then to the "Higher Institute of Affliction." "For it was fitting that he . . . should make the pioneer of their salvation perfect through suffering" (Heb 2.10). For it is impossible to share his glory without first sharing with him in his sufferings.

But all who were made perfect in the school of the Lord's sufferings have become mighty in faith:

> Who through faith conquered kingdoms, enforced justice, received promises, stopped the mouths of lions, quenched raging fire, escaped the edge of the sword, won strength out of weakness, became mighty in war, put foreign armies to flight . . . Some were tortured, refusing to accept release, that they might rise again to a better life. Others suffered mocking and scourging, and even chains and imprisonment. They were stoned, they were sawn in two, they were killed with the sword; they went about in skins of sheep and goats, destitute, afflicted, ill-treated . . . wandering over deserts and mountains, and in dens and caves of the earth . . . all these [were] well-attested by their faith." (Heb 11.33–39)

And so every one who wishes to be made perfect in faith has to be first made perfect and purified by the Spirit. He has to undergo the various kinds of discipline to become fit to witness to faith in God amidst sufferings and tribulations, and before the fiercest threats of death. For as one's sufferings bear witness to one's worthiness of glory, so will God also bear witness: "Come, O blessed of my Father, inherit the kingdom prepared for you from the foundation of the world" (Mt 25.34).

Therefore, the experience of prayer is not only for the sake of him who prays, giving him renewal and growth, but is ultimately reflected on others as well. It gives them light: "Let your light so shine before men" (Mt 5.16).

The value of prayer is thus transcendent and unlimited, overflowing from him who prays to all people. Its light extends beyond time, in proportion to the depth of experience, to give light to all generations and to bear witness to God in every country.

People of prayer could only remedy the lack of testimony due to the short-comings of professional preachers. This is done through the witness of their lives, the power of their faith, and the certainty of their hope. Likewise, the effect of the sweeping flood of falsehood, injustice, and love of money with which the world is plagued cannot be effaced nor its sharpness blunted except by the existence of these men, women, and young people. By their lives and prayers, they give a new meaning to the world and a new hope to life. Such hope is renewed in proportion to the impressive testimony that they show by their renunciation of everything and the total dedication of their lives to God and the truth. The world is now in dire need of a living witness of faith issuing from a soul that has a true relationship with God. Such a witness outweighs and outshines a thousand books on doctrine, faith, or prayer.

As for the menace of nuclear weapons and their threat to destroy the world, we have no path to peace, security, or hope except through people of prayer. By means of the divine power stored like treasure within them, these people can create within us a transcendent vision of a world that evil cannot overcome.

We have thus no choice but to enter the inner room of prayer, not to isolate ourselves from the perishing world, thus escaping destruction and saving ourselves, but to attack the destruction that is in the world and redeem it. For when we die to ourselves and to the world, the world lives and is renewed. Through bended knees not only can other souls be changed, but also the fate of the whole world.

The soul that bears its cross is never attracted alone to Christ; without realizing, it attracts many after it: "Draw me in your footsteps, we will run after thee" (Song 1.4). The human soul is by no means isolated from other souls. The arrival of any soul at the kingdom of God is a gain for the world in a mystical way. A trodden way is easy to walk along; and people of prayer are firm landmarks that shine along the way for ever more.

PART ONE

The Nature of Prayer

CHAPTER ONE

A Definition of Prayer and Its Efficacy

WHAT IS PRAYER?

"Lord, teach us to pray." (Lk 11.1)

"You have said, 'Seek my face.' My
heart says to you, 'Your face, Lord,
do I seek.'" (Ps 27.8)

PRAYER THAT IS SPIRITUAL AND GENUINE is both a call and a response: a divine call and a human response.

This definition of prayer rests on an important fact: Prayer does not reach its power and efficacy as an actual communion with God until man is fully aware that his soul is created in God's image. He should feel that it derives its very being from him. In this being, nothing is more vital than this self-awareness. Once man's soul becomes sure of this, it will have laid hold of the source of such awareness—which is God. Thus, the soul realizes, sees, and touches God's self.[1]

There is only one true, realistic, and honest way for man to be aware of himself. It is to be first aware of God. For it is God who has created man's soul in his own likeness. When man then becomes aware of himself, he finds himself at once facing God's likeness. Even self-consciousness, a faculty that God has granted to man's soul, is but an image of God's consciousness of himself. And so the way leading man to a true and honest awareness of himself is a

---

[1]St Antony the Great says, "He who knows himself has known God. . . . As for the heretic Arius, he has been stricken with an incurable plague. Had he truly known himself, he would never have uttered anything contrary to the truth. It is clear that he has not known himself, and for this reason he presumed against the mystery of the Only Son" (Chitty, *Letters of St Antony the Great* 4).

simple one. It is the same way, and the only way, which leads to his awareness of God. This becomes especially true in the renewal of creation through the Holy Spirit by baptism. In baptism, this self-consciousness reverts once again to its original divine image after wiping out the blemish of sin.

Prayer, then, has become the stance of the soul toward its Maker in and through the awareness of its renewal by the Holy Spirit. In this renewal, the soul recovers through Christ the image of its original sonship that was lost through sin. It henceforth approaches God the Father boldly and at all times in answer to his open invitation. The soul actually becomes a creation ever attracted to its Creator. It is a son who finds no rest except in his Father's bosom. This rest lies in simultaneously hearing and heeding his Father's call.

Prayer, then, is a mystery forming an integral part of our being and psychic consciousness. Mystically, it is God's perpetual call within us drawing us toward the fulfillment of the ultimate purpose of our creation, our union with God.

In its outward form, prayer is the free response of man's good will. It awakens from time to time to heed God's call to stand before him and speak to him. Prayer then has two forms: a perpetual, vague urge, and an open, intermittent response. In both its forms together, prayer is made whole as a divine-human action: a call and a response.

According to St Gregory of Nyssa, prayer is a heart-to-heart talk, forever active on God's part, forever slow on ours. In fact, both parties call, and both respond. However, the initiative is always God's: "I spread out my hands all day long" (Is 65.2).

The temporal purpose for this divine-human dialogue is to ensure man's safe existence under God's providence during his life on earth and to guarantee his growth. The eternal purpose, however, is man's re-acceptance of the communion of God's love, once and forever.

God thus appears as a benefactor every time we pray, for it is he, as Creator and as Father, who calls us to pray. Therefore we should always begin our prayer with overflowing thanks. O, the humility of God, who seeks to talk with us in spite of our sins!

Therefore, to exalt God to his proper place, we must give him his due glory. We must confess our sinfulness and repent, for as much as our hearts are pure, God finds his rest in us.

God's willingness to share in man's temporal life, with all its failings, is certainly striking. He undertakes to bear with man the responsibility for the imperfections of the whole temporal order. He accepts with him the oppression of nature that has been "subjected to futility" (Rom 8.20).

During our prayer and daily life, we will eventually comprehend this amazing condescension on God's part in calling us to stand before him and speak with him. He is willing to share all our difficulties with us: "In all their affliction he was afflicted" (Is 63.9). This will open up for us the mystery of how God's greatness and humility are in harmony.

Through our sense of God's greatness, the fact of our sinfulness will be revealed to us, together with the condemnation we deserve, leading us to repent. Through his humility in dealing with us, all our sense of pride will be burnt up within us. We will feel contrite in his presence and will experience an overwhelming sense of self-abasement. The sacrifice of our humility and our love to him will thus become perfect. Through this, the nature of prayer will be revealed to us as an effective means of communion with God that brings sure and definite results.

Thus, prayer begins on God's part as a secret call to stand before him. We then carry it as a free response in our yearning to speak with him. Afterward, prayer assumes its divine purpose as an act of repentance and purification. It subsequently attains its ultimate goal as a sacrifice of love and humility that prepares us for fellowship with God.

Although prayer is a spiritual sense implanted in man's soul, in the very core of its self-consciousness, many people never pray. Prayer thus remains dormant for a whole lifetime. A man may die without ever having been aware of the self or of its affinity to God. St Jude the Apostle described such souls as "wandering stars for whom the nether gloom of darkness has been reserved for ever" (Jude 13).

This is a very serious matter. Prayer is not merely a sense to be used to organize our lives in this age alone. It is implanted in our nature that, through it, we may ascend to God and achieve union with him. We may thus pass from this fleeting perishable life to an eternal life with God.

It seems as if we were created for prayer. Prayer is the only bond that links us to God. It stands before our hearts as the eternal life, which is our hope. Prayer is the condition in which we discover our own divine image, on which the stamp of the Holy Trinity is impressed.

When we lose prayer, we actually lose the glory of our image, and we no longer resemble God in any way. God draws us to himself through prayer, and through prayer we mysteriously travel toward him in a manner too deep to understand. In fact, through prayer we draw God to ourselves, and he comes to us and makes his home with us.

To God, love is not an emotion but a self-offering. In prayer, God offers us himself. God offered us himself when he created us in his own image. Through prayer, he offers us union with himself so that he may become totally ours, and we may become totally his.

Prayer opens up our lives toward God: "In all their affliction he was afflicted, and the angel of his presence saved them" (Is 63.9). Prayer also opens up God's life to us: "The Spirit himself intercedes for us [during prayer] with sighs too deep for words" (Rom 8.26).

In this chapter, we present what the saints have said about prayer. Each of them defined prayer as he saw it and tasted it, not as a concept or as intellectual knowledge, but as experience and life. One of them saw it as raising the mind and confining the thought within God; another as reconciliation with God; another as an experience of tears of repentance; another as a weapon against the enemy; another as a source of grace and blessings; another as conversion of the heart; another as seclusion with God; another as too great to be confined to words or expressions. So every sentence of these sayings carries with it an experience or, rather, a part of the life of every saint.

Therefore, you should pause at each of these sayings and consider the lives of these heroes—how they gained prayer for themselves as if it were everything. Their lives became prayer and their prayer became life. Compare your life with theirs and your experience with theirs. If your spirit burns within you, lay down this book, worship, and pray, and thus mingle your reading with prayer.

SAYINGS OF THE FATHERS ON THE NATURE OF PRAYER

1. We ought to pray, neither according to any bodily habit nor with a habit of loud noise nor out of a custom of silence or on bended knees. But we ought soberly to have an attentive mind, waiting expectantly on God until he comes and visits the soul by means of all of its openings and its paths and senses.

And so we should be silent when we ought and to pray with a cry, just as long as the mind is concentrated on God . . . so also the soul should be totally concentrated on asking and on a loving movement toward the Lord, not wandering and dispersed by its thoughts but with concentration wait expectantly for Christ.

And thus he will enlighten, teaching one how to ask, giving pure prayer that is spiritual and worthy of God and bestowing the gift of worship "in spirit and in truth" (Jn 4.24). . . . God who teaches us how truly to pray. In this way the Lord finds rest in the well-intended soul, making it a throne of glory and he sits on it and takes his rest. (St Macarius the Great, *Homilies* 33.1, 2, in Maloney, *Intoxicated with God: The Fifty Spiritual Homilies of Macarius*)

2. Prayer is the lifting up of the mind to God. (St John of Damascus, in Moore, "Some Aspects of Orthodox Prayer," p 1)

3. Prayer is by nature a dialog between man and God. It unites the soul with its Creator and reconciles the two. Its effect is to hold the world together. (St John Climacus, *Ladder of Divine Ascent* 28.1, p 274)

4. Now, my children, do not neglect to cry out day and night to God, entreating the bounty of the Father, and in his bounty he will give you help from heaven, teaching you until you know what is good.

. . . God will have pity upon him who follows these instructions, and will grant him that invisible fire which will consume all his impurity. His spirit will be purified; and then the Holy Spirit will dwell in him, and Jesus will abide with him, and so he will be able to worship God as he should. (St Antony the Great, in Chitty, *The Letters of St Antony the Great* 4, 5, pp 12, 14, 15)

5. We must also know, beloved brethren, that every secret converse, every good care of the intellect directed toward God and every meditation upon spiritual things is delimited by prayer, is called by the name of prayer, and under its name is comprehended; whether you speak of various readings, or the cries of a mouth glorifying God, or sorrowing reflection on the Lord, or making bows with the body, or psalmody in verses, or all the other things from which the teaching of genuine prayer ensues. From genuine prayer the love of God is born, for love comes of prayer. (St Isaac the Syrian, *Homilies* 63, in *The Ascetical Homilies of Saint Isaac the Syrian,* p 303)

6. Sometimes during a long-continued prayer only a few minutes are really pleasing to God, only a few moments constitute true prayer and true service to God. The chief thing in prayer is the nearness of the heart to God, as proved by the sweetness of God's presence in the soul. (Fr John of Kronstadt, in Moore, "Orthodox Prayer," p 3)

THE GREATNESS OF PRAYER

"The prayer of a righteous man has great power in its effects." (Jas 5.16)

"Let my prayer come before thee." (Ps 88.2)

"Let my prayer be counted as incense before thee." (Ps 141.2)

"Holy, holy, holy is the Lord of hosts; the whole earth is full of his glory." (Is 6.3)

THIS LAST QUOTATION is the transcendent essence of prayer that the Seraphim declared in a vision to the prophet Isaiah.

In its true essence, prayer is a communion with the heavenly host in praising their Creator. It will surely end up as such when all things are put in subjection to God the Father.

Prayer, originally, is not the work of man alone. Neither is it performed for his comfort or for the fulfillment of his needs or demands. The greatness of prayer lies in its being the work of spiritual beings in general. It is neither of this age, nor for this age. Thus, if we restrict prayer to the satisfaction of man's needs and demands or to responding to his pleas in this life, it loses its essential greatness. Through hallowing the name of God, paying homage to him, thanking and honoring him with pure praise, man is transformed into a spiritual being. He thus joins the heavenly host in their transcendent ministry.

However, we ask God for temporal things because we have fallen from our original spiritual status in which we lacked nothing. Although this is alien to the original concept of prayer, God in his graciousness has come down to our level and promised to listen to our prayers when we bring him our needs and complaints, which he knows only too well. He thus assures us that he will never abandon us for our sins and that our tribulations are a matter of concern to him.

But when we delve deeply into the life of prayer, we end up with the conviction that it is an act of glorifying God, a divine ministry of transcendent honor. This was the conclusion reached by all the saints at the end of their understanding and practical experience of prayer.

The foundation of prayer is paying absolute honor to God's will: "Thy will be done, on earth as it is in heaven." For this reason, prayer inevitably demands that man relinquish his own will: "Not my own will, but thine be done" (Lk 22.42). The glorifying and hallowing of God implied in doing so resemble the office of the Seraphim. (It should be borne in mind that the glory of the Seraphim springs from their office and not from their nature.) So the corruption of our nature does not hamper the glory of our office, as long as this office is prompted by the power of love and is pure and clear from the blemishes of egotism and selfishness.

Total surrender to the will of God is an entry into a covenant with him. This is done in preparation for our final union with his will. As for the corruption of our nature, God has taken upon himself the task of lifting this curtain between him and man by the blood of his Son: "By his knowledge shall the righteous one, my servant, make many be accounted righteous" (Is 53.11).

For this reason, prayer, as a glorifying of the Creator, transcends the limits of our shortcomings and unworthiness. It is a perfect action by itself able to make up for every imperfection and to heal every disability.

When faithfully performed for hallowing the name of God, prayer takes upon itself, with grace as a mediator, to turn us into saints: "For he who sanctifies and those who are sanctified have all one origin" (Heb 2.11). So when we stand in God's presence to glorify him, the angels hover around us with great joy, although the weight of our sins still sticks to us. For it is well known that the angels rejoice over the return of one penitent, and as sinners, we are called to repentance every day.

When addressed to God directly to hallow him, prayer endows man with holiness and purity. Man's eyes are then opened anew to see, in the spirit, the tree of life, which is Christ: "The holiness without which no one will see the Lord" (Heb 12.14). So, by pure prayer, man's hand stretches forth in heartfelt repentance to pluck the words of the gospel from the tree of life and to eat them at all times. Thus he is renewed and lives, never to die.

In this same sense, St Isaac the Syrian, bishop of Nineveh, says that prayer is the kingdom of God! For this reason, Christ presses and urges us to pray: "[You] ought always to pray and not lose heart" (Lk 18.1). For it is in constant prayer that God's kingdom is secretly revealed within us. As St Antony the Great says, "I love you with all my heart and spirit because you have obtained the presence of God within you" (*Letters* 13, in "The Letters of St Antony the Great," Manuscript 23, Arabic version).

SAYINGS OF THE FATHERS ON THE GREATNESS OF PRAYER

7. But the head of every good endeavor and the guiding force of right actions is perseverance in prayer. By means of it we can daily obtain the rest of the virtues by asking God for them. By this means are engendered in those deemed worthy the fellowship of God's holiness and of spiritual energy and the attachment of the mind disposed toward the Lord in ineffable love. For the person who daily forces himself to persevere in prayer is enflamed with divine passion and fiery desire from a spiritual love toward God, and he receives the grace of the sanctifying perfection of the Spirit. (St Macarius the Great, *Homilies* 40.2, in *Spiritual Homilies*)

8. Every monk (who looks for the perfect way) aims at uninterrupted prayerfulness ... The keystone in the arch of all virtues is perfect prayer. (Abba Isaac, *Conferences of John Cassian* 9.2, in Chadwick, *Western Asceticism: Selected Translations of Christian Classics,* p 214)

9. Question: "What is the apex of all the labors of asceticism, which a man recognizes on reaching there as the summit of his course?"

Answer: "When he is deemed worthy of constant prayer. When he has reached this, he has touched the end of all the virtues, and has become an abode of the Holy Spirit." (St Isaac the Syrian, in Moore, "Some Aspects of Orthodox Prayer," p 27)

10. I have received this great fiery Spirit: receive him now yourselves. If you wish to receive him that he may dwell in you, first offer hard labors of the flesh and humility of the heart. Raise your thoughts up to heaven night and day. Ask in uprightness of heart for this fiery Spirit and he will then be given you. . . . Persist in prayer diligently, with all your heart, and he will be given you, for this Spirit dwells in upright hearts. He will reveal to you higher mysteries and other things which I cannot express in ink and paper. . . . Celestial joy will then be your portion day and night. (St Antony the Great, *Letters* 8, Arabic version)

THE NECESSITY OF PRAYER

"Apart from me you can do nothing."
(Jn 15.5)

"Pray that you may not enter into temptation." (Lk 22.40)

"Call upon me in the day of trouble; I will deliver you, and you shall glorify me." (Ps 50.15)

"For such the Father seeks to worship him." (Jn 4.23)

THE HUMAN SOUL'S RELATIONSHIP with God and the longing to speak with him are essential elements of man's very being. In the same way, ministry and praise are essential elements in the nature of angels. The tree that is ordained to bear fruit according to its kind does so in its proper season. So, too, does the man who responds to the spirit of worship within his soul also bear good fruit in good time.

The tree appeals to the eyes of the gardener as one of good quality when it yields the expected fruit. So does the man who prays in good season appeal to

God. The fruit, in fact, is the gardener's ultimate hope in planting the tree, then watering and tending it. Fruit is the relationship that binds the tree to the gardener's heart and thought. It is also the main purpose that motivates him to care for it and keep it in his garden.

Prayer functions in much the same way. God is the good vine dresser who bought us with his blood and acquired us for his vineyard. He planted us in his kingdom. He thus expects us to bear fruit. This is the ultimate aim of his enduring hardship and suffering on the cross. The ripe fruit of the blood that was shed, and the conscious response to the work of his love and suffering, is our prayer.

But is prayer vital to our existence in this world?

First, we should know that the world in which we now live is one that has fallen back to the worship of idols—money, greed, and sensual pleasure. It is a world from which the fear of God has withdrawn. The race for gathering wealth; the use of power, cunning, guile, and bribery for reaching distinguished positions; the resorting to lies for self-vindication; the use of force and oppression for establishing supremacy—all have now become commonplace. Such is the case both in the world and in the Church alike.

As for how to "save myself" in such a world, it has become a very critical problem. It demands much struggle and dissociation from this corrupt environment. One has to take refuge in prayer as the first and only weapon. In this age, more than in any other, prayer has become the vital need on which hang the loss or the salvation of one's soul. In such an age, man may live without a God and escape the notice of everyone. He may even be praised and commended! In the midst of this world—which teems with atheism, sin, and injustice— prayer now stands as a reminder for all of us that we have a living God, a kingdom prepared for us, another glorious life, and a judgment we have to face.

Prayer also reminds us day after day that we are not of this world. We are the children of light. Prayer reminds us that we ought not to have communion with the dissolute, the wanton, the lewd, or the immoral.

Prayer restrains our hearts from coveting injustice. It keeps our feet from wandering down the path of sin and our tongues from flattery and lies. Prayer supplies us with a deep insight, so that we may refrain from involvement in wrongdoing or condoning improper behavior or praising wayward or wicked actions.

Prayer grants us every day with a new heartfelt peace in return for that which we lose as a result of the provocations and injustices that we face in the world. Had it not been for God's grace, we could have been blighted with anxiety and morbidity.

Prayer is an inward light that exposes the blemishes and defects of our daily conduct. This saves us from being driven into the abyss of hell.

But God does not seek mere believers. Rather, he seeks "true worshippers . . . who worship him . . . in spirit and truth" (Jn 4.23, 24). Here, Christ refers to the lawful state of prayer that is recognized by the Father. For God is truth, and he accepts no prayer except in truth. Such a prayer knows him well and surely believes in him. God is Spirit, and he accepts no prayer except in spirit. Such a prayer knows what eternal life is and submits to the Spirit of God. Therefore, the prayer that is in spirit and truth is the only prayer acceptable to God. It is thus an expression of true spiritual contact with God. This definition is actually the summary of the whole clear-cut theological concept of true prayer, or spiritual prayer.

Moreover, Christ's words that God "seeks" such worshippers, or prayerful people, reveals the value and need for prayer from God's point of view: God seeks (Jn 4.23). The word *seeks* implies that God looks for man's prayer and shares in providing the circumstances and possibilities for its success. It is as if the existence of man hangs ultimately in the eyes of God on the existence of those who worship him in spirit and truth! True prayer here appears as the only channel or bond between man and God. Without prayer, man loses the meaning of his existence and the purpose of his creation.

Oh that we should always remember that God ever seeks our worship! It is as if he awaits the hour of our prayer.

SAYINGS OF THE FATHERS ON THE NECESSITY OF PRAYER

11. God does not need our prayers! He knows what we need even before we ask. He is the all-merciful, and he pours his abundant bounties even on those who do not ask him. It is for us that prayer is indispensable; it appropriates man to God. (Bishop Ignatius Brianchaninov, in Moore, "Some Aspects of Orthodox Prayer," p 21)

12. Virtues are formed by prayer. Prayer preserves temperance, suppresses anger, restrains pride and envy, draws down the Holy Spirit into the soul and raises man to heaven. (St Ephraim the Syrian, in Moore, "Orthodox Prayer," p 22)

13. Hold on to the staff of prayer and you will not fall. And even a fall will not be fatal, since prayer is a devout, persistent coercing of God (cf Lk 18.5). (St John Climacus, *Ladder of Divine Ascent,* 28.63, p 281)

14. Prayer heartens the conscience, invests the mind with power, strengthens one's hope, fires one's confidence. Thus is man made able to withstand the tribulations and evils of this world, for when he compares them with the glorious things he is to inherit, he can defy torture and all manner of affliction. (St Isaac the Syrian, in "The Four Books of St Isaac the Syrian, the Bishop of Nineveh," 1.1.118, Arabic version)

15. Perfect prayer guides man to heaven. It disdains the love of this world. By prayer we draw to us that grace which is termed "the Kingdom of Heaven," and once we feel it exists, we forget earth and all that belongs therein. All we remember is our invisible, powerful Helper. (St Isaac the Syrian, "The Four Books," 1.119–122)

16. By means of words we find access to mysteries, for prayer draws the mind near to God. (St Isaac the Syrian, "The Four Books," 1.134, 135)

17. It is not by reason of our requests that God dispenses his gifts and blessings. No, he made our petitions and requests as a channel to lead our mind to contemplate his eternity that by doing so we may realize how much concern he has for us. (St Isaac the Syrian, "The Four Books," 1.144, 145)

18. Prayer that is not accompanied by sublime and devout thoughts is no more than immature words that have no power in God's presence. But prayer coupled with virtuous conduct turns into flames of fire, for mighty is the prayer of the righteous.

The power of prayer lies not in its words but in righteousness: Moses, Joshua and Elisha used to work miracles without prayer [but this is an exception, it is for those who have reached the stage of prophecy and of miracle-working]. (St Isaac the Syrian, "The Four Books," 2.40, 41, 42)

19. Prayer is superior to all other virtues. (St Isaac the Syrian, "The Four Books," 2.44)

THE EFFICACY OF PRAYER

> "If you then, who are evil, know how
> to give good gifts to your children, how
> much more will the heavenly Father
> give the Holy Spirit to those who ask
> him!" (Lk 11.13)

THE TRANSCENDENT GIFTS of the Christian life are manifold. Some are general, like the new second birth, redemption for the forgiveness of sins, justification by grace, sanctification by the blood of Christ. Others are personal, like the gift of love, humility, piety, the glowing of spirit in constant intimacy with the Lord, and so forth. The strength and efficacy of all these gifts, however, can never be manifested except by prayer.

By prayer, the effect of Christ's nature becomes manifest in us. By prayer, the power of his death and life appears in our works and behavior. By prayer, the sweet savor of Christ is scented in our words and thoughts. It is even scented in our quietude and silence as well.

The work of Christ to redeem from sin, to save from sin, and to bring victory over evil can never appear except through a life of prayer. Neither can the living testimony of the new birth be brought about without such life. Without a life of prayer, all attempts to declare these divine actions in man's nature become false, theoretical, and a product of the ego or self-will. In such a case, the old Adam remains as he is with his inclinations, passions, and earthly nature.

We should then accept these facts about prayer and set our hearts to them. We should resolve firmly to apply them with all our strength, which will cost us much effort and sacrifice. But whatever the sacrifice or effort, we will surely attain to all the transcendent mysteries of Christ—such mysteries as were previously only a matter of hearing.

This can be realized only when prayer becomes our supreme concern, our main preoccupation, which outweighs all other cares; our duty, which challenges all other duties; our pleasure, which surpasses every other pleasure. We would then pray at all times, in all circumstances, in all places, in all conditions. We would pray in an insatiable hunger for constant contact with Christ. In all this we would be urged by his words, deeds, actions, and character—as he said, "Learn from me" (Mt 11.29).

There is a purpose for all the works of our life and all its circumstances. Ultimately, they should lead to the pleasure of the Father in our obedience to him through the person of Jesus Christ. Christ then should fill our lives and minds. He should always be before our mind's eye, in our sleep and in our wakefulness, in our talk and in our silence. Thus, he may truly be the one who is alive within us and not our own selves. It is then that we will feel how Christ can be born within us. We will know what it means to be changed from day to day. We will be renewed like a new creation to conform to his image and likeness according to his will. It is also then that we will see how he works out within us all that we crave for in the spirit. He never denies us any desire or petition at all, whatever we may wish or ask in prayer.

We will also come to feel within ourselves how our lives are changed; how the bleeding sources of sin dry up; how the motions of evil die down; how a new ear is created in us every morning through which we come to learn the mysteries of the gospel. The Spirit will reveal to our minds these mysteries together with insight and power to understand the inspired truth.

The farther we advance in the life of prayer, the more we relish the sense of union with God. The more our hearts are anchored to the passion for an intimate life with Christ, the more we feel the eternal chains that now fetter us to his person—the chains that henceforth hold sway over all our senses and thoughts. Formerly, we sought in tears and sorrow and struggled in sweat and grief, wishing that our thoughts, words, acts, and passions could acquiesce to the will of Christ. But now we find all this at our disposal, as if in a dream or a vision. God now sets a guard over the mouth and lips and a censor over the eyes. The ears become like the gate of a divine fortress, never to be opened except for pure things alone. The heart desires nothing but to please God and enjoy his love.

While proceeding in the life of prayer, man becomes suddenly aware that he has found the priceless gem in the field of the gospel after he had plowed it in diligence, fervor, and perseverance. For the spiritual, psychological, and physical gains that suddenly descend on man while persisting in prayer make him sure that he has truly found the gem of the gospel. In his great joy, it indeed becomes easy for him to sell everything in order to retain the indescribable gifts of Christ that transcend reason.

Something of the passions or glories of this world might have clung to our heart, mind, or flesh. The value of all this eventually drops to nothing in one's eyes. Whether it be riches, learning, respect, fame, glory, power, leadership, pleasure—everything becomes like a handful of dust. It becomes like an impurity of which one wishes to be rid. Even a man's own self becomes as nothing to him.

The mystery of the efficacy of prayer is shown in Christ's appeal when he urges us to pray: "[You] ought always to pray and not lose heart" (Lk 18.1); "Watch and pray" (Mt 26.41); "Whatever you ask in prayer, you will receive, if you have faith" (Mt 21.22).

In prayer, God's personal will and ours meet. Christ's will is sharply focused upon our own salvation, renewal, and rescue. Nothing can thwart Christ's will for us except our failure to pray. All the sick, blind, lame, and paralyzed who prayed and asked Christ to heal them are those whom he healed. Never did Christ cast out any man who believed in him and asked him. The will of Christ, which is ever present, is always willing and able to save completely all those who come to him by prayer in faith. Through prayer, our will becomes like that of Christ. Through prayer we gain his Spirit and are conformed to his will. His power thus rests upon us.

Without prayer, man cannot know what the will of Christ is in relation to himself. Neither does the Spirit accept knowledge of the will of man except through prayer: "Have no anxiety about anything, but in everything by prayer and supplication with thanksgiving let your requests be made known to God" (Phil 4.6).

For this reason, let him who does not pray expect nothing whatsoever from God—neither salvation nor renewal nor direction nor grace. Rather, he is consigned to the whims and fancy of his own mind, the will of his own ego, and the direction of his own thinking. He is like one who has rejected the intervention of the Lord Jesus in his life, like one who hides himself from the Spirit of God. A man who does not pray is one who is content with his own condition. He wishes to remain as he is and not be changed, renewed or saved. His life unconsciously changes from bad to worse. He recedes spiritually day after day. The ties that bind him to the earth and the flesh increase without his awareness. His ego remains the source of all his desires and ambitions.

As for his relationship with Christ, it remains only superficial and outward. It has no power to change or amend anything. The possibility even to deny Christ at times of danger, temptation, illness, or poverty becomes imminent.

So if man does not pray, he can never be changed or renewed, and he who is not changed or renewed can have no genuine or effective relationship with Christ. His worship, however active, is nothing but an outward protrusion or a superficial growth. In the end it breaks off, bearing no fruit.

We do not pull Christ toward us from heaven by prayer. Rather, we discover him within ourselves. For Christ has been pleased to dwell in our new man by the sacrament of baptism. He takes the initiative in offering himself for the salvation of our lives, according to his supreme mercy and love. In prayer, we discover that he stands within us at the door of our hearts. He is always knocking until we open our door to him. If we respond, he will enter our lives, beginning immediately to raise us from the dead and to bring us out from the world of darkness.

The new man created after the likeness of Christ cannot live, grow, or become strong except by the indwelling of Christ in his very heart. This can only be brought about by prayer, faith, and will: "That Christ may dwell in your hearts through faith" (Eph 3.17). Christ is the Word of life that can be embraced by man in his heart through prayer and through the gospel.

Christ is the self-same eternal life that becomes a true kingdom within man. This takes place when man accepts the person of Jesus Christ in his heart by prayer and by the sacrament of the Body and Blood.

Christ is the true light that illumines the mind of man. This comes about when man accepts, through prayer, to live according to the truth and commandments of Christ.

Christ is the vanquisher of the devil, the old serpent. He is thus able to bruise his head, defeat his counsel, and foil his seduction of man. This can be carried into effect only by prayer. For through prayer there now exists a true, constant, and intimate bond between man and Christ.

Therefore, without a life of prayer with Christ, there can be neither life nor kingdom nor light nor victory over the devil.

Prayer is an effective power that brings us into contact with the Christ who is actually present within us. He is the source of every power, blessing, and life: "Whom God made our wisdom, our righteousness and sanctification and redemption" (1 Cor 1.30). He who does not use the power of prayer never makes contact with the Christ who is within him. He thus lives alienated from God's wisdom. He remains deprived of his righteousness, sanctification, and redemption. However hard we may try to know Christ without prayer, we would only know him as a Savior of people, a Redeemer of others, a Sanctifier of saints, a Justifier of sinners. We would remain deprived of all these gifts and graces. We will not receive them unless we first receive Christ through prayer within our lives. We should first make him at rest in our hearts so he may live with us. He should share everything with us and manage all our affairs.

Christ will never unite with one's thought, emotions, will, or senses unless he first unites with one's soul. So man should first open his whole being in prayer that Christ may rest within the recesses of his soul. God has created this soul in his own image for himself that he may own it and rule it completely. He is thus able to manage man's life and command his thoughts, emotions, will, and senses.

Christ becomes king over man's soul through man's frequent prayer and the outpouring of his self. He becomes the true center of its being and movements. At that stage, man will never find rest in anything except in Christ alone, where the image would rest in its own likeness. Since the soul has been created for immortality, it will thus find in Christ, when it unites with him, its ultimate joy. Through his existence, he consummates its own existence and immortality.

SAYINGS OF THE FATHERS ON THE EFFICACY OF PRAYER

20. For this reason we must first beg of God with struggle in the heart through faith that he grant us to discover his riches, the true treasure of Christ in our hearts, in the power and energy of the Spirit. In such a way, first, by finding the Lord to be our help within us and our salvation and eternal life, we may be of help and profit to others also, insofar as it is possible and attainable, by drawing upon Christ, the treasure within, for all goodness of spiritual discourses and in teaching the heavenly mysteries.

Thus the goodness of the Father was pleased to wish to dwell in every believer who asks this of him. Christ says: "He that loves me, he will be loved by my Father and I will love him and I will manifest myself to him" (Jn 14.21). And again: "I and my Father will come and make our mansion in him" (Jn 14.23).

Thus the infinite kindness of the Father decreed; thus the incomprehensible love of Christ was pleased. Thus the ineffable good of the promised Spirit. Glory to the ineffable compassion of the Holy Trinity.

Those, who have been deemed worthy to become children of God and to be reborn by the Holy Spirit from above, who have within themselves Christ, illuminating and bringing them rest, are guided in many and various ways by the Spirit. They are invisibly acted upon in the heart, in the spiritual tranquility, by grace. (St Macarius the Great, *Homilies* 18.6, 7, in Maloney, *Intoxicated with God: The Fifty Spiritual Homilies of Macarius*)

21. If anyone is naked and lacks the divine and heavenly garment which is the power of the Spirit, as it is said—"If anyone does not have the Spirit of Christ, he does not belong to him" (Rom 8.9)—let him weep and beg the Lord that he may receive from heaven the spiritual garment. Let him beg that he, now stripped of any divine energies, may be clothed, since the man who is not clothed with the garment of the Spirit is covered with great shame of "evil affections" (Rom 1.26)....

The very first man, seeing himself naked, was filled with shame. So great a disgrace accompanies nakedness. If, therefore, in physical matters, nakedness carries with itself so great a shame, how much more shame for the person that is naked of divine power, who does not wear nor is clothed with the ineffable and imperishable spiritual garment, namely, the Lord Jesus Christ himself? Is he not really covered with a greater shame and the disgrace of evil passions? ...

Let us, then, beg and implore God to clothe us with "the garment of salvation" (Is 61.10), namely, our Lord Jesus Christ, the ineffable Light, which those who have borne it will never put off for all eternity....

For if the Lord had such concern for perishable bodies when he came into this world, how much more does he concern himself with the immortal soul, made according to his own image? ...

Let us, therefore, believe in him and approach him in truth so that he may speedily bring us to full and authentic health. For he promised that he would give to those who asked him the Holy Spirit and that he would open to those that knocked and by those seeking he himself would be found (Lk 11.9–13; Mt 7.7). And "He cannot lie who promised" (Titus 1.2). To him be glory and power forever. Amen. (St Macarius the Great, *Homilies* 20.1–8, in *Spiritual Homilies*)

CHAPTER TWO

Degrees of Prayer

"For now we see in a mirror dimly, but then face to face. Now I know in part; then I shall understand fully, even as I have been fully understood." (1 Cor 13.12)

"And we all, with unveiled face, beholding the glory of the Lord, are being changed into his likeness from one degree of glory to another; for this comes from the Lord who is the Spirit." (2 Cor 3.18)

"In every degree they ascend toward glory, they think they have reached the end. But if they ascend further and become illumined with a brighter light, they forget their first degree and think that this is the end! This is because it is not they who are moving toward glory, but it is the action of the Holy Spirit within them." (St John of Dalyatha, *Homily on the Greatness of the Rank of Angels*, in "The Homilies of the Spiritual Elder [John of Dalyatha]," Manuscript 12.23)

MANY OF US DO NOT KNOW about praying except in its most simple forms: reciting before God a few words improvised according to what the occasion may inspire us; or reciting some words set by the saints or selected from the Bible, like psalms or pieces from the gospels, and so on. Yet, in point of fact, all these should only serve as a preparation for true prayer in spirit and truth. There is a hidden splendor and exaltation contained in the advanced degrees of prayer. They bring about many graces and blessings. If people knew this, they would not hesitate for a moment in beginning to practice them.

It is not easy to divide prayer into separate degrees, for they are united by strong bonds. Nevertheless, it is possible to classify prayer into two types: vocal and mental. From this division, prayer then falls into three degrees.

The first degree is vocal prayer, the second and third degrees are mental prayer. In vocal prayer, we utter words and sentences. As we have mentioned before, they are either of our own improvisation or parts memorized from the Bible or set by the Fathers. This kind is, in fact, the foundation on which we build the other types of prayer. It is the introduction that ushers us into a realistic dialogue with God.

Vocal prayer, however, calls for mental effort to follow the meaning of the words we utter. It also requires an inward interest in their subject matter. We should not merely recite words as if they proceeded from others to God. They should pass through our own selves and then proceed directly from our own persons.

Prayer may be recited or sung, privately or chorally, in church. But whatever the manner, it may suddenly burst into a state of contemplation and rapture of mind. Man would then feel at once that he is standing in God's presence. For, in truth, the stance of prayer by itself, whether in one's chamber or in church, is indeed a standing before the presence of God. It is entering into the sphere of the heavenly hosts as they praise and minister.

Man should approach vocal prayer with a contrite heart. He should humbly worship God with the sense that he is ministering before the Holy Trinity. If this be done, such vocal prayer would instantly qualify him, as it were, for initiation into the knowledge and contemplation of the divine mysteries. His prayer and praises would then be blended with fervor, purity, and a pleasure beyond description.

But this does not mean that every vocal prayer has to turn into mental contemplative prayer. Vocal prayer is a special degree of its own. It is a divine ministry that has its value and effect on man's spiritual life. It is by no means of less value than contemplative prayer.

The second degree is meditation. It is sometimes called inward prayer, as it issues from the depth of one's heart. In this degree, prayer is shared by the mind and the heart, linking thought and feelings. It may sometimes be expressed in a few words. But usually it is offered in silence and quietude. This could be defined as a dialogue with God. In this dialogue, man recalls some of God's works in his creation. He lays bare the condition of his soul before God. He regrets his negligence and sin when regret is due. He expresses his thankfulness to God when thankfulness is due. He also resolves to mend his ways in full accordance with God's pleasure.

This stage is also called discursive prayer. It includes many and various things among which there may exist no particular linkage. The best example of this kind is the Psalms. They are select portions of David's meditations with God: sometimes on the irrational creation, other times on the rational; sometimes on the law, other times on the soul. All this might perhaps be contained in one psalm. At any rate, it does not go beyond a deeply moving, realistic dialogue in which the soul expresses its feelings toward God.

The third degree is contemplation. Here, prayer is a mode of concentration. This applies to its theme, like focusing one's prayer on a certain commandment or on one of Christ's evangelistic or redemptive works. But it also applies to man himself. Man would be under a strong influence of love, making his mind extremely alert. All his senses would be controlled by, and his will focused upon, prayer. His heart would also be spiritually ready for receiving any directions from the Holy Spirit.

Contemplative prayer is divided into two correlative parts:

1. *Acquired Contemplation.* The success of acquired contemplation depends on the amount of love a man bears in his heart for Christ. It also depends on man's readiness to employ all his mental powers in meditating on a particular theme deep in his mind and heart. He should also be in utmost readiness to accept any spiritual directions.

This part, however, is not without a hidden support from grace, adhering to man's will. It offers him the ability to follow up, persist in, and delve deep into the theme of prayer. It also opens up before him the scope for enlightenment. Thus, man emerges with considerable spiritual gains from his prayer.

2. *Infused Contemplation.* In infused contemplation God's heart lovingly welcomes man in return for man's warm feelings of love in prayer. Here, there intervenes a divine factor that pushes prayer out of the confines of human will and abilities. For this reason, it is rather difficult to term this degree as "prayer." We would rather call it "the gift of prayer," or "the grace of prayer."

This part appears esoteric and lofty at the beginning. Yet once God grants it to man, it becomes a matter of habit to him. Rather, he becomes a matter of habit to it, as it were, and so it becomes easy and usual. Normally, whenever he seeks it, he finds it. This is due to the modesty, the easygoingness, and the amazing readiness of the Holy Spirit to answer every plea of love. For man to abide in this degree of prayer, nothing is required except to remain always in compliance with the will of the Holy Spirit as to love, simplicity, and purity of heart. He should stop concerning himself with earthly matters and worries and should be willing to carry out the commandments and the spiritual advice given him.

But a man should bear in mind that nothing he can do in terms of preparing himself can make him worthy of initiation into the grace of this degree of contemplation. Neither can he be made worthy of God opening his heart toward him in love. It is a sheer gift. However, he has to ask for it in tears and supplication. As St John of Dalyatha says, "Love me God, though I am not worthy of thy love."

But man should not believe that he is worthy of it even if he experiences it every day. He might be qualified for all other virtues, whether they be purity, asceticism, humility, or constant prayer. But still, that does not qualify him for infused contemplation. For the gift of infused contemplation, God opening his heart in love toward the human soul, surpasses all other virtues.

Yet this does not mean that the stage of infused contemplation is a miracle. It is grace. The evidence for this lies in the accompanying gift of discernment and wisdom. The stage of infused contemplation is in fact the perfection of prayer and of all graces and gifts.

Those who are qualified for abiding in this degree are entrusted with other gifts—such as ecstasy—which surpass the limits of prayer. Ecstasy is absorption in contemplating God in a spiritual semi-trance in which one beholds divine truths too great for words. This and other gifts surpassing the limits of prayer will be dealt with in a special chapter.

In simple terms, the first degree of prayer, vocal prayer, can be described as "standing before God in fear"; the second, meditation, as "moving toward God in longing"; the third, contemplation, as "resting in the arms of God in love." We may also simplify further by distinguishing these three degrees from each other by the words of the Lord Jesus: "Ask, and it will be given you," which is vocal prayer; "Seek, and you will find," which is meditation; "Knock, and it will be opened to you," which is contemplation, or the degree of attainment.

In the rest of this chapter, we shall discuss mental prayer with its degrees and exercises.

MEDITATION (μελέτη)

"Let the words of my mouth and the
meditation of my heart be acceptable in
thy sight, O Lord, my rock and my
redeemer." (Ps 19.14)

"Blessed is the man . . . [whose] delight is
in the law of the Lord, and on his law he
meditates day and night." (Ps 1.1,2)

"I revere thy commandments, which
I love, and I will meditate on thy
statutes." (Ps 119.48)

"As I mused (meditated), the fire burned
[within me]." (Ps 39.3)

"Practice these duties, devote [μελέτα]
yourself to them, so that all may see your
progress." (1 Tim 4.15)

MEDITATION IS AN OLD, TRADITIONAL term closely linked to profound and heartfelt Bible reading. Such reading leaves an indelible impression upon one's memory, emotions, and tongue.

According to patristic tradition, meditation is the key to all graces. It makes him who practices it biblical in every thought, word, and feeling. He also becomes advanced in every gift and full of divine understanding. When he opens his mouth, the words of the Bible flow spontaneously from his lips without embellishments. Divine thoughts proceed from his mouth in amazing succession. They are like waves of light that submerge the hearer's mind in the light of divine knowledge. They stir his heart and set aflame his emotions.

The word *meditation* in its Hebrew origin is *hagîg,* and in its Greek is μελέτη. The verb is μελετάω, which indicates studying and delving deep into meanings, together with mental and inner exercise. Meditating on wisdom (μελετᾶν σοφίαν), then, means studying it in depth and with diligence as well as putting it into practice.

In patristic tradition, the usage of the word *meditation* was confined to the way in which the mind and heart were diligently handed over to the word of God. This was done to renew the mind and heart through that word. The fathers maintain that it is not proper for man to engage in meditating on anything other than the written word of God, that is, the Bible. For inward meditation can imprint its impression on the emotional and intellectual makeup of man. Man, therefore, should not be so stamped except by the holy word of God, which accords with God's will and mind.

From this, the word *meditation* became particularly associated with Bible reading. Its usage came to be confined to studying the word of God with an inner depth. In this way, the soul may be imbued with the word of God and the spirit stimulated by it.

According to patristic tradition, the first degree of meditation begins with reading the words slowly, relishing them, and repeating them in an audible voice. Reading, to the fathers, always meant doing so in an audible voice and was called reiteration. The word of God is reiterated in an audible voice and relished in our inner consciousness. In this manner, it can find rest in our innermost recesses. Reiteration here is like rumination. After a while the words actually become one's own words. Man, then, becomes a faithful storehouse for the word of God. His heart becomes a divine treasury for it. He brings "out of his treasure what is new and what is old" (Mt 13.52). This is what is originally meant by "keeping the gospel" or "keeping the word." The gospel, or the word, is thus kept safely inside one's heart as a precious treasure. According to the prophet David, "I have laid up thy word in my heart" (Ps 119.11). Man then withdraws himself into God's word as if into a strong room inaccessible to thieves.

For this reason, extempore prayer, to the Fathers, was tinged with a purely biblical color. Their hearts were replete with God's word to the point of overflowing. Extempore prayers, which "man himself fits together," according to St Isaac the Syrian, are nothing but a coherent and integrated recital of God's memorized word. They express the condition of the human soul when moved and impressed by his word and will.

It is thus that meditation becomes closely linked to prayer in its first formal degree. When man applies it, he grows before God in all confidence and safety, since it is a prayer that proceeds from the core of the Bible. It is henceforth able to transform and renew man's emotional makeup, his thought and his expression, in a radical way. Extempore prayer, in Orthodox tradition, cannot, therefore, be counted as prayer unless man is imbued with the word of God. He has to be well trained in correct meditation. Otherwise, his words will come forth unbiblically, and his ideas will fall short of expressing the will of God and his thought.

The meaning of meditation is not restricted to the manner of profound audible reading as such. It also extends to include the sense of reiterating that reading silently and inwardly more than once. This is carried on until the heart is ablaze with divine fire. Such a sense appears most strikingly in the prophet David's words in Psalm 39: "And as I meditated, the fire burned [within me]." It is here that the fine, mystical thread that links practice and diligence with grace and divine fire can be discerned.

Merely meditating on the word of God in quietude and slowness for several times will surely end up with inflaming one's heart. Thus, meditation is the first, formal link that connects sincere effort in prayer and worship with God's gifts and his transcendent grace. For this reason, meditation is accounted first among the degrees of prayer of the heart through which man can ascend to a warm spiritual condition. He may live therein throughout his life.

We should notice here that *haga,* the Hebrew word for *meditate,* originally means "to spell" or "to pronounce in a primitive way." It implies an earnest effort on one's part to learn or understand the will of God and the mysteries latent in his word and commandments. And so we hear the prophet David saying in his first psalm, "Blessed is the man . . . [whose] delight is in the law of the Lord, and on his law he meditates day and night." He would surely be a man who conforms to God's will, as did David himself.

The result of this kind of meditation, or *haga*, on God's law, David says, is that "in all that he does, he prospers" (v 3). This shows that meditation can well serve as a degree for the spiritually perfect. But *haga* also means to spell, as it were, the law. Meditation is, thus, a degree that also suits beginners in their faithful friendship with God.

This means that meditation by itself can actually serve as a beginning and also as an end. The word of God is actually a beginning and also an end. Through the word of God, man is initiated into truth, and with the word of God, he ends up in truth.

For this reason, meditation was a profitable undertaking for the Fathers. They lived it and practiced it to their last breath. We thus hear from Palladius, the author of the *Paradise of the Fathers*, that St Mark the Ascetic, who was a hundred years old at that time, recited before him the four gospels! He also says that St Aaron memorized the hundred and fifty psalms by heart, together with the Letter of St Paul to the Hebrews, the whole Book of Isaiah, part of the Book of Jeremiah, the Gospel of St Luke, and the Book of Proverbs! The traveler Rufinus also saw and bore witness to the like.

But this does not mean that meditation for the Fathers merely meant memorization. It was only an inevitable result, since they habitually relished the books of the Bible. They reiterated them daily, which left an indelible impression upon their memory. Thus, the words of the Bible flowed easily from their tongues.

The ability to persevere in the continual practice of inward meditation on the Bible is an actual expression of the life that genuinely flows in one's heart. For the word of God is spirit and life, as the Lord defined it for us. Hence, persistence in meditation on God's word inevitably reveals a mystical affinity and, therefore, a true life flowing within one's heart. On the other hand, the heart to which meditation on the word of God is repellent betrays an impasse and hardness of spirit. We hear the prophet David showing the contrast between the heart that meditates on God's law and that which refrains from meditation thus: "Their heart is gross like fat, but I delight in thy law" (Ps 119.70). This means that meditating on the law of God keeps the heart warm and glowing with the fire of the divine word, for meditation intrinsically implies a continual delving into the spirit of the Bible. It is also a continual discovery of one truth after another, each hidden behind the commandments. This brings about a perpetual renewal in man's ideas. His emotions become, as it were, biblical and refined and his conduct easygoing, flexible, and successfully adaptable to all contingencies.

For this reason, we find that meditation, in its advanced stages, becomes gradually detached from reading. It eventually enters upon conceiving divine truths as well as the interactions of God's commandments and his discipline for the ascetic life. Meditation introduces us into the first stage of contemplation. It moves from delving deep into the word of God to fathoming the truth that that word contains.

Continual meditation on the living word of God inevitably fills the heart and mind with sacred thoughts and images. These later become the raw material from which contemplation forms its airy wings. By these wings, it soars up in the heaven of spirit without the agency of reading. However, there has to be perpetual meditation on the divine word and the commandments and promises of the Lord. Otherwise, one cannot possibly have holy thoughts and images that fill and overflow from one's heart and mind.

It should be also borne in mind that we will glean an immense harvest of holy thoughts and images from continual meditation on the Bible. This is considered a bliss by itself, which enriches man with spiritual wealth. Besides, it is for him a flaming sword of fire, which cuts off all the sources of evil thoughts and images. It also counts for him as a mental offering, always acceptable and pleasing to God: "Let the words of my mouth and the meditation of my heart be acceptable in thy sight, O Lord, my rock and my redeemer" (Ps 19.14).

A monk went to his master in the morning, sad after a long night he had spent in meditation counting the virtues of one of his fellow monks. He said to his master, "Father, I have wasted the night in vain—sitting the whole night and counting the virtues of brother so and so, and found that they were thirty virtues; and I grew sad, since I found that I own nothing, not even one virtue of them." But his master said, "Your sadness because your soul is void of virtues and your meditation on the virtues of another is better than thirty virtues."

This is a practical example of the impression that the Lord's commandments make on man's mind and conscience. They encourage and prompt him in spirit to seek after virtue and guide him where to find it and where not to find it. This actually shows how meditation on the law of God engenders meditation on and scrutiny of the virtues. It spurs man to seek after them, inciting his soul and knocking hard and persistently at its door to search itself and measure it against the gospel. Never will his soul find rest except in the truth on which it meditates. Nowhere shall it find pleasure or happiness except in applying the law of God. Meditation then is the teacher of truth, who takes man by the hand to raise him above his own self. It is a lamp that illumines man's insight and leads his steps toward eternity.

But the highest degree of meditation is that on the economy of the divine incarnation and what relates to it. Meditation on the redemption that was perfected on the cross and the resurrection that has given us the power of life is called meditation on the mystery of divine economy. The Bible describes this in clear and plain terms.

When man ponders these mysteries for a long time, their hidden implications open up within his heart. From them a flaming power pours forth to grant him a new life: "That I may know him and the power of his resurrection, and may share his sufferings, becoming like him in his death" (Phil 3.10);

"that Christ may dwell in your hearts through faith; that you, being rooted and grounded in love, may have power to comprehend with all the saints what is the breadth and length and height and depth, and to know the love of Christ which surpasses knowledge, that you may be filled with all the fulness of God" (Eph 3.17–19). Here meditation adheres to the same words and expressions and is confined to their plain meaning in the Bible. This is what distinguishes meditation from contemplation. Contemplation becomes free and no longer restricted to the written word. It depends on the totality of personal perception and the extensive horizons of insight and knowledge.

For this reason, meditation on the mysteries of divine economy as exactly recorded by the Bible is the necessary base for proper contemplation. Thereby, the power and light of these mysteries become manifest. Successful, perpetual meditation thus makes contemplation also successful and ever growing.

Meditation is then a desirable spiritual activity of the essential nature and obligation of worship. It is incumbent on everyone without exception. For man simply cannot be nourished by the word of the gospel without reiterating it in his heart and mind. This is the import of meditation. It is also difficult for man to enter upon a fervent and true prayer with God without reiterating before him the words of his promises. He should cling to them and clarify his standpoint in their perspective. This, too, is the import of meditation.

Meditation, therefore, is a prayer that depends on reiterating the words of God and his promises in the heart and mind. In this manner, they become an inseparable part of man's faith and hope. They become a true power on which to rely in time of need: "I have laid up thy word in my heart, that I might not sin against thee" (Ps 119.11).

Meditation as an Inward Overflowing of Prayer

When one is fervent and ardent in spirit, meditative prayer becomes very simple to him and spontaneous. It needs no concentration or mental effort or any stimulation beyond one's abilities. It is called in this case simple prayer. It is an intimate and fervent discourse in which the soul speaks with God, its creator, expressing its feelings. Such feelings may be glorification of his works, attributes, or wisdom, or thankfulness for his mercy and his transcendent and humble care.

Here, the soul might be afire during this silent meditation and thus could not bear to keep silent any longer. It breaks forth into unchecked words that express love, worship, and submission, as a child expresses in his feeble words his strong feelings. The heart, which quakes with the touches of the hidden hand of God, is thereupon laid open before him.

Meditation as a Voluntary Act of Prayer

Man might wish to enter upon meditation without previously having enough fervor to push him at once up to the level of prayer of the heart. The need is then for some psychological effort and mental concentration. Such effort and concentration is required that the soul may be released from its impasse. The mind likewise should relinquish its preoccupation with outward affairs to enter upon a sober spiritual reading, enabling man to reach to a state of prayer. Here, the inner recesses of man must act. The conscience must stand alert to counteract freely all the psychological and mental preoccupations that have brought the worshipper to an impasse. Such preoccupations have served only to distract him from worship, prayer, and communion with God.

The action of one's conscience depends on love in overcoming this impediment and superficial preoccupation. When man moves inwardly and willfully to love God, even though somewhat coercively at the beginning, divine love starts to flow on the spot. Divine work always supports human work, becoming one with it at the end.

For this reason, man's will has to remain active, patient, and in anticipation until divine power descends upon it and spiritual warmth flows into it. It is then that man is launched inwardly and begins his prayer and meditation with all joy and facility.

This spiritual action takes place during spiritual reading. It transports man from a state of psychological deadlock and mental preoccupation with visible things to a state of interior depth, fervor, and prayer. It is the most important and most subtle spiritual action in the whole life of prayer. This is the only gate that provides access to all the mysteries of the spiritual life. It is the first step in the heavenly ladder, which connects the soul with its maker.

At this point, man may face a certain stubbornness on the part of his soul. The soul may be distracted by various concerns or cares that have no real value or meaning. Man may encounter some dodging on the part of his mind. It might jump from one thought to another and from one image to another. It thus becomes distracted by exceedingly trivial matters.

Here, the will needs to be armed with a sincere inward intention. This would help it persist firmly and cling fast to love. It must head toward Christ's face in supplication and anticipation. The time will come for divine grace to set it free and infuse it with love through and through.

The profuse source that the Holy Spirit draws upon to supply the student with material for meditation is the Holy Bible. The Bible is indeed the great school in which there is no end of lessons. However much we may grasp, we can only but little do so. This school is rich in three courses. The first is historical, which covers the period from the beginning of creation up to the end of all ages. It deals with the irrational and rational creation from every aspect. The second is legal, which includes all the commandments of God, his ordinances, and his laws, which he has set for mankind. The third is the dealings of God with his beloved, his discourse with them, and theirs with him. These three courses are enough to satisfy all the needs for our meditation with God. They do not deal with matters that have passed away, but with matters that are ever present here and now. They do not tackle them as merely objective facts, but as regards the actual state of our own souls.

The prophet David has left us a gorgeous harvest in his psalms. This is the best example of free and all-inclusive meditation. It includes all these courses together. The Psalms are artistic pieces for meditation. They contain a deeply moving and continuing dialogue between the psalmist and God.

As regards the creation, the psalmist never fails to praise any of its creatures. He talks to God about his creation of the heavens, of the earth, and what is under the earth, of mountains, hills, seas, rivers, springs, valleys, fields, plains, trees, forests, grass, fruits. He sings of the sun, moon, stars, planets, clouds, mist, snow, frost, heat, cold, rain, storms. He speaks of living creatures in the sea, birds of the air, beasts of the earth, wild beasts of the forest, cattle of the field, creeping things that crawl on the face of the earth. He speaks of peoples, nations, tongues, and every creation on the face of the earth. Out of the exuberance of his spirit, he cries aloud for each by name to sing with him and praise the Creator and the Most High God.

The psalmist then goes back in several places in his psalms, especially in the immortal Psalm 119, to speak to God about his law and commandments. He describes to him their broadness, beauty, and sweetness. He testifies before his Creator that they are sweeter than honey and the honeycomb to his mouth and that they enlighten his eyes. They are the joy of his heart and the richness of his soul. They are his meditation day and night and have thus become a lamp unto his feet and a light unto his way. He testifies to the young man that they are the means of keeping his way pure and to the child that they are his understanding. He then speaks to God of the depression that overwhelmed him at seeing the sinners who neglect God's law and the insolent who transgress it. At this point, he grows furious in his discourse with God at those who wander from his law. He curses them. He then offers thanks to God that he has taught him his commandments better than he has taught his enemies. Through them he has given him more understanding than the aged.

The psalmist then goes back to tell his Creator about himself. He regards himself as a worm and not as a man. He is contemptible and despised more than all people. In remembrance, he recalls his young days and the sins he committed in folly, and thus cries to God for mercy. He beholds his present iniquities depicted before his eyes. His soul becomes depressed and thus cries out to God for mercy. He describes how his eyes have wasted away, how his flesh has become gaunt and has cleaved to his bones. He has become like an owl or a lonely bird on a desolate housetop. He then beseeches his Creator not to rebuke him in his anger. He is ready for chastisement, but in love and mercy as from a kindly Father. He implores him not to take away his life in the midst of his days, but to allow him time patiently until he has given God due praise, glory, and thanksgiving.

With that, David can be said to have digested the lessons of the Holy Spirit in full, and so deserved God's attestation: "The Lord has sought out a man after his own heart" (1 Sam 13.14). He also gained Christ's testimony: "David, inspired by the Spirit, calls" (Mt 22.43).

Thus, David has set down for us, in the Spirit, a living and immortal model of meditation according to God's pleasure. Every psalm stands by itself as a magnificent piece of meditation that suffices as a whole lesson. It forms, with the rest of the psalms, an articulate image of the intimate life that David spent in discourse with God. The secret behind David's progression was his accurate knowledge of the law of the Lord and his regularity in meditation on it.

One should also know that meditation is an art that one needs time to master. However, progress is easy and rapid, though invisible, as it is in all spiritual virtues. The more we progress, the more we feel our deficiency and disability. So much so that when we reach a high point we look around as though we have not made any progress. Such is the action of grace; it hides our progress from our eyes that we might not fall into pride or vanity.

Paradoxically, inasmuch as we become more dominated by a feeling of deficiency, we have good reason to believe that we have covered a good distance. This we learn from the teachings of the Fathers, who were inspired by the Spirit. But still, we have before us a hill, which we must prepare to surmount.

SAYINGS OF THE FATHERS ON MEDITATION

22. Meditation on the scriptures teaches the soul the discourse with God. (St Isaac the Syrian, in "The Four Books of St Isaac the Syrian, Bishop of Nineveh," 1.3.69, Arabic version)

23. There is one kind of reading that teaches you how to behave. There is another that fires the soul with the zeal for virtue. Be diligent in meditating on the holyscriptures and the lives of the saints, for constant reflection upon them fosters thoughts of fervor, makes prayer easy, makes tribulations endurable. (St Isaac the Syrian, "The Four Books," 3.73, 75)

24. Reading is a sublime work, for it is the gate through which the mind finds access to divine mysteries. Reading is the reserve of strength upon which the mind draws to gain strength for pure prayer and meditation. (St Isaac the Syrian, "The Four Books," 5.86)

25. Without the perusal of holy scriptures, the mind can never approach God. (St Isaac the Syrian, "The Four Books," 5.87)

26. The gate through which man finds access to wisdom is meditation on the scriptures. (St Isaac the Syrian, "The Four Books," 4.132)

27. If you are a seeker of truth, know for sure that true meditation consists in purity of prayer and in recollection of mind. (St Isaac the Syrian, "The Four Books," 7.3)

28. When man advances in the practice of meditation with the help of grace, he begins little by little to understand the mystical subtleties in the word of God and in the psalms. He understands all that goes on around him and within him. He sees the ship of his life sail onward day after day. (St Isaac the Syrian, "The Four Books," 7.32–34)

29. Persist in prayer more than [in singing] the psalms, but do not give up your psalms on the pretext of meditation. Only give more time for prayer than recital. . . . While observing the canonical hours give allowance for prayer, and you will find yourself after a while to be another person! (St Isaac the Syrian, "The Four Books," 7.40)

30. Nothing invests the mind with modesty and chastity like speaking with God. (St Isaac the Syrian, "The Four Books," 3.85)

31. Throughout the mind's activity, which begins with meditation on divine things and ends up with contemplation and ecstasy, nothing is needed more than constraining the mind in prayer. (St Isaac the Syrian, "The Four Books," 4.186)

32. Constant meditation on God qualifies us for constant prayer. And prayer in its turn stirs the heart to meditate on God without tiring. (St Isaac the Syrian, "The Four Books," 1.109)

33. Constant meditation on God, with quietude of the mind, enables man to live out all kinds of prayer, to derive sublime knowledge of God himself. (St Isaac the Syrian, "The Four Books," 1.133)

34. Prayer draws the mind near to God. By means of meditation the mind gains the courage to gaze at him searchingly, and to become purified and sanctified. This is the kind of meditation that rules over, which masters all thoughts. The mind is thus illumined by hidden inward mysteries, which inspire it with the knowledge of God. (St Isaac the Syrian, "The Four Books," 1.135–38)

35. By speaking to God in prayer, we are raised to behold the kingdom of heaven—the place in which we are to worship in spirit and truth, the place that is confined by neither physical limit nor any of this world's bounds. (St Isaac the Syrian, "The Four Books," 1.140)

36. Fervent prayer and meditation burn up the passions and evil thoughts like a consuming fire. It gives wings to the soul, it creates a spiritual mind whose ministry before God is not by the lips but by the spirit. (St Isaac the Syrian, "The Four Books," 6.52–53)

37. Not only do wars [of the flesh] become nothing, but the flesh itself, which is the cause of such warfare, becomes despicable to us. Such is the effect of prayer and the benefit of divine meditation. (St Isaac the Syrian, "The Four Books," 1.130)

38. I advise you to sit down in solitude . . . without reciting psalms and without prostrations. If you are able to do so, pray with your heart alone, and by all means spend the night sitting in your delightful meditation [an exercise for those who are advanced in vigil]. (St Isaac the Syrian, "The Four Books," 3.97)

39. If anyone loves Jesus and really gives himself attentively, not superficially, to him: if he perseveres in love, God is already planning to reward that soul for that love. (St Macarius the Great, *Homilies* 12.16, in Maloney, *Intoxicated with God: The Fifty Spiritual Homilies of Macarius*)

40. Hush your tongue that your heart may speak [which is meditation], and hush your heart that the Spirit may speak [which is contemplation]. (St John of Dalyatha, *Homily on the Gifts of the Spirit*, in "The Homilies of the Spiritual Elder [John of Dalyatha]," Manuscript 19)

41. Hold him in your arms like Mary his mother. Enter with the Magi and offer your gifts. Proclaim his birth with the shepherds. Proclaim his praise with the angels. Carry him in your arms like Simeon the Elder. Take him with Joseph down to Egypt. When he goes to play with little children steal up to him and kiss him. Inhale the sweet savor of his body, the body that gives life to every body. Follow the early years of his childhood in all its stages, for this infuses his love into your soul. Cleave to him: your mortal body will be scented with the spice of the life in his immortal body. Sit with him in the temple and listen to the words coming from his mouth while the astonished teachers listen. When he asks, when he answers, listen and marvel at his wisdom. Stand there at the Jordan and greet him with John. Wonder at his humility when you see him bow his head to John to be baptized.

Go out with him to the desert and ascend the mount. Sit there at his feet in silence with the wild beasts that sought the company of their Lord. Stand up there with him to learn how to fight the good fight against your enemies.

Stand at the well with the Samaritan woman to learn worship in spirit and truth. Roll the stone from the tomb of Lazarus to know the resurrection from the dead. Stand with the multitude, take your share of the five loaves and know the blessings of prayer. Go, wake him up who is asleep at the stern of your boat when the waves beat into it. Weep with Mary, wash his feet with your tears to hear his words of comfort. Lay your head on his breast with John, hear his heart throbbing with love to the world. Take for yourself a morsel of the bread he blessed during supper to be one with his body and confirmed in him forever.

Rise, do not keep your feet away that he may wash them from the impurity of sin. Go out with him to the Mount of Olives. Learn from him how to bend your knees and pray until the sweat pours down. Rise, meet your cursers and crucifiers, surrender your hands to the bonds, do not keep your face away from the slapping and spitting. Strip your back to be lashed. Rise, my friend, do not fall to the ground, bear your cross, for it is time for departure. Stretch your arms with him and do not keep your feet from the nails. Taste with him the bitterness of gall.

Rise early while it is still dark. Go to his tomb to see the glorious resurrection. Sit in the upper room and wait for his coming while the doors are closed. Open your ears to hear the words of peace from his mouth. Make haste and go to a lonely place. Bow your head to receive the last blessing before he ascends. (St John of Dalyatha, *Homily on Meditation on the Economy of the Lord*, in "Spiritual Elder")

CONTEMPLATION (θεωρία)

> "I will pray with the spirit and I will
> pray with the mind also." (1 Cor 14.15)

VERY FEW PEOPLE SPEND ANY TIME practicing being with God. Fewer still enjoy the greater blessing, by God's grace, of interior prayer. Interior prayer is, in fact, the fruit of the spiritual life. It is a return of Adam to the beauty of his former spirituality.

We have dealt with meditation as the first degree of mental, or inward, prayer. We should note here, however, that no clear-cut boundaries divide meditation from another activity of the spirit: contemplation. Meditation sometimes overlaps with this activity of contemplation. Meditation serves, in fact, as a foundation on which the contemplative life stands. This will be clear from the sayings of the fathers that follow. In clearer terms, meditation is the practice by which we begin the state of contemplation. Meditation is an activation of one's spirit by reading or otherwise, while contemplation is a spontaneous activity of that spirit. In meditation, man's imaginative and thinking powers exert some effort. Contemplation then follows to relieve man of all effort. Contemplation is the soul's inward vision and the heart's simple repose in God.

The idea that the contemplative life consists in doing nothing but contemplating is certainly erroneous, for this means restricting it to hermits and ascetics. Rather, contemplation is a kind of prayer accessible to everybody. It is free from any restriction to a particular class of people. It is for the man of the world as it is for the monk, for the married as it is for the celibate, for the young as it is for the old.

Meditation requires delving deep into mental investigation, requiring excessive mental and intellectual activity. Contemplation, on the other hand, needs total quietude of man's mental powers and the cessation of all investigation or deep penetration. In meditation, the mind seeks after truth and investigates it. In contemplation, it is truth that actually begins to surround one's mind and to overwhelm it. The more the mind is quiet and silent, the more divine truth radiates, shines, and is transfigured within it.

As a spiritual experience, contemplation is by no means beyond the capacity of the ordinary nature of the soul in its normal collected condition. According to its first creation, the soul in its original state can contemplate divine truth when it stands quiet and silent before its Maker. In its normal and natural condition, the soul is not presupposed to be positive or negative. No work is demanded of it to qualify it for receiving divine truth except that it should not be preoccupied with things other than God—evils, passions, or trifles. Otherwise, it cannot be receptive to divine truth.

In its normal condition, and when it gets rid of all its evils and fantasies, the soul enters upon a state of interior watchfulness and poise. The Fathers call this state νῆψις, that is, sobriety. So it should not be preoccupied with anything at all. It should be in a state of wakefulness and attention of heart (ἡ καρδιακὴ προσοχή, as the Fathers term it).

This is the basis of contemplation, which qualifies man for receiving divine truth and contemplating it. Its demonstration in one's soul consists in gaining discretion and good behavior and judging things from a spiritual point of view. The fathers call this the faculty of discernment (διάκρισις).

Contemplation is simple. It totally depends on quietude and the cessation of all mental and psychic activity, be it positive or negative. It demands nothing other than the stance of the soul and the mind in attention and readiness: "My heart, O God, is ready, my heart is ready" (Ps 56.7, LXX).

But in spite of all that, many souls find this simple surrender, interior quietude, and the cessation of their psychic and mental commotion rather difficult. In such cases, the soul should be trained in what qualifies it for entering upon contemplation. This training in itself is a form of contemplation. We shall name it practical, voluntary contemplation, or acquired contemplation.

All these aspects of contemplation are intricate and overlapping. For the Spirit ascends and descends from one level to another without being restrained by a fixed rule. These various degrees of contemplation only clarify the state of the soul before God, but they never determine God's position in his relation to us. They are experiences that we undergo in our human life, but they are not degrees upon which our salvation depends. Neither are they regulations to which God must strictly adhere in instructing us. They are simply things that have taken their course in the lives of the saints who followed them. These saints reached the end, delineated them, and described their nature for our own instruction.

Voluntary Contemplation

Before presenting the different stages of contemplation, we have to note as well that all classification on the subject of prayer has only a relative value.

Voluntary contemplation is that which mostly concerns us. It is a spiritual work that can be mastered by the exertion of will. But though it depends in the beginning on human effort, to persist in it requires the support of grace.

But before discussing this kind of contemplation, we should remark once more that contemplation in any of its states or forms is not originally based on mental activity. Neither does it depend on any positive work on man's part.

Rather, it is a state of inward readiness of the mind and soul to accept the action of divine truth and its sway over them.

For this reason, the aim of voluntary or acquired contemplation should be restricted only to the attainment of a certain measure of interior quietude and mental tranquility. This is tantamount to the attainment of the mere qualifications for true contemplation. So contemplation acquired by the will is a process that truly prepares us for accepting contemplation in full, that is, the spiritual theoria.

This contemplative exercise that leads up to the spiritual theoria is a very ancient patristic tradition. We hear of it frequently in the teachings of such early fathers as St Macarius the Great in Scete and St Theonas in Nitria. Also, Cassian dedicated a whole chapter to it, discussing it in the minutest details (*Conferences* 9 and 10, in Chadwick, *Western Asceticism: Selected Translations of Christian Classics*).

The exercise could be summarized as focusing the mind upon a small verse, which is called *monologistos*. Man repeats it constantly without stopping for long hours every day. He should restrict his mind to the narrowest confines of the meaning of the verse. Or he might choose a single supplication in the name of the Lord Jesus, which is called here *Onomatolatreia*. He should train his mind not to step out of its bounds. Whenever his mind transgresses, he summons it back without boredom. This goes on until the mind learns how to stop meandering here and there, to calm down, and to be at peace.

At the time of the early Fathers, this exercise was merely a spiritual training that led to spiritual repose. From it man might strike out toward pure spiritual contemplation, that is, the spiritual theoria. The later Byzantine fathers, however, turned it into a spiritual work on its own. They laid down for it technical requirements and many bases and stipulations. It thus evolved until it became a point of serious theological controversy. It is still a matter of great interest to the Byzantine, Russian, and other eastern churches in our day. What concerns us in this spiritual exercise is its amazingly rapid success in calming down the soul—the feelings and thoughts. It constrains the mind, confining it to the narrowest limits of prayer.

The first aim of this exercise is to enter a state of spiritual quietude, which the Fathers named the prayer of *hesychia* (ἡσυχία), or repose. But we should note that it is a prayer that is totally void of any reading, meditation, singing, or any positive spiritual activity.

In this exercise, there are some instructions of an exterior nature laid down by the Fathers to attain the state of interior repose, such as sitting in a quiet place without moving and fixing one's mental sight upon the heart that the mind may first share with the heart in reiterating the prayer. The mind will finally fall under the sway of the heart and relax its grip. The exercise in this form is nothing more than an attempt or a trial to break loose from those exterior and interior elements that oppress man's mind and soul. These elements may have become part of man's activity as if they were of his very nature. They deprive man of the spiritual quietude and repose that are originally of the very nature of his human soul.

In the prayer of repose, man repeats the name of Christ or a short verse, according to what the early Fathers have set. This is nothing but a spiritual attempt to restore to the human soul and mind their original natural and spiritual state of repose. In such repose, man may hear the voice of God and see his light in the heart. In short, it restores to man his authentic spiritual and contemplative state. Maybe this was the end the Lord Jesus had in mind when he urged us to persist in prayer, saying, "[You] ought always to pray and not lose heart" (Lk 18.1). To this effect, the apostle Paul also said, "Pray constantly" (1 Thess 5.17).

This voluntary or acquired contemplation is available to everyone, whether he be of the clergy or of any secular occupation. Contemplation, in this respect, is, as it were, an impregnable fortress. It protects God's people against the vices of the environment in which they are forced to live and work. It enhances man's will and strengthens his personality, supplying it with transcendent powers of profundity, insight, and discernment. It qualifies man, furthermore, for leadership. For this reason, regular contemplation is considered one of the richest means for building up the soul. It makes it competent for positions of leadership at all levels.

Access to Contemplation

There are certain basic conditions stipulated for the initiation of the soul into a genuine and successful state of contemplation.

1. Before anything else, one has to be free of earthly cares, sins, or bad habits. In other words, one has to be free to combat sin. Those who have experienced meditation and made some progress in it will find this struggle quite easy, for speaking with God is a most vital and powerful means that sets man free. It burns his sin and wipes away its lust and power, as we have learned from the sayings of St Isaac on meditation.

At this point, I would like to stress the importance of practicing meditation. Man has to progress in meditation until he reaches a state of purity and repentance that befits contemplation. In contemplation he meets God face to face, as St Augustine says. We can sum up this phase of readiness into two elements: self-denial and victory over passions and evil desires, with all the meanings implied.

As for the way to release the soul from its bondage to passions and lusts, this falls within the domain of ascetic discipline (ἀσκήσις). Asceticism is the positive activity of the soul by which it counteracts negative activity. It is an exercise in practicing virtues to root out vices and evil habits. The Fathers call this exercise the practical stage (πρᾶξις).

Success in contemplation, or in spiritual life in general, cannot be attained without effort. One has to be disciplined by acts of asceticism and virtue. St John Cassian says, "In vain does one strive for the vision of God, who does not shun the stains of sin" (*Conferences* 14.1, 2, Butler, *Western Mysticism: The Teaching of SS Augustine, Gregory and Bernard on Contemplation and the Contemplative Life*, p 36).

2. There are people who have managed to subdue their ego and conquer sin with its passions, pleasures, and images. For these, it is easy to subdue the mind as well. Keeping still is an essential condition for the mind to enter into contemplation. St Gregory the Great says, "[The mind] must first have learned to shut out from its eyes all the *phantasmata* of earthly and heavenly images, and to spurn and tread underfoot whatever presents itself to its thought from sight, from hearing, from smell, from bodily touch or taste, so that it may seek itself interiorly as it is without these sensations" (*Homilies on Ezekiel* 2.5.9, in Butler, *Western Mysticism,* p 97).

St Gregory also says that the first step is that the mind recollect itself— gather itself to itself (*se ad se colligit*). The second step is introversion: that it should see itself as it is when recollected. It should turn its eyes inward upon itself, and consider itself thus stripped of sense perceptions and free from bodily images. In this way, the soul makes of itself a ladder for itself (*sibi de seipsa gradus ascensionis facit*) and mounts to the third stage, which is contemplation (Butler, *Western Mysticism,* p 97).

There is a philosophical and spiritual rationale that underlies the need to summon one's mind preliminary to contemplation and beholding God. This rationale is that we can reach God only from the depth of our souls. True, God exists everywhere, but not in relation to us. He exists everywhere only in relation to his own nature, which fills the whole universe. But there is no place at all in this vast universe where we can meet God except within ourselves. Here, he waits for us; here, we face him and talk to him; here, he answers us.

In a magnificent piece of meditation on seeking God, St Augustine proves that man can only find God in the depths of his own soul:

> **42.** Thou remainest unchangeable over all, and yet has vouchsafed to dwell in my memory since I learnt Thee. And why seek I now in what place thereof Thou dwellest, as if there were places therein? Sure am I that in it Thou dwellest since I have remembered Thee, ever since I learnt Thee, when I call Thee to remembrance. Where then did I find Thee that I might learn Thee? For in my memory Thou wert not before I learnt Thee. Where then did I find Thee that I might learn Thee but in Thee above me? ... Too late loved I Thee, O Beauty so old, yet ever new! Too late loved I Thee. And behold, Thou wert within, and I abroad, and there I searched for Thee. Thou wert with me, but I was not with Thee. Thou calledst, and shoutedst, burstedst my deafness. Thou flashedst, shonedst, and scatteredst my blindness. Thou breathedst odors, and I drew in breath, and panted for Thee. I tasted, and hungered and thirsted. Thou touchedst me, and I was on fire for Thy peace. (*Confessions* 10.36, 37, 38, in Butler, *Western Mysticism*, pp 40, 41)

3. There must be an incentive of love. Gregory the Great stresses a certain degree of love as a prerequisite for contemplation. In this respect, he says, "It is necessary that whoever eagerly prosecutes the exercises of contemplation, first questions himself with particularity how much he loves. For the force of love is an engine of the soul, which, while it draws it out of the world, lifts it on high" (*Morals on Job* 6.58, in Butler, *Western Mysticism*, p 96). He also says, "The greatness of contemplation can be given to none but them that love" (*Homilies on Ezekiel* 2.5.17, in Butler, *Western Mysticism*, p 96). There is a magnificent piece on love by St John of Dalyatha that we will meet later when quoting excerpts from the Fathers' sayings.

4. After being released, the soul should start to settle down. It should cease to concern itself with many things. It should relinquish its dependence on its own self and its own mind in approaching God. Prayer, in this case, does not

depend on any mental effort or psychic activity. It is merely a silent and quiet stance before God. In this stance, the soul accepts divine truth without struggling, seeking, investigating, or employing any intellectual dialectic. This prayer, the Fathers call pure prayer (προσευχὴ καθαρά), that is, pure from all mental images. St Isaac the Syrian calls it spiritual prayer. The attainment of pure prayer would be the clearest proof of man's success in the stage of action or ascetic struggle. Arriving at pure prayer means that the soul has definitely got rid of all its negative activity. It has become emancipated and is no longer enslaved to anything at all.

But man does not reach pure prayer as soon as he finds access into contemplation. Pure prayer represents the last stage of a continuous struggle during contemplation. Man undergoes such struggle to be freed from the mental activity that falsifies spiritual knowledge and corrupts the truth. After this, contemplation truly becomes spiritual contemplation.

Yet man has to undergo long periods during his prayers and contemplation in which the mind may interfere with divine truth. However, by perseverance, simple surrender, and ardent love, the mind calms down little by little and its commotion subsides. It gives way to divine truth that it may hold sway over the mind and not vice versa: "You will know the truth, and the truth will make you free" (Jn 8.32).

So long as the mind holds sway and is active and influential, the will remains constrained and subject to human desire. The will always remains fastened to the mind. But, when the mind begins to calm down and give way, the will is thereupon released and heads straightforwardly toward God. It acts under the immediate influence of grace. The soul, here, penetrates into the sphere of the spirit. Its prayer and contemplation thus become spiritual. It becomes dominated by a sort of divine repose, which the Fathers call ἡσυχία. In this repose, it moves, as St Isaac says, under the influence of the Holy Spirit.

Contemplation, or *theoria*, in its integral and correct form, does not depend on mental activity. On the contrary, it is proportionate to the stopping of that activity. Instead, it depends on quietude and interior silence. Hence, its extreme simplicity and facility. Nothing throughout man's experience in his spiritual life is more delightful or enjoyable than contemplation. So much so is it that the Fathers have described contemplation as *the* kingdom. This is due to the exquisite happiness and joy, which baffle one's mind, when the soul draws near to God and tastes him.

As a sheer gift of grace from beginning to end, this form of contemplation

does not stipulate anything on man's part: It requires neither being in a particular state nor seeking a particular state by feelings or by the exertion of the will.
Instead, it is a work of grace that God dispenses at will, as he chooses and sees
fit. This second kind of contemplation is mostly that which extends beyond the
usual limits of prayer. It is often manifested as divine ecstasy, visions, revelations, prophecy, and the transcendent gifts of miracles and healing.

The State of Contemplation

For us who meditate regularly, there comes a time when we no longer feel a
need to summon ourselves to spiritual attention. No sooner are we inwardly
ready to take up mental prayer than we find ourselves in the very heart of
prayer. So our feelings are instantly focused, and our minds promptly recalled.
Hereupon lies the threshold of contemplation that is soon reached without
exerting any effort whether by reading, imagination, or discourse. Thus,
prayer becomes spontaneous and no longer in need of being devised by some
medium or other.

This quick initiation into the heart of prayer, and the feeling of God's presence, means that our relationship with him has been firmly established. The
short period in which we used to enjoy meditation in God's presence has
expanded to include all the period we spend in contemplation. We have taken
up a new kind of prayer that is simpler in its nature than the previous ones.

But the main problem here is to believe that it is simple. When we believe
it and rid our minds of all the delusions of this being a state of esoteric spirituality, we shall surely make progress.

Since this spiritual exercise is simple, it requires a simple and easygoing
soul that can go on caring little how or where it goes. This may be likened to
walking in the dark in simple faith, making no use of the senses, mind, or
imagination. It is as though a blind man were guided to walk along a path free
of stumbling blocks or other impediments without boundaries on the left or
right—a path that is seldom trodden by anyone. This blind man may have a
simple heart, a clear conscience, a serene mind, and a calm imagination. In this
case, he would advance rapidly forward in faith without confusion as an open-
eyed man would do. But if the blind man were a sophisticated, skeptical, and
fanciful philosopher, he would grope his way with a stick. Imagining the
existence of ditches, barriers, or wild beasts, he would stumble on the way.
After a while he would prefer to sit down rather than walk on.

Such is the way of contemplation: an easy way demanding an easygoing soul. All it has to do is simply believe and walk along easily, guided by faith.

There will come a time when your soul is quiet and prayerful, your senses tractable, and your mind collected. Your soul will then move on gradually to shake off the sway of the senses and break loose from the mind's turmoil. It is as if the soul were elevated above the body, not in distance or space, but in quality and entity. It contemplates itself adhering to a spiritual truth or an attribute of God. During its progress, it meets new things and wondrous realities, some perceptible to the mind, others imperceptible to it. We are thus overwhelmed by a sweet sense of joy, amazement, and pleasure all together. We find ourselves entrusted with hidden realities and mysteries. Thus, faith and trust increase, inspiring the soul all the more and strengthening our hope.

The spirit, henceforth, becomes more active and militant in its continuous progression farther and farther along this easy and difficult way. This progress goes on until it approaches the source of light, which inspires it with all these feelings. Once it faces it, the mind stops in a flash, and all the senses are brought to a halt. The soul then falls into a state of ecstasy before the one whom St Augustine describes as the "Unchangeable," that is, God.

During this easy tour, the mind may stop to investigate any of the realities presented to it and discuss it with concern. In such case, contemplation immediately stops. In vain we try to carry on with it. However, the mind has receded, our feelings have become confused, and chaos reigns once again.

For this reason, after we begin to pray—whether by meditation or contemplation—as soon as the heart becomes on fire with love and the joy of liberty overwhelms it, we have to lay aside at once all the means we employ in prayer, whether it be reading, thinking, psalms, prostrations, or the like. We must be calm and quiet, happily waiting for the release of the soul. We must not try to resume or think upon these means again. For by trying to do so, we will only hamper the soul's release. We will impede its initiation into the stage of contemplation. This is like turning on the engine of one's car manually. As soon as it starts, will it not be useless to keep on moving one's arm? One only has to feel happy, get into the car, and drive away uninhibitedly.

We have thus passed on to a kind of prayer that relates to the spirit rather than to the heart or mind. Instead of speaking to God in our own words and with our own feelings, we now stand before him that he might speak to us, not in words but in matters too great for words. In the words of St Paul, who tasted the highest degrees of contemplation and revelation, no ear can hear, nor eye can see, nor can the heart of man conceive such experience.

Our feelings then can find no better expression than in the words of the psalmist: "My heart, O God is ready, my heart is ready" (Ps 56.7, LXX, the second psalm in Sext in the Coptic canonical hours).

While proceeding in the contemplative life slowly but surely, the willingness of our minds, senses, and hearts to enter into contemplation will gradually increase. Contemplation will become habitual as well as delightful. We will thus seek contemplation at all times easily and without effort. Our prayer will become warmer, nay, burning with love and longing. The existence of God will be a tangible reality to us, so much so that some of us might see visions. However, we will continue to doubt that we have seen anything. But what is undoubtable is that God will be actually present before us and we will be cleaving to him. Though the inner senses may not fully perceive him, his effect on the soul will be striking. For the soul will experience a sense of delight it had never tasted before. The commotion of feelings and thoughts will die down. The mind will cease to roam about. Everything will calm down and hold its peace in expectation of him who is coming soon that it might offer him obeisance, as St Isaac says.

The soul waits in anticipation and is longing to see its lover as if he were coming from afar. It suddenly feels his presence within when he invisibly alights upon it. The soul is thus filled with delight and pleasure. It will then try to discern its lover, but he will, as it were, have laid his hands upon its eyes that it may not see him. However, it actually feels his presence and is burning with love and joy. It is most certainly sure that it is God himself!

Out of all this, the soul tries to understand something, but the mind stands powerless and the senses remain numb, unable to discern anything. This is nothing but the incomprehensible union. The soul thus becomes contented with what befalls it but remains apprehensive of losing this mysterious joy.

Meanwhile, a sort of translucent cloud isolates us from the surrounding world. If anything happens around us, like someone calling us, we hear the voice but cannot, without great difficulty, answer spontaneously. It is as if we are locked up in our great holy quietude, unable and strongly unwilling to leave it. Minutes, or even hours, may pass while we are unaware, feeling comfortable in our contemplative state.

End of the Contemplative State

Contemplation passes away, but some of its aftereffects upon the soul may last for several days. Calmness pervades all the members of our bodies. Every movement that we make is slow. The concentration of our thought is hard to maintain. The look of our eyes is fixed and absent. We are be reluctant to take part in conversation or exchange compliments. During this period, entering into contemplation may recur, or it may end, not to return again except after the lapse of a long time, perhaps years. But there are souls that are well disposed to contemplation. If no earthly inhibitions occur, they may get used to entering into it daily and continually. An example of this is St Macarius the Great. Palladius and Serapion, contemporaries of his, wrote that he was in a constant state of rapture and contemplation. Anyone who wanted to talk to him had to draw his attention to receive spiritual answers from him.

SAYINGS OF THE FATHERS ON CONTEMPLATION

43. Make me worthy, O Lord, to know you so as also to love you, not with knowledge arising from study's exercise and joined to the intellect's dispersion; but make me worthy of that knowledge whereby the intellect, in beholding you, glorifies your nature in divine vision which steals the awareness of the world from the mind. Account me worthy to be lifted above the will's wandering eye which begets imaginings and to behold you in the constraint of the cross's bond in the second part of the crucifixion of the intellect, whose liberty ceases from the activity of its thoughts by abiding in your continuous vision which surpasses nature. (St Isaac the Syrian, *Homilies* 36, "On the Modes of Virtue," in *The Ascetical Homilies of Saint Isaac the Syrian,* p 161)

44. Those upon whom you shed a ray of your love could no longer bear to live among people. In search of their Beloved, they renounced every physical love, becoming foreigners to all. They gave up all the pleasures of this life, seeking the way of their Beloved in tears. They felt unworthy of his beauty; finding themselves on this blessed quest, they wept . . . They shook off every bodily pleasure and disdained all human joy. And instead, they loved the toil and fatigue which prompted the compassion of their Beloved.

They abandoned father and mother, brother and friend, seeking him whose love is rich. They knew that in his heart much love, and therefore much comfort was stored for them, this love, this comfort surpassing any other. When they felt this passionate love for the Only Begotten, they could not bear to abide a moment longer in the pleasures of this world. And when they found that they owned nothing worth offering, in love they offered their own selves upon his altar. In joy they surrendered their own bodies to death, for by so doing they found something to sacrifice to their Beloved.

They ran impetuously along the way of sorrows, bearing the torments of their own hearts. They crucified their members and passions contentedly. They drank the bitterness of gall with pleasure. Beloved! You robbed them of everything, even their own selves. They felt no longer alive, for it was you who lived in them . . . When hardships surrounded them on every side, they no longer sought to be exempted from them. Instead, they asked for more sufferings, they pleaded for the patience to endure them for their Beloved's sake.

These people were drunk with love. When they heard their Beloved say, "Blessed are those who mourn now," they could not stop mourning.

What mourning! The man's heart would ignite with love, would explode with living water! When his knees could no longer support him in his prayer he fell on his face. Trying to stand up, he would fall down again. His eyes streamed with flaming tears, burning his cheeks with their fire and flowing down on the earth to purge it from its curse.

How shall I describe you, divine love! You have elevated the human soul and seated her in the light of her Maker. You have washed her until she looked like her Master. The loving soul tamed the wildest beasts; they saw in her the image of her Maker, they could breathe his heavenly fragrance.

It is not only wild beasts who submitted to the [saintly] human soul, but even demons were terrified at seeing her illumined with love. They fled when they saw in her the image of God's authority. (St John of Dalyatha, *Homily on Love and the Love of God*, in "The Homilies of the Spiritual Elder [John of Dalyatha]," Manuscript 19)

45. The soul does not pray a prayer, but she perceives the spiritual things of that other age which transcend human conception; they are understood by the power of the Holy Spirit. This is noetic divine vision—this is not the movement and entreaty of prayer, although prayer initiates [and prayer is the means.]

Some have already reached the perfection of purity, and there is no time when their prayers move within them, as we said above. And when the Holy Spirit visits them, he always finds them in prayer. He brings them forth from prayer into *theoria* [or contemplation], which means "vision of the spirit" [or spiritual contemplation]. They have no need of the form of prolonged prayer, nor of the fixed and definite order of liturgy: it is sufficient for them to remember God and at once they are taken captive by the love of him.

However they do not neglect to stand at prayer, so as to render honor to prayer; in addition to their unceasing prayer they stand on their feet at the prescribed times. (St Isaac the Syrian, *Homilies* 37, in *Ascetical Homilies*, pp 182–83)

46. Beyond this boundary there is awestruck wonder and not prayer. For what pertains to prayer has ceased, while a certain divine vision remains, and the mind does not pray a prayer. Every mode of prayer originates from a motion, but once the intellect enters into spiritual movements, there is no longer prayer. Prayer is one thing, and the divine vision of prayer is another, even though each takes its inception from the other. For prayer is the seed, and the divine vision is the harvesting of the sheaves. (St Isaac the Syrian, *Homilies* 23, in *Ascetical Homilies*, pp 116–17)

47. To certain persons the sign of the cross appeared as light and plunged itself deep into the inner man. At another time a man, while praying, was thrown into a trance . . . Sometimes indeed the very light itself, shining in the heart, opened up interiorly and in a profound way a hidden light, so that the whole person was completely drowned with that sweet contemplation. He was no longer in control of himself, but became like a fool and a barbarian toward this world, so overwhelmed was he by the excessive love and sweetness of the hidden mysteries that were being revealed to him. The result was that the person was granted liberty and arrived at a perfect degree of purity and freedom from sin. (St Macarius the Great, *Homilies* 8.3, in Maloney, *Intoxicated with God: The Fifty Spiritual Homilies of Macarius*)

48. The highest spiritual state of the soul in this life consists in the vision and contemplation of Truth, wherein are joys, and the full enjoyment of the highest and truest Good, and a breath of serenity and eternity, such as great and incomparable souls have described in some measure, who, we believe, have seen and see such things. And I dare aver that if we with constancy follow the course that God commands, we shall by the Power of God and his Wisdom arrive at the First Cause of all things, and intellectually see It. (St Augustine, *De quantitate animae,* in Butler, *Western Mysticism,* pp 59–60)

49. To some it has been granted by a certain holy inebriation of mind, alienated from fleeting temporal things below, to gaze on the eternal light of Wisdom. (St Augustine, *C. Faust.* 12.42, in Butler, *Western Mysticism,* pp 59–60)

50. What is it that I love when I love you? Not the beauty of a body nor the comeliness of time, nor the luster of the light pleasing to the eyes, nor the sweet melodies of all manner of songs, nor the fragrance of all flowers, ointments and spices, not manna and honey, nor limbs welcome to the embrace of the flesh—I do not love these when I love my God. And yet it is a kind of light, a kind of voice, a kind of fragrance, a kind of food, a kind of embrace, when I love my God, who is the light, voice fragrance, food, embrace of the inner man, where there shines into the soul that which no place can contain, and there sounds forth that which time cannot end, where there is fragrance which no breeze disperses, taste which eating does not make less, and a clinging together which fulfillment does not terminate. It is this that I love when I love my God. (St Augustine, *Confessions* 10.6, in Blaiklock, *The Confessions of Saint Augustine,* p 244)

51. The sweetness of contemplation is worthy of love exceedingly, for it carries away the soul above itself, it opens out things heavenly, and shows that things earthly are to be despised; it reveals things spiritual to the eyes of the mind. (St Gregory of Rome, *Homilies on Ezekiel* 2.2.13, in Butler, *Western Mysticism*)

52. And while all those virtues which we say St Paul the Apostle possessed are most splendid precious gems, yet their value seems poor and trifling when they are compared with that most beautiful and unique pearl which the merchant in the Gospel sought to acquire by selling all that he had . . .

What then is that one thing which is so incomparably above those great and innumerable good things? That which alone should be acquired while all

the others are scorned and rejected. Doubtless it is that truly good part which
Mary chose in disregard of the duties of hospitality and courtesy . . .

So it is contemplation then, it is meditation on God which is the one
thing, whose value leaves wanting all the merits of our righteous acts and all
our aims at virtue fallen short . . . Likewise, all those merits of holiness
(although they are not merely good and useful for the present life, but also
secure the gift of eternity) if they are compared with the merit of divine contemplation, are considered trifling and, so to speak, fit to be sold. (*Conferences
of John Cassian* 23.3, NPNF, 2nd series, 11.520)

53. He who sees the beauty of such revelations and visions no longer finds
beauty in this world of ours. There is none who has tasted God's richness and
does not regard money as dung; none who has enjoyed the company of angels,
none who has got drunk with their rapture, none who has shared their secrets,
who does not hate the company of this world and its intrigues. There is none
whom the love of Christ has pierced who can any longer bear the filth of abom-
inable lust; none whose mind has been captivated by God's beauty who can be
captivated by any of the passions of this world; none who has found God and
known him who has not proudly forgotten this world. These precious stones
he collects and keeps in the treasure of his heart.

This is the merchant who finds solace in prayer. He always swims in its
waters. He sits down to examine himself that he may be purified in the sea of
light, and radiate that light: a royal robe for the everlasting Christ. This is the
man who labors quietly, his mind transported by his love for the waters that
wash away his sins. Blessed are those who, while captive still in the unfath-
omable depth which encloses all, soar above the crests of light with the wings
of the Holy Spirit. Blessed are those who have washed in the waters of purity,
in waves of light, in cataracts of refining fire, fire which cleanses all who seek
it. Blessed are those whose Creator has become their Teacher, whose wealth lies
in his Spirit, whose nourishment is to see God, whose drink is the delights of
the Spirit. Blessed are they whose sun never sets, whose eye shall never see darkness, whose light, the splendor of Christ, shall never quit their souls. Blessed are
they who have become spiritual beings while still on earth, who converse with
their Creator. Blessed are those who labor in prayer, whose rest lies in the wakefulness of the Holy Spirit inside them. In their souls they always listen to his
hidden secrets. It is the Spirit which sanctifies the joy of their heart. (St John of
Dalyatha, *Homily on the Greatness of the Rank of Angels*, in "Spiritual Elder")

CHAPTER THREE

Beyond Prayer

"Yet among the mature we do impart wisdom, although it is not a wisdom of this age or the rulers of this age who are doomed to pass away. But we impart a secret and hidden wisdom of God, which God decreed before the ages for our glorification. None of the rulers of this age understood this; for if they had, they would not have crucified the Lord of glory. But, as it is written, 'What no eye has seen, nor ear heard, nor the heart of man conceived, what God has prepared for those who love him,' God has revealed to us through the Spirit . . . For what person knows a man's thoughts except the spirit of man which is in him? So also no one comprehends the thoughts of God except the Spirit of God. Now we have received not the spirit of the world, but the Spirit which is from God, that we might understand the gifts bestowed on us by God. And we impart this in words not taught by human wisdom but taught by the Spirit, interpreting spiritual truths to those who possess the Spirit.

"The unspiritual man does not receive the gifts of the Spirit of God, for they are folly to him, and he is not able to understand them because they are spiritually discerned. The spiritual man judges all things, but is himself to be judged by no one. 'For who has known the mind of the Lord so as to instruct him?' But we have the mind of Christ" (1 Cor 2.6–16).

ECSTASY (ἔκστασις)

> "And they went out and fled from the
> tomb; for trembling and astonishment
> (ἔκστασις) had come upon them."
> (Mk 16.8)

T HE BIBLE DESCRIBES THE STATE OF ECSTASY as ἔκστασις. In its linguistic origin, this word indicates the sense of bafflement, rapture of mind, or losing of one's consciousness or awareness. It was translated into Arabic as *heera*, or "bewilderment" and into English as *dismay*. This word occurs in David's Psalm 116.11, "And in my dismay I said, 'All men are liars.'" Unfortunately, the Arabic word for bewilderment connotes confusion and was understood as such, but the original meaning purports a state of spiritual elation or ecstasy. This postulation rests on the following verses, which account for this meaning. David says afterwards: "What shall I render to the Lord for all his bounty to me? I will lift up the cup of salvation and call on the name of the Lord" (Ps 116.12, 13). So he acknowledges the level of grace to which his soul has been elated during ecstasy. He says that in his ecstasy he saw that all men are liars (v 11). This resembles Solomon's saying in Ecclesiastes, "All is vanity and a striving after wind" (Eccl 1.14). So it was revealed to David during his spiritual ecstasy that all that relates to man is vain.[1]

In several places in the New Testament, the word *amazement* occurs as a translation of ἔκστασις, indicating the sense of spiritual ecstasy. It purports unusual astonishment and baffling wonder due to deep spiritual emotion or overflowing joy: "And amazement (ἔκστασις) seized them all, and they glorified God and were filled with awe, saying, 'We have seen strange things today'" (Lk 5.26).

It also occurs in another place, where the power of the word is striking: "Moreover, some women of our company amazed us (ἐξέστησαν ἡμᾶς). They were at the tomb early in the morning and did not find his body; and they came back saying that they had even seen a vision of angels, who said that he was alive" (Lk 24.22).

---

[1]St Gregory of Nyssa comments on this by saying that when David says that "all men are liars" (Ps 116.11), he means that any attempt by man to describe transcendent vision is a lie (*On Virginity* 10).

Finally, the meaning of the word *ecstasy* as "amazement" becomes most clear in the following occurrence: "And they went out and fled from the tomb; for trembling and astonishment (ἔκστασις) had come upon them; and they said nothing to anyone (they were dumb with amazement), for they were afraid" (Mk 16.8).

In the same vein, amazement also occurs in the Book of Acts: "And all the people saw him walking and praising God, and recognized him as the one who had sat for alms at the Beautiful Gate of the temple; and they were filled with wonder and amazement (ἐκστάσεως) at what had happened to him" (Acts 3.10).

Ecstasy, or spiritual trance, is a state of rapture. The Bible describes it in different terms, such as "the Spirit of the Lord came upon him" (Judg 3.10; 11.29); "The hand of the Lord God fell there upon me" (Ezek 8.1); "I know a man in Christ who . . . was caught up to the third heaven—whether in the body or out of the body I do not know, God knows" (2 Cor 12.2, 3); "falling down but having his eyes uncovered" (Num 24.4); or "I was in the Spirit on the Lord's day" (Rev 1.10).

This experience stipulates a state of inward spiritual readiness on man's part to accept God's revelations. Hence, ecstasy is always correlative with a state of total quietude or repose (ἡσυχία). After this, communication between man and himself and the surrounding world is cut off. He thereupon becomes connected to God with all his being. In ecstasy, man loses the freedom of control over his mind and senses. It is the Holy Spirit who takes over the lead at these moments. Man's freedom is thus swallowed up in that of the Spirit. He then becomes subject to its management and revelation.

In the Old Testament, ecstasy is most clearly mentioned in all the cases in which the prophets receive the voice, commands, and warnings of God. The prophet's mind is suddenly caught up in rapture, and he enters into a trance. He afterward returns to himself to utter the word of God in all sobriety, poise, and lucidity, or he may utter it during his ecstasy while half-conscious, describing what he is seeing or hearing. He may also write with his pen—while in his ecstasy—all that God may dictate to him. Such is the case with the prophet Daniel: "But you, Daniel, shut up the words, and seal the book, until the time of the end" (Dan 12.4). Such also is the case with John in the Book of Revelation in the New Testament: "And he said to me, 'Do not seal up the words of the prophecy of this book, for the time is near'" (Rev 22.10).

Now, the Son of God is incarnated. The Holy Spirit has descended upon the Church. It has been poured over all flesh. This has been done in fulfillment of God's promise in the Book of Joel and of Christ's promise before his ascension. The Book of Acts testifies to all these facts in its description of the first Pentecost. Therefore, through the divine mystery poured over him by the Holy Spirit, every man is now qualified to be subject to the power of that Spirit. He can become subject to its direct instruction and control just like the prophets of old.

This grace is offered to every man. However, the purpose is not to receive new revelations of faith as the prophets or the apostles did. It is to know what relates to one's self in the light of the same faith. What is now given to man is to realize his own salvation. He can rediscover the secret of the love of Jesus Christ reserved for him in person. He receives from God revelations that concern him personally, according to Christ's promise: "And I will love him and manifest myself to him" (Jn 14.21). For being under the control and management of the Holy Spirit differs in its effect on the human soul from one person to another.

Ecstasy is still, as it used to be in the Old Testament, one of the direct means of communication between God and man. It may, however, vary now in its degree or purpose. Although it can reach the highest stage, the purpose now is different. The purpose of ecstasy in these times is to increase knowledge and strengthen the ties of personal love relationships between God and his faithful beloved ones. God has promised to let this knowledge or love grow from day to day and for evermore.

At this point, the following question may be asked: Why are all the transcendent divine mysteries that relate to the knowledge and love of God not capable of being revealed to the conscious mind of man? The answer is simple and plain. The makeup of man's conscious mind is based on material, conceptual, and logical measurements. This mind has been brought up, has developed, and has matured under the influence of these dimensions. It has thus developed almost foreign to a genuine and comprehensive knowledge of God. God's nature is not subject to material, conceptual, or logical measurements. The knowledge of God then becomes a matter that inevitably transcends man's mind. He who truly wishes to believe in God must be lifted above himself, his mind, and even the whole world.

For this reason, the value of faith is considered higher than the value of man. It is even higher than the value of the whole world. Therefore, the reward of faith should be higher than all of man's possessions along with the glories of his world. The reward of faith is God. The value of faith, then, is higher than that of ecstasy, visions, or revelations: "Blessed are those who have not seen and yet believe" (Jn 20.29).

But to show his love for the man who loves him and believes in him, God needs sometimes to reveal himself to man. God's love must then be personal and subjective at the human level: "He who loves me will be loved by my Father, and I will love him and manifest myself to him" (Jn 14.21). For man to receive these manifestations from God, it is vital to ignore whatever his eyes may fall upon or his ears may happen to hear or his thought may think of. In a word, he must discard all his conceptual and physical perception. This should be done in order not to allow conceptual and physical perception to interfere with or falsify the reality of God, who transcends them. God here appears to man and manifests his love to those who love him, but this appearance stipulates the cessation of all the activity and functioning of the mind that are related to one's senses. Such silence of the mind and senses takes place only for a time. During this time, the transcendental contact that surpasses our sensory nature occurs. Such ecstasy in God is what earlier in this book we have called absolute ecstasy, due to its elevation above the limited and the sensible.

The experience of ecstasy in God demands no particular worthiness on man's part in order for God to reveal himself to him. What is needed is only deep love from the heart, mind, and soul, according to God's commandment. It is strange indeed that the strong and basic relationship between warm, sweeping love and ecstasy in God appears only most strikingly at the level of experience. For all who have experienced ecstasy in God are those who have entered into a state of absolute love for him. As soon as love reaches a certain level of intensity, it foreshadows man's entering into ecstasy. Ecstasy is thus sometimes described as an exquisite pleasure or as rapture.

Nevertheless, grace remains unbound even by this prerequisite. For grace may suddenly visit man without any worthiness or readiness on his part. It may transport him at once into a state of ecstasy. It is as if he has suddenly fallen as a beloved prey to a sweeping love. This love strips him of his freedom and self-consciousness to let him enjoy ineffable delight and knowledge.

Hence, we are not so much in favor of considering ecstasy a degree for the spiritually advanced. Some of the Fathers, such as Simeon the New Theologian, are even disposed to consider it a stage suitable for beginners. Beginners, he claims, are unfamiliar with the interior divine light. This makes them liable to sudden and violent collision with the reality and splendor of that transcendent light. They become at once bereft of their awareness. They are just like a man who is used to darkness and is suddenly blinded by a powerful light.

In our opinion, beginners are indeed in a state that, even in their inexperience, qualifies them for ecstasy. But such is the case not because they are not used to seeing the divine light. They are qualified for ecstasy, rather, because of the extreme fervor of their first experience, which surpasses all comprehension. For it is well known from practical experience that the fervor of the beginner and his love for Christ start from the very top. The first moments of his new life are the zenith of his spiritual experience. This makes a man live in a state of joy and spiritual ecstasy that transcends the whole world. It transcends reason itself. One almost lives in constant bafflement.

We thus hear time and again from the early Fathers and teachers that man should always live in the feeling, fervor, and love of the first day on which he repented and threw the world behind his back. Many of the Fathers have proved their ability to live constantly in a fervent life imbued with love and ecstasy. An example of this is St Macarius the Great. We read of him in Palladius that he lived in a constant state of rapture.

St Dionysius the Areopagite believes that ecstasy is an involuntary process through which man approaches God. This, he claims, is a reward in return for a man's forsaking the world. What he gains is proportionate to what he gives up when he leaves the world. Insofar as he dies, he lives. Ecstasy, indeed, demands submission like that of the dead man as he surrenders himself to God.

For spiritual writers in general, ecstasy signifies a process of evolution. It is a mystical ascent of the human nature toward a better state. To this state man was called in his first creation. He was created to change for the better. He was called to ascend spiritually upward to be closer to God.

But involuntary ecstasy is not the only access into this mystical evolution or ascension of the human nature toward God. There exist souls with a deep and wide spiritual sphere who have a powerful mental structure. While still in their full awareness, they can reach a certain level of self-deliverance. Here, they can meet with the divine truth and contemplate the face of Jesus Christ within the basis of their consciousness. Here, they can face God with all their power and potentials, whether spiritual, intellectual, or sensory. This may take place for a single moment, when the soul reaches a state of sincere love. Such conscious experience in which the soul faces God may be of less power or depth than the state of ecstasy or unconscious, insensible spiritual trance. However, it is more attached to the life of prayer. It is also more realistic so far as the beauty of worship is concerned. In it the soul tastes the blissful pleasures of the spirit and becomes, as it were, in a state of wakeful drunkenness.

There are cases in the Bible where the soul is described as inebriated with wine. The work of the Holy Spirit in the soul is compared with the effect of wine on man's mind. Such cases are depictions of the state of ecstasy in its different stages. These stages can be experienced in many different ways, in a range of degrees from the conscious to the unconscious, just like the variant effect of wine upon man's mind.

SAYINGS OF THE FATHERS ON ECSTASY

According to St Augustine, there are three kinds of perception: sensory perception, conceptual perception, and pure intellectual perception (*De Gen. ad litt.* 12.6–9). He who is elevated to conceptual perception needs to dispense with sensory perception. Imagination is one thing, and the sphere of the physical senses is another. Likewise, he who reaches absolute mental perception needs first to lose both sensory and conceptual perception: this, in order to perceive the truth clearly and without the falsehood resulting from the interference of the senses or imagination. In other words, it is to perceive the truth as it is, not as pictured by one's fancy.

Losing both sensory and conceptual perception together is what we call ecstasy. St Augustine compares it to a state midway between sleep and death:

54. When the attention of the mind is wholly turned away and withdrawn from the bodily senses, it is called an ecstasy. Then whatever bodies may be present are not seen with the open eyes, nor any voices heard at all. It is a state midway between sleep and death. The soul is rapt in such a way as to be withdrawn from the bodily senses more than in sleep, but less than in death. (St Augustine, *De Gen. ad litt.* 12.12.25 and 26.53, in Butler, *Western Mysticism*, p 71)

In another place, Augustine explains clearly how the mind leaves the sphere of the senses, and the significance of this phenomenon: "Ecstasy is a departure of the mind, which sometimes happens by fright, but sometimes by a revelation, through an alienation of the mind from the senses of the body, in order that the spirit may be shown what is to be shown." (St Augustine, *Enar. in Psalm* 67.36, in Butler, *Western Mysticism,* p 71)

Regarding this, a question may occur to us: How can the soul take leave of the physical senses? Is it by departing from the body? And if so, would the body be in such case really dead? St Augustine tackles this problem when discussing the vision of the apostle Paul:

55. When rapt to the third heaven, he (St Paul) did not know whether he was in the body, as the soul is in the body when the body, awake or asleep, is said to live; or when in ecstasy the soul is alienated from the bodily senses: or whether his soul had altogether gone forth from his body, so that the body lay dead until, when the revelation was over, his soul was restored to the dead members. So he did not awake as one asleep, nor, as one alienated in ecstasy, return to his senses; but as one dead, came to life again. When his soul was alienated from his body, it was uncertain whether it left his body quite dead; or whether after some manner of a living body the soul was there, but his mind carried away to see or hear the unspeakable things of that vision—for this reason, perhaps, he said: Whether in the body or out of the body, I know not; God knows. (St Augustine, *Enar. in Psalm* 12.5.14, in Butler, *Western Mysticism,* p 71)

For St Augustine, the question is not unanswered. What he means is that rapture or ecstasy falls into two kinds: First, ecstasy can be rapture of mind only. In this case, the mind is rapt beyond the physical senses, but the body remains with the soul. The body, without the leadership of the mind, remains receptive to external stimuli in a spontaneous way. One sees and hears but does not respond. One is in a state of rapture, as is clear from the words of St Augustine. St Seraphim of Sarov says in this respect:

56. When a person inwardly contemplates the eternal Light, then his mind is pure and he has no sensible representations within him but, wholly absorbed in contemplation of the uncreated beauty, he forgets all the things of sense. He does not even wish to see himself, but desires to hide himself in the heart of the earth, if only he may not be deprived of that true food—God. (St Seraphim of Sarov, in Moore, "Some Aspects of Orthodox Prayer," pp 85–86)

On this topic, other saints also say:

57. The mind may be transported by its Guide, the Spirit, to an eternal ocean of light. A brother once said to me, "When my mind is enraptured with these brilliant visions, I can see it [my mind] gazing at the ocean of life, swimming in the billows of light, inhaling the savor of life, falling into ecstasy, transfigured with great joy. Immersed in light, my mind surges with the action of love and joy in splendor ... It gazes at the choirs of angels shining, it enjoys their holy and splendid company. They carry it away to swim with them in the upper regions of light. There it is entrapped and overwhelmed by the sight of the glory which surrounds the Great Light ... There the mind may remain a moment, an hour, a whole day or a whole night—according to the will of the Spirit, and the portion of the gift dispensed by God." (St John of Dalyatha, *Homily on the Theoria which Severs the Mind from this World*, in "Spiritual Elder")

58. [The mind] enters into the mystic Darkness of Unknowing wherein it renounces all the perceptions of the understanding, and abides in That Which is wholly intangible and invisible, belonging wholly to Him that is beyond all. By the quiescence of all cognition, [all sensory and conceptual perception] it is united in its highest part to Him Who is wholly Unknowable, and by knowing nothing, knows in a manner that which is above understanding. (St Dionysius the Areopagite, in Lossky, *The Mystical Theology of the Eastern Church*, 1.3; PG 3.1001A)

59. Wherefore he even forgets himself and his nature, he becomes like a man in ecstasy, who has no recollection at all of this age. With special diligence he ponders and reflects upon what pertains to God's majesty and he says, "Glory be to his divinity!" ... And so the ascetic, being engrossed in these marvels and continually struck with wonder, is always drunken and he lives as it were in the life after the resurrection. (St Isaac the Syrian, *Homilies 37*, in *The Ascetical Homilies of Saint Isaac the Syrian*, p 179)

The second kind of ecstasy or rapture is the release of the soul from the noose of the flesh, a total release. It is the withdrawal of the soul, its departure and freedom from any relationship binding it to the body, so much so that the body lies down half in death. It does not respond to external stimuli at all, not even to the mutilation of its members. The mind becomes the soul's companion in its heavenly vision. In this state, man remains until his soul returns to his body. This is the experience that the apostle Paul underwent when he was caught up to the third heaven. He returned not to know whether he was in the body or out of it!

In this vein, St Augustine says:

60. In a fully religious ecstasy the subject "is withdrawn from the bodily senses and is carried away unto God and afterward is restored to his mortal members." (St Augustine, *Serm.* 52.16, in Butler, *Western Mysticism*)

61. It is not incredible that even this transcendent revelation has been granted to certain holy men not yet dead in the full sense, in the sense that they were actual corpses for burial. (St Augustine, *Liber de videndo Deo*, Ep 147.31, in Butler, *Western Mysticism,* p 82)

In the sayings just quoted, St Augustine tempers the overstatement of the claim that the body is completely dead—that the soul, the source of life, has definitively left the body. The body, he says in commenting on the vision of St Paul, would be still alive one way or another (Moore, "Orthodox Prayer," p 15).

62. But sometimes a certain divine vision is born of prayer, and the prayer of a man's lips is cut short. Stricken with awe by this vision one becomes as it were a body bereft of breath. This (and the like) we call the divine vision of prayer. (St Isaac the Syrian, *Homilies* 23, in *Ascetical Homilies,* p 116)

63. There is no human weakness, nor prayer nor supplication nor petition nor thoughts nor movements nor the moving of human life nor a mention of things which are or which shall be. Instead, he [i.e., the praying person] is united with the Spirit of the Son who speaks within him, and he knows within himself that he is God's son. Like a son he speaks to his Father with intimacy, and so becomes not like one who prays but like one who receives prayer . . .

O the unexplainable mystery! Neither can my hand put my intended meaning to writing. I wish the Creator of this mystery himself would explain it to you . . . For if man reaches this degree he does not pray for those who asked him to pray, rather mercy alone moves him to pity toward all who are in need.

It is the Spirit, who is in him and is one with him, who heals their ailments and satisfies their needs . . .

At the time when this gift is active within man, even if the whole creation turns into noise and tumult, it cannot force him to come to himself or return out of his rapture or ecstasy. (St John of Dalyatha, *Homily on the Assurance Acquired by the Servants of God*, in "Spiritual Elder")

Thus, we can see that some of the saints believe that in ecstasy the soul leaves the body and sojourns in heavenly places. The body is left lying in a state of death in which the soul does not function—for it has left the body. Others believe that the body remains in a state midway between sleep and death—although more motionless than in sleep. However, breath remains in the body some way or another. We conclude now with these words of St Augustine, who tends to hold the former view:

64. But unless [man] be in some way dead to this life, whether as having wholly departed from the body, or as being so withdrawn and alienated from the carnal senses that he knows not whether he be in the body or out of the body, he is not rapt and uplifted to that vision. (St Augustine, *De Gen. ad litt.* 12.27.55, in Butler, *Western Mysticism*, pp 80–81)

VISION OF GOD

'Αποκάλυπσις

῎Ορασις

'Οπτασία

> "For he endured as seeing him who is invisible." (Heb 11.27)

> "But I will go on to visions and revelations of the Lord." (2 Cor 12.1)

> "And we all, with unveiled face, beholding the glory of the Lord." (2 Cor 3.18)

> "Behold, I see the heavens opened, and the Son of man standing at the right hand of God." (Acts 7.56)

VISION IN THE CONTEXT OF PRAYER does not belong to the bodily eye. Neither is it concerned with a visible object. It is the vision of knowledge. Here, vision involves all the potentials and depths of knowledge. This includes mind, heart, soul, spirit, and all emotions. Knowledge in its turn is acquaintance with the person of God. To this kind of knowledge belong perception, love, confidence, and communion.

Man is invited to see God. He is invited to know him with all his available potentials together with the utmost capabilities of love and communion that human knowledge can bear. But we should make it clear from the first that vision of God does not mean encompassing him. Vision of God is possible only insofar as acquaintance is concerned. Encompassing God is absolutely impossible. God is a perfect, perceptible being. However, man's faculties of perception do not extend as far as God's perfection.

This does not mean that God may be partially perceived. There is no part or whole in God. He is simply one and perfectly whole. His simplicity is unlimited and infinite. But man's perception is weak. His knowledge is divisive due to transgression. There is a dark veil of sin severely obstructing his power of a clear, inward vision of the truth. This makes him unable to see God as he is in his perfect simplicity. Conversely, inasmuch as man is chaste, loving, obedient and humble, God is unveiled to him and he becomes acquainted with God. Furthermore, inasmuch as man grows in these virtues, the scope of his vision of God widens and God reveals himself to man more perfectly.

In other words, vision of God is always based on man's inward potentials. Such potentials qualify man for the unveiling of God in proportion to man's holiness: "The holiness without which no one will see the Lord" (Heb 12.14). So long as man is not perfect in holiness, he shall never see God as he is. He who is not perfect in his chastity, love, and humility will remain unable to see God in his perfect simplicity. He will see God sometimes cruel, at other times merciful. He will sometimes confide in God's extreme love, but at other times remain in fear of his justice. He will sometimes realize the depth of God's wisdom and his transcendent care for his creation, but at other times he will suspect God's care or condemn it. Man will thus remain, in his relationship with God, unable to form a perfect vision of him as he is. This will go on until he reaches the holiness that qualifies him for perfect vision.

The apostle John informs us in his first letter that we will never reach this complete holiness except at the appearance of the Lord: "But we know that when he appears we shall be like him, for we shall see him as he is" (1 Jn 3.2).

As we have said, the appearance of God does not mean seeing his form or image with the physical eye. Rather, it means seeing God's attributes and works, understanding the divine wisdom and knowing the divine love, which transcends all knowledge. Yet, due to the corruption of our nature, we cannot fully or clearly perceive this form of vision. This corruption, however, is not total. Our nature still retains some incorruption. Hence, there always remains for us a partial opportunity for knowing God. Besides, there also exists another partial potentiality within the very nature of our being, which was created to overcome the elements of this corruption. This too allows us to grow in the knowledge of God.

The existence of these two factors—that is, the partial incorruption and the partial potentiality for overcoming corruption—opens for us the sphere of faith in God. "Without having seen him you love him; though you do not now see him you believe in him and rejoice with unutterable and exalted joy" (1 Pet 1.8).

Therefore, faith, in reality, is a kind of vision. But this vision is somewhat blurred, or rather, it is a partial vision, since it is not perfectly understood. This is due to the divisiveness of our knowledge: "For our knowledge is imperfect and our prophecy is imperfect . . . For now we see in a mirror dimly" (1 Cor 13.9, 12). These words of St Paul are a realistic statement of our condition, for man now, however his faith, still asks why God did this, and why he did not do that. So many matters are incomprehensible and unknowable to him. There is a cloud of mental darkness hanging around them.

This human condition has a remedy, however. The remedy is faith. By faith man can transcend his lack of knowledge. By faith he can transcend the divisiveness of his knowledge. By faith he can transcend this mental darkness. Although faith is an incomplete and somewhat incomprehensible vision of God, its reward is tantamount to perfect and clear vision. Faith actually prepares for vision. By faith we receive here and now the power of resurrection in which we will see God face to face: "For now we see in a mirror dimly, but then face to face. Now I know in part; then I shall understand fully, even as I have been fully understood (that is, I shall understand God as he understands me). And now these things remain: faith" (1 Cor 13.12, 13).

When considering faith and vision, we may wonder, Are we never to see God in a clear vision? Can we not know God perfectly in this age? To answer these questions we must examine them spiritually and logically.

We have already said that seeing God in a clear vision rests basically and totally on man's holiness. If man reaches perfect holiness and is totally rid of the corruption of his nature, he will certainly see God most clearly as he is. The question must then be asked another way: Is it possible for man, in this earthly existence, to reach a state of utter holiness and put on a totally new nature? The answer encompasses the very essence of Christianity.

Christ came to the world, sacrificed his body, and shed his blood. He vouchsafed his union with us through the mystery of faith and the work of the Holy Spirit. This was done that we might attain through him total holiness. Such holiness qualifies us not only for seeing God but even for uniting and living with him as well: "But you were washed, you were sanctified, you were justified in the name of the Lord Jesus Christ and in the Spirit of our God" (1 Cor 6.11).

Therefore, we are sanctified through the mystery of faith in Christ and the action of the Holy Spirit which was poured on our nature. This sanctification qualifies us for seeing God, that is, knowing him in his very being. Such knowledge is one of union and communion: "So that they may have the full riches of complete understanding, in order that they may know the mystery of God, even the Father, and of Christ" (Col 2.2).

Sanctification, ablution (washing), and justification are the main elements in vision. They are all associated with faith. Faith, by its nature, decreases and increases, grows and stops growing. This is due to its affinity to man's fickle nature, which is liable to growth and change. In its turn, the vision of God—that is, knowing him—becomes liable to change and growth. Hence, inasmuch as man grows in his faith in God, confides in him, relies on him, and loves him, he grows also in his vision of God.

We return to the original question in another form, then: Is it possible for faith to grow to a perfect degree with man? Is it possible for man to reach a state of perfect holiness? Can he see God in a clear vision here in this existence?

From the theoretical point of view, clear vision resulting from perfect holiness is not only a possibility but also an obligation: "If you would believe you would see the glory of God" (Jn 11.40). But from a practical point of view, clear vision is not possible. This is due to the interference of man's senses and reason. Man's senses and reason rest on divisiveness, skepticism, and investigation. All of these interfere with vision. They corrupt knowledge and blur the clarity of vision. They may even abolish knowledge and vision altogether by doubt: "Lord, by this time there will be an odor, for he has been dead four days" (Jn 11.39). Man's nature, however renewed in this age, will still keep a certain amount of corruption. This corruption is represented in the physical senses and in reason. Both prevent a clear vision of God. Nothing will wash away this remaining element of corruption except the grave and then the resurrection. Thus, man can never see God clearly in this earthly existence.

What about God? Is he unable to show himself to man? The logical answer, which is supported by theological proof, is that since God is omnipotent he can show himself to man. God has actually materialized such vision in a transcendent manner in the mystery of the divine incarnation. Effective with the incarnation, man has been endowed with the mystery of seeing God, with Christ as the mediator. Christ has taken upon himself the task of clearing the way from all impediments of corruption in man's nature upon the moment of his appearance. He has done so by neutralizing all negative activity from the senses and the mind. He has purified them completely with a transcendent sanctifying power. This power makes man, as it were, a new transfigured creation located within the sphere of God's holiness. It is then that man, being transfigured as such, may see God in a clear vision as he is: "Am I not free? . . . Have I not seen Jesus our Lord" (1 Cor 9.1)?

So in this existence, contrary to our first conclusion about faith, we see there does now exist a new way of clear vision. But this vision is not through human faith; it is through God's manifestation. Here God manifests himself according to the absolute pleasure of his own will. This is the only means for clearing away all the obstacles that block the way of a clear vision of God. By such vision man becomes sanctified through and through.

But we must keep in mind that even this vision through God's sanctification is a temporary vision. Its effect does not last perpetually, compared to the clear vision in the afterlife, which will be completed by perpetual union.

We are now able to discern the great difference between seeing the Lord and having the Lord appear to us. Seeing the Lord indicates what man may discover of divine attributes in proportion to his abilities and saintliness. In this sense, man can never attain a perfect vision of God. As for the Lord appearing to us, in this he unveils his own self to us according to the abundance of his love, mercy, and goodwill. In his appearance, God reveals himself in all his depth to man. He takes upon himself the task of sanctifying man and offering him all the power by which he may discover God's glory: "For the Spirit searches everything, even the depths of God" (1 Cor 2.10).

With this distinction between vision that results from endeavor and saintliness and vision that results from the gratuitous appearance of the Lord, we may understand the difference between the verses occurring in the Old and New Testaments that confirm at one time the impossibility of seeing God and at another time the possibility of seeing him. On the impossibility of seeing God, we find God saying to Moses, "Man may not see me and live" (Ex 33.20). We find the Spirit saying, "No one has ever seen God" (Jn 1.18). St Paul, moreover, says, "I charge you to keep the commandment unstained and free from reproach until the appearing of our Lord Jesus Christ; and this will be made manifest at the proper time by the blessed and only Sovereign, the King of kings and Lord of lords, who alone has immortality and dwells in unapproachable light, whom no man has ever seen or can see. To him be honor and eternal dominion. Amen" (1 Tim 6.14–16). At the same time, we find verses that prove that God actually revealed himself to Moses, Isaiah, Job, and others in the Old Testament. As for the New Testament, "all flesh have seen him" (cf Is 40.5; Lk 3.6) in accordance with prophecy. According to St John, "the life was made manifest" (1 Jn 1.2). Christ says, "He who has seen me has seen the Father" (Jn 14.9), also promising that "he who loves me . . . I will love him and manifest myself to him" (Jn 14.21). Again St Paul also preaches, "For the Spirit searches everything, even the depths of God" (1 Cor 2.10).

From all this, it becomes clear that what had been impossible for man to reach by effort or worthiness, that is, to see the Lord, has become possible with the appearance of the Lord. The appearance of the Lord is an act of love and a gratuitous work of grace, for the attempt to see the Lord is impossible for man to realize except for a small part. This part is proportionate to man's chastity, love, and obedience to God's commandments. As for the appearance of the Lord, it is granted to man unconditionally and without any effort or worthiness on his part. For God grants ability and saintliness to man by which he may see God as he is, that is, as God may wish to reveal himself at will. This fact is clear from the saying of the Lord: "All things have been delivered to me by my Father; and no one knows who the Son is except the Father, or who the Father is except the Son and any one to whom the Son chooses to reveal (ἀποκαλύψας) him" (Lk 10.22). The word *reveal* here indicates appearance by vision.

From these words of the Lord, what is being explained is that the appearance or revelation of the Father or the Son, which is the same as knowing the essential attributes of God, is a matter that inevitably and necessarily hangs on the will of Jesus Christ and his mediation. Vision through the revelation of Christ in his manifest human appearance leads to clear knowledge. By Christ's true appearance and manifestation in human form, man perceives the truth that exists in God, and with this truth, he reaches ultimate joy and comes to the very core of communion and abiding with God.

To see fully the importance of vision in Orthodox belief, we should refer to the early church fathers and trace their ideas, experiences, and expressions on the life of vision in Christianity. The Christian life of vision is considered the direct expression of faith. It likewise directly expresses the efficacy of the incarnation. For their ideas on vision, we have chosen to cite three of the early theologians who held both to the gospel and also to patristic tradition without deviation.

Theophilus of Antioch

This saintly father wrote a letter to a pagan in about A.D. 178, explaining to him what seeing God means. He wrote this letter to answer the man's challenge to show him the God of the Christians if he could:

> **65.** But if you say, "Show me thy God," I would reply, "Show me your-self, and I will show you my God." Show, then, that the eyes of your soul are capable of seeing, and the ears of your heart able to hear . . . For God is seen by those who are enabled to see him when they have the eyes of their soul opened . . . So also when there is sin in man, such a man cannot behold God . . . The appearance of God is ineffable and indescribable and cannot be seen by eyes of flesh . . . When thou shalt have put off the mortal and put on incorruption, then shalt thou see God worthily. For God will raise thy flesh immortal with thy soul; and then, having become immortal, thou shalt see the Immortal, if now you believe in him. (Theophilus to Autolycus, 1.2, 3, 7, ANF 2.89, 91)

These words of Theophilus of Antioch are an extension of those of St Paul about God, "Who alone has immortality and dwells in unapproachable light, whom no man has ever seen or can see" (1 Tim 6.16). He speaks explicitly of the eschatological vision for which man will be qualified when he puts on incorruptibility or immortality. It is then that he becomes at the same level with the nature of God "who alone has immortality."

It is noteworthy here that the attribute of immortality belongs to God alone. Man will only put on immortality that is of the nature of God and of his very essence. Thus, true vision of God can never be attained unless man reaches the stage of incorruptibility, that is, immortality. This applies not to the soul alone but to the flesh as well in the resurrection. For vision cannot be complete to man except as a whole, that is, body and soul together. In immortality there will be no struggle or contradiction between lucid reason and bodily senses.

But Theophilus of Antioch also expounds the capability of knowing God and holding to the splendor of his glory here and now. This takes place in preparation for the perfect eschatological vision:

> **66.** All things God has made out of things that were not into things that are, in order that through his works his greatness may be known

and understood . . . For as the soul in man is not seen, being invisible to men, but is perceived through the motion of the body, so God cannot indeed be seen by human eyes, but is beheld and perceived through his providence and works. (Theophilus to Autolycus, 1.4, 5, ANF 2.90)

Here, the words of Theophilus of Antioch are an extension of St Paul's words: "For what can be known about God is plain to them, because God has shown it to them. Ever since the creation of the world, his invisible nature, namely, his eternal power and deity, has been clearly perceived in the things that have been made. So they are without excuse" (Rom 1.19–21).

Theophilus then proceeds to form a live mental vision of God out of his works in creation as a practical application of the words of St Paul:

67. The appearance of God is ineffable and indescribable and cannot be seen by eyes of flesh . . . For if I say he is Light, I name but his own work; if I call him Word, I name but his sovereignty; if I call him Mind, I speak of His wisdom; if I say he is Spirit, I speak of his breath; if I call him Wisdom, I speak of his offspring; if I call him Strength, I speak of his sway; if I call him Power, I am mentioning his activity; if Providence, I but mention his goodness; if I call him Kingdom, I but mention his glory; if I call him Lord, I mention his being judge; if I call him Judge, I speak of him as being just; if I call him Father, I speak of all things as being from him; if I call him Fire, I but mention his anger . . . and all things God has made out of things that were not into things that are, in order that through his works his greatness may be known and understood. (Theophilus to Autolycus, 1.3, 4, ANF 2.89, 90)

Thus, Theophilus of Antioch has given us the contents of the present vision, which suits the life of this age. He has revealed the attributes of God that we have to recognize through his works in the creation. This is an inevitable preparation for the eschatological vision that suits the life of immortality. Though it be an indirect vision now, it nevertheless unveils the essential attributes of God as Father, Son, and Holy Spirit.

In short, St Theophilus of Antioch indisputably proves from the very essence of the gospel that God, although now directly imperceptible in himself, can yet be perceived in his works. This takes place in proportion to one's faith to a degree that may result in direct perception. For so the Father is: though he is totally hidden from every mind and eye, yet he is manifest in his

Son and by his Holy Spirit. As the Bible says: "No one has ever seen God; the only Son, who is in the bosom of the Father, he has made him known [or made clear and explained: ἐξηγήσατο]" (Jn 1.18). As Christ says, "He who has seen me has seen the Father" (Jn 14.9). This means that the works of Christ and his attributes reveal the truth and nature of the Father as being his own Father who had sent him.

St Irenaeus

St Irenaeus also supplies us with apostolic teachings, which he wrote about A.D. 190, in which he explains the meaning of seeing God. He begins his teachings by clarifying the gradual appearances that God has completed in the Word since the beginning. He considers the Word—that is, the Logos—"a true manifestation of the Father who can never be physically seen."

> **68.** And who, as regards his greatness, is indeed unknown . . . but as regards his love, he is always known through him by whose means he ordained all things. (*Against Heresies,* 4.20.4, ANF 1.488)

Wherefore the Son reveals the knowledge of the Father through his own manifestation. For the manifestation of the Son is the knowledge of the Father.

> **69.** For the Father is the invisible of the Son, but the Son the visible of the Father. (*Against Heresies,* 4.6.6, ANF 1.469)

> **70.** Peter says in his Epistle: "Whom, not seeing, ye love; in whom, though now ye see him not, ye have believed, ye shall rejoice with joy unspeakable" (1 Pet 1.8), neither do we receive another Holy Spirit, besides him who is with us, and who cries, "Abba, Father" (Rom 8.15), and we shall make increase in the very same things [as now], and shall make progress, so that no longer through a glass, or by means of enigmas, but face to face, we shall enjoy the gifts of God. (*Against Heresies,* 4.9.2, ANF 1.472)

St Irenaeus proceeds further to explain that after the incarnation, the manifestation of God in man as regards man's gradual spiritual progress has become the responsibility of man. By the Holy Spirit, he materializes in himself this likeness which God has offered him. This gradual growth in the Spirit surpasses man's ability—physical, psychic, and spiritual—all together. For this reason, God gave man his own Holy Spirit to endow him with the ability to grow. He raised him to the level of God's life on account of the image and likeness that are deeply rooted in him and that have been blurred by man's weakness and sin.

Thus, God granted man, through his Son and his Holy Spirit, to grow and progress in the spirit. This growth is meant to go on until man reaches the life of communion and union with the Father:

> **71.** If therefore, at the present time, having the earnest, we do cry, "Abba, Father" what shall it be when, on rising again, we behold Him face to face; when all the members shall burst out into a continuous hymn of triumph, glorifying him who raised them from the dead and gave the gift of eternal life? (*Against Heresies,* 5.8.1, ANF 1.533)

To St Irenaeus, the vision of God is always a revelation on the part of God, which he perfects according to his will. God, to Irenaeus, is not a topic to investigate or know. God is a self with which one cannot be acquainted unless he declares and reveals it. He but reveals himself by his own choice only because of his love and as a kind of vouchsafing.

Thus, when God says he "cannot be seen," this saying is as true as "I reveal myself." For what man cannot achieve by effort and ascension, God can do by love and condescension. For this reason, God says he is ready to declare himself to him who loves him and is truly humble. In this vein, St Irenaeus says:

> **72.** For man does not see God by his own powers; but when he pleases he is seen by men, by whom he wills, and when he wills, and as he wills. (*Against Heresies,* 4.20.5, ANF 1.489)

It is as if St Irenaeus wants to say that God, although he cannot be physically seen, can nevertheless be spiritually seen through grace.

In examining the entire teachings of St Irenaeus we can find three kinds of visions:

1. That which occurs through the inspiration of the Holy Spirit. St Irenaeus calls this *prophetic vision*. It is a vision in which the likeness of God's glory is manifested.

2. That which occurs through Jesus Christ. This St Irenaeus calls *vision of sonship*. This kind of vision is only for the elect.

3. That which comes by seeing God. St Irenaeus calls this *vision of the Father*. It is a face-to-face vision of life in the kingdom of heaven.

The three visions are directly linked. The prophetic vision through the Holy Spirit prepares for the vision of sonship in Christ. This in turn ushers man into a complete vision of the Father. The Father then grants immortality to man. During this progression, man can be quite certain that he is actually seeing God, for these three visions are very intricate. Each conceals the other behind it.

> **73.** The Spirit truly preparing man in the Son of God, and the Son leading him to the Father, while the Father, too, confers [upon him] incorruption for eternal life, which comes to every one from the fact of his seeing God. (*Against Heresies,* 4.20.5, ANF 1.489)

From this teaching, we can see that St Irenaeus is certain that the vision of the Father in the kingdom of heaven imparts a communion in eternal life. It grants man immortality. Here is a magnificent elucidation of the relationship that exists between total vision and immortality. From this, how man cannot see the face of God and live (Ex 33.20) becomes clear. It means the sinner has to die first so that the corruptible may change to uncorrupted and incorruptible. It is only then that man may see God's face and live forever.

Man cannot see the face of God without death. In the life to come and the resurrection from the dead, this face becomes a fountain of new life. To this effect, St Irenaeus says:

> **74.** Men therefore shall see God, that they may live, being made immortal by that sight and attaining even unto God. (*Against Heresies,* 4.20.6, ANF 1.489)

> **75.** It is not possible to live apart from life, and the means of life is found in fellowship with God; but fellowship with God is to know God and to enjoy His goodness. (*Against Heresies,* 4.20.5, ANF 1.489)

> **76.** The manifestation of God which is made by means of the creation, affords life to all living in the earth. (*Against Heresies,* 4.20.7, ANF 1.489)

St Irenaeus then turns again to this life and considers it a partial communion with God. So it is a partial vision, which has been most clearly manifested by the incarnation of the Son of God. It has become a mutual vision. On the one hand, God declared or revealed himself with the incarnation of the Word, who is Christ. On the other hand, the Word revealed man, manifested him and presented him to God.

77. Revealing God indeed to men, but presenting man to God. (*Against Heresies,* 4.20.7, ANF 1.489)

Such is the essential vision mutually exchanged between man and God that has been substantially effected by and in the incarnation. This vision was granted to mankind through Jesus Christ and through his body: "He who eats me will live because of me" (Jn 6.57). Consequently, the sphere of quickening vision, or the sphere of actual communion with the Father through the Son and the Holy Spirit, has been opened to us.

78. For the glory of God is a living man; and the [eternal] life of man consists in beholding God. For if the manifestation of God which is made by means of the creation, affords life to all living in the earth, much more does that revelation of the Father which comes through the Word [Logos] give life to those who see God. (*Against Heresies,* 4.20.7, ANF 1.490)

The cornerstone on which St Irenaeus builds his notion of total vision is the transfiguration of Christ on Mount Tabor.

79. And that the paternal light might meet with and rest upon the flesh of our Lord, and come to us from His resplendent flesh, and that thus man might attain to immortality, having been invested with the paternal light. (*Against Heresies,* 4.20.2, ANF 1.488)

The will of Christ to declare his glory through clear vision on the Mount of Transfiguration expresses the will of God in making man a partaker in the invisible light of God. This light will be granted to him afterward forever to make him no longer subject to death and so live forever. To this effect, St Irenaeus says:

80. For as those who see the light are within the light and partake of its brilliancy; even so, those who see God are in God, and receive of His

splendor. But [his] splendor vivifies them; those, therefore, who see
God, do receive life. (*Against Heresies,* 4.20.5, ANF 1.489)

St Irenaeus considers vision a knowledge of God that extends to infinity,
even in eternal life:

> **81.** But also in that which is to come, so that God should for ever teach,
> and man should for ever learn the things taught him by God. (*Against
> Heresies,* 3.28.3, ANF 1.399)

In short, St Irenaeus considers the vision of God to be realistic and essential to man whether in this life or in the life to come. Now it is by partial
communion. We see the invisible and imperceptible God in the light of Jesus
Christ. He is the imparter of resurrection and eternal life. The vision of Jesus
Christ now is a life-giving vision. It dresses man in the potentiality of immortality. It thus inevitably prepares for seeing the Father. This is the very essence
of eternal life or immortality.

St Cyril of Alexandria

The theology of St Cyril is a lucid and agreeable orthodox theology that satisfies one's spirit and sets it ablaze. To St Cyril, vision is an essential merging
with God that is pleasing to one's faith, bringing to man the joy of salvation
rather than gratification for his intellect. Knowledge is not the means to reach
God. On the contrary, knowledge is the result, fruit, and gift of the indwelling
of the Holy Spirit within us. St Cyril thus turned all the standards of Ori-
genism topsy-turvy.

Perhaps one of the direct influences that oriented the theology of St Cyril
the Great and St Athanasius before him was the life of St Antony and his
attainment of full grace and virtuous perfection, together with all the spiritual
gifts, which derive not from speculative contemplation, but from faith, life,
simplicity of heart, and practical application of the gospel. St Antony, from this
simple life of faith and belief in the gospel, managed to acquire all the qualifications for partaking of the divine nature by direct communication with
Christ in the intimacy of love, sacrifice, and prayer.

One of the gorgeous attributes of St Cyril's theology is that he does not
set down union with God as a result of ascetical struggles, purgation, or

contemplative thoughts. Our union with him has been already accomplished and perfected in us by the incarnation; we are sons of the living God through Christ, or sons by "partnership" (*De recta fide,* 30, PG 76.1177), one might say. Our *union* with divine nature is an expression exactly tantamount to our *sonship* to God. This we acquire as a gift from God by faith in Christ and the indwelling of the Holy Spirit, who immediately testifies to our spirits that we have become sons to God.

St Cyril the Great says that our communion in the divinity of Christ means our union with the Trinity, which in its turn allows the divine nature to pervade and permeate us, just as fire heats a piece of iron and makes it glow. All we have to do after believing in Christ and discovering our communion with him is to give the divine, ineffable beauty of the nature of the Trinity the chance to dawn within us, to glow and to shine (*On St John* 17.19, PG 74.544).

To St Cyril, ascetical struggle is nothing but an attempt to be in conformity with the Holy Spirit, which is actually within us, and to be in harmony with the thought of Christ, which actually fills us. The Holy Spirit, which God gives us as soon as he dwells in us, qualifies us for acquiring the likeness of Christ, and consequently, we become a real image of the Father (*On St John* 17.18, 19, PG 74.541). When we acquire the likeness of Christ by the indwelling of the Holy Spirit in us, we become "sons by partnership," and when we partake of the divine nature as sons with Christ we become in union with God through the Holy Spirit.

82. If it should happen that we would lose our intimacy with the Holy Spirit—which is a matter so improbable even in the direst conditions—we should never hope for the dwelling of God within us. (*On St John* 17.19, PG 74.545A)

The Holy Spirit is not only the fountain of spiritual life in the soul but is also the source and foundation of spiritual knowledge; it is he who makes us sense what grace is in this life. Thus, total knowledge of God, that is, vision in its utmost sense, is not a final objective of our life to seek after now or in the age to come. It is integral to the life of partnership we live, within the essence of the divine nature by faith from the very first moment the Holy Spirit dwelt in us.

83. For to the pure in heart the mystery of the vision of God (θεοπτίας) will be clearly revealed . . . Therefore it is true that knowing these things well, the Saints sometimes say, *Unto us God revealed them through the Spirit;* sometimes, *But we have the mind of Christ,* meaning by his mind his Spirit. (*On St John* 14.21, PG 74.284–5)

As to our growth in the complete perception of God, it is bound to our sacramental life: Total knowledge of Christ begins with baptism, where we acquire enlightenment by the Holy Spirit (*On Exodus* 2, PG 69.432A). Even the flesh—in this present life—partially partakes of the mystery of union with God, particularly in the sacrament of the Eucharist in a mutual bodily communion with Christ (*On St John* 6.54, PG 73.577).

We notice here that the total perception of St Cyril, which is nothing but vision in its brightest sense, and the mystical union with God, which St Cyril time and again calls "deification," are not so much objectives to seek after as truths that man attains in spirit in the sacraments as gifts of grace. Vision does not stand on the top of a meticulous contemplative method, but is an enlightenment accomplished by the indwelling of the Holy Spirit. Union, which is the end of all ends, is not a faraway goal to reach, but is treasured in the sacrament of Holy Communion. It is as easy and realistic as eating the morsel or drinking the cup. Man has nothing to do afterward except to realize what is latent within it, abide in what has been granted to him, manifest by act and deed the mercy that he has gratuitously received, and respond to the debt of love that has been poured into his heart by the Holy Spirit.

In the theology of St Cyril, we find no reference to the method of Dionysius the Areopagite, whom the majority of theologians in the East and West, including Western mystics in particular, drew upon. This apophatic method is engrossed with describing the abstract way to the knowledge of God in darkness, nothingness, namelessness, and nonexistence in relation to God. St Cyril sees God in the brightness of his light, which is manifested in the face of Christ, who came to disperse every sense of darkness and to enlighten every man in the world. St Cyril reiterates the words *light* and *enlightenment* in all his definitions and cognitions of God.

St Cyril acquaints himself with God's perfections by that shining vision in his heart which is the work of the Holy Spirit, where man is originally granted the mind of Christ, by which he sees, loves, and approaches the Father with all the boldness and courage of the Son and with the faith and intimacy of Christ.

We never find St Cyril so presumptuous as to search for God without the guidance of the Spirit or his illuminating leadership, which enlightens man's heart and mind. Hence, St Cyril's theology never bumps into the darkness that envelops God and conceals the glory of the godhead from the human mind undeified by Christ or the Holy Spirit.

For St Cyril, Christ is the Sun of Righteousness who came to us, we who were dwelling in darkness, to enlighten our souls with the light of the true knowledge of God. For he revealed the Father to us in himself and qualified us for the transcendent mysteries (*On Malachi* 4.2–3, PG 72.360AC).

In the theology of St Cyril, we find that the only difference between the vision of God in the present and that in the life to come is that Christ in the present life grants us his light and mind in proportion to the needs of our salvation and in a manner that qualifies us for the first resurrection. In the life to come, he will lavish on us his light and thought to the uttermost needs of our life with the Father, together with what the total vision of the Father may require where "we shall see him as he is" (*On St John* 16.25, PG 74.464B).

It is thus evident from the profound but easy theology of St Cyril that it is absolutely impossible for us to acquire a clear and complete vision of God without the mediation of Christ. It is Christ who works in us through his person and the mystery of his incarnation, and then through that of his death, and last of all through that of his resurrection and glorification. The glory of the Father, to St Cyril, cannot be seen except through the glory of Christ, since the glory of Christ is nothing but the manifestation and power of the glory of the Father: "Christ was raised from the dead by the glory of the Father" (Rom 6.4). Likewise, the glory of the Father cannot be manifested except through the manifestation of the glory of Christ: "When he comes in his glory and the glory of the Father" (Lk 9.26).

St Cyril often focuses upon the point that the essence of vision is the manifestation of the Father's nature, which in terms of feelings and from our contemplative point of view is a transcendent beauty "the beauty of the divine nature," and what we partake of is this very beauty through the mediation of the Holy Spirit (*Thesaurus* 34, PG 75.612A).

As for the glory of Christ, it shines in the mind as new knowledge or vision. St Cyril the Great calls it "divine insight" (in Greek, Θεία σύνεσις), which is the same way of expression used by St Paul: "that the God of our Lord Jesus Christ, the Father of glory, may give a spirit of wisdom and of revelation in the knowledge of him, having the eyes of your hearts enlightened, that you may know what is the hope to which he has called you, what are the riches of his glorious inheritance" (Eph 1.17, 18), which takes place when the Holy Spirit sets afire the soul and deifies human nature. Man would then see Christ face to face through the mediation of the Holy Spirit. The vision of Christ leads us to a mystical communion in the Trinity, which will be manifested by total enlightenment in the age to come.

We can also notice in Alexandrian theology in general, which St Cyril the Great represents, a recurrent focusing on the glory of Christ and that of the Father as the essence of manifestation and vision. St Cyril expresses the vision-ary description of the glory of Christ most magnificently with his theological feelings as "the beauty of the divine nature" and considers this beauty an object of communion and ineffable joy, just as the Bible says: "That you may also rejoice and be glad when his glory is revealed" (1 Pet 4.13).

SAYINGS OF THE FATHERS ON THE VISION OF GOD

What Is the Vision of God?

St Antony the Great dwells on the definition of vision of God, its action in the soul, and its fruits. He draws upon the experience of the apostle Paul, in which he says that he has seen the Lord as the other apostles saw him. This, St Antony claims, was not the conjuring of the facile eye, which sees nothing in Christ except a feeble man. No, it was an unveiled mental vision, which sees him as a glorified God:

84. For he (the apostle Paul) was freed from evil and then he was not enslaved to any kind of passion for he had become an ascetic, and last of all, he was liberated by seeing the Lord Jesus Christ. And when he saw him, he at once followed his word, reaching the utmost perfection and humility. Likewise, all those who hold fast to the word of the Lord know the truth, and the truth makes them free, and it frees their souls from all evil, just as the apostle Paul was freed. For our Savior proclaimed him free. For this reason St Paul said of himself: Am I not free? . . . Have I not seen Jesus our Lord, I saw him as the first [disciples] did (cf 1 Cor 9.1).

Many say, in their ignorance, that they have seen the Lord Jesus as the apostles saw him. These people, my children, are deceived and have no eyes to see: they do not see the Lord as the apostle saw. For the apostle (Paul) saw the Lord just as the disciples saw him, just as the people of the Lord's time who believed in him saw him, just as any one in the crowds around him saw him, a man. When the woman who was afflicted with a flow of blood saw him with the eyes of her heart, and believed he was God and touched the edge of his garment in faith, she was delivered . . . But Pilate and Annas and Caiaphas saw the Lord just as the rest of the crowd saw him, with the eyes of the body only. They did not look at him trustingly as the apostle had done. For that reason they gained nothing from the sight of him.

The apostle saw him with the eye of his heart, with his strong trust, just as the woman with the flow of blood saw him, the woman who touched him in faith and was healed. In the same way, our Lord Jesus Christ appeared to his apostle Paul after he had overcome his passion and made him free. Likewise, whoever is freed from affliction looks to the Lord with the eyes of his heart and is freed, but he cannot look at that radiant light that Paul saw, with the eyes of his body . . . For the Lord does not appear to those who are not subject to affliction, for so it is written of Isaiah the prophet: That the Lord forbade him from prophesying and no longer appeared to the prophet because he had not censured King Uzziah. After the death of Uzziah the angel of the Lord appeared to him and purified him with the burning coal and the fiery tongs.

Know then, my beloved children, that if a man has died to the authority of sin, then God appears to his soul and purifies it and his body together. If the authority of sin is still alive in the body, man cannot see God. For his soul is in darkness, and light, the vision of God, cannot appear in it. David says: "In thy light do we see light" (Ps 36.9). What is this light by which man sees God? It is the light that our Lord Jesus Christ mentioned in the gospel: "If then your whole body is full of light, having no part dark, it will be wholly bright" (Lk 12.36). Again he said: "No one knows the Father except the Son and anyone to whom the Son chooses to reveal him" (Mt 11.27). My children, the Son does not reveal his Father to the children of darkness but only to those who abide in light, the children of light. He has illumined the eyes of their hearts with the knowledge of the commandments . . . When Moses was delivered from the bondage of Pharaoh, he was freed and made worthy to look upon the burning bush which was not consumed. He said that it was a glorious vision with a beginning, a central mystery, and a final perfection.

Know my children that these visions of God are for the imperfect, as glanc-
ings in a mirror (cf Jas 1.23–24). But as for those who have reached perfection:
the eyes of their hearts are opened and a glorious light is revealed to them in
ease and not in toil. For the eyes of those who are perfect retain none of the
darkness of sin. As the apostle Paul says, we will, with unveiled faces, behold
the glory of God as one looking into a mirror, and our selves will be changed
from one glory to another (cf 2 Cor 3.18) . . . from virtue to more perfect virtue.
This transition, this progress, is what brings us near to the Lord. We reach a
powerful, compelling vision of knowledge, for the Lord says that those who
draw near to him know his power (cf Lev 10.3). In the mind that has not yet
drawn near to God the devil grows, like a cedar of Lebanon; but if the mind
draws near to God and unites with him, he becomes one with him. The Hypocrite [that is, Satan] having once towered over the mind like a Lebanese cedar,
no longer appears. David says: "I have seen a wicked man overbearing, and
towering like a cedar of Lebanon. Again, I passed by, and lo, he was no more;
though I sought him, he could not be found." David sought the Hypocrite only
because he was in fact pursuing the knowledge of God [and wanted to rid himself of the devil], and when he says "I passed by," meaning "I passed over and
progressed," as he says in Psalm 42: "I passed from the miraculous tent to the
house of God" (Ps 42.4 LXX). This is the passing over that reveals the raising of
the soul to perfection, after being away from God . . .

Therefore, my children, do hard to reach to see God by the spiritual *theoria*, by the grace of our Lord Jesus Christ, he who is glorified by all beings, with
his Father and the Holy Spirit, from now and to the end of all ages. Amen.
(St Antony, *Letters* 17.1–11, in "The Letters of St Antony the Great," Manuscript 23, Arabic version)

From this experiential account by St Antony the Great, we find the bases of
spiritual sight and vision of God clearly set in order:
    1. To prepare for seeing God man should get rid of all passions and sins,
and their effects.
    2. He should practice the kinds of virtues that lead to a state of asceticism.
    3. He must have a yearning for God and a love for truth.
    4. Through the vision of truth, which is God, he is delivered from bondage
to sin and promoted to the status of child of God, who does not sin.

Saint Antony also describes the meaning of vision of God. He distinguishes
between bodily and spiritual vision. The latter is an absolute mental vision that

occurs through the eye of faith. He explains how this gift may be withdrawn once man returns to violating God's commandments. This he illustrates by the example of the prophet Isaiah, who had to be purified by the burning coal from God's altar, that the gift of vision might return to him. St Antony also distinguishes between the unclear vision of those who have not reached perfection and the unveiled vision of those who have.

Saint Antony attaches great importance to the experience of the mind when it approaches God and attains this vision. He also explains how this mind may become a dwelling place for the devil if it strays away from the knowledge of God or gives up contemplation.

St Antony was the first to sketch the way to the contemplation of truth and the vision of God. He has opened this wonderful gate to the saints who succeeded him both in the East and in the West.

In Search of the Absolute

85. I entered even into my inmost self, Thou being my Guide. I entered and beheld with the eye of my soul, above the same eye of my soul, above my mind, the Light Unchangeable, not this ordinary light which all flesh may look upon, nor as it were a greater of the same kind, as though the brightness of this should be manifold brighter, and with its greatness take up all space. Not such was this Light, but other, yea, far other from all these. Nor was It above my soul . . . as heaven [is] above earth: but higher than my soul, because It made me; and I below It, because I was made by It. He that knows the Truth, knows what that Light is; and he that knows It, knows Eternity. Love knoweth It. O eternal Truth, and true Love, and lovable Eternity! Thou art my God, to Thee do I sigh day and night. (St Augustine, *Confessions* 7.16, in Butler, *Western Mysticism: The Teachings of SS Augustine, Gregory and Bernard on Contemplation and the Contemplative Life,* pp 42, 61)

86. I search for God not only to believe in him, but also to see something of him. (St Augustine, *On the Psalms* 41.7, in Butler, *Western Mysticism,* p 62)

87. Moses, as we read in Exodus, had yearned to see God, not as he had seen him on the mountain, nor as he saw him in the tabernacle, but in his divine essence without the medium of any bodily creature that might be presented to the senses of mortal flesh. (St Augustine, *The Literal Meaning of Genesis* 12.55, in Butler, *Western Mysticism,* p 79)

88. It was his desire to see God, not by imaginary likenesses of bodies in the spirit but by a vision of the divine essence as far as this can be attained by a rational and intellectual creature. (St Augustine, *The Literal Meaning of Genesis* 12.55, in Butler, *Western Mysticism*, p 82)

In these selected sayings, we can see a yearning for the absolute, mental knowledge of God. It is a longing to see God as he is in his absolute reality, to see him without the mediation of senses, thought, or imagination. We find this yearning clear in St Augustine's narration of his own life. He adduces the example of Moses to prove that this yearning is a truth of the human condition. The desire to see God is something that stirs in the souls of all men. It is a sense that from time to time beguiles our hearts. However, the boldness to declare our need or to ask for its fulfillment differs according to the intimacy that binds each man to God. This intimacy depends on the holy life that he leads before God.

There is nothing strange in man's longing to see God. For he bears within him the Spirit of God: "God's Spirit dwells in you" (1 Cor 3.16); "In him we live and move and have our being" (Acts 17.28). Man will never find rest so long as he is far from God. He will never settle down until his soul feels close to its Maker. In this vein, St Seraphim of Sarov says:

89. If you do not know God, it is impossible for you to have love for him. You cannot love God if you do not see him. And the vision of God comes from the knowledge of him. (St Seraphim of Sarov, in Moore, "Some Aspects of Orthodox Prayer," p 85)

Here we find a nice gradation toward vision. We begin our relationship with knowledge, and knowledge evolves into love, and love aspires to vision, to be strengthened and made fast.

St John of Dalyatha concurs, allowing, to a certain extent, the possibility of seeing God clearly:

90. Beholding the glory of God, filled with assurance and unquestioning reliance on him. They see the nature of God and gaze at that nature which is hidden from all, with a sense of sweet meekness blended with joy. (St John of Dalyatha, *Homily on the Grandeur of Spiritual Beings*, in "Spiritual Elder")

91. Because the glory of his nature, not the essence of his nature, appears to those who love him, it is said that God was never seen by man. St John of Dalyatha, *Homily on the Grandeur of Spiritual Beings*, in "Spiritual Elder")

92. Thus he appeared to each of the holy fathers, exactly as he wished and as it seemed helpful to them. In one manner he appeared to Abraham, in another to Isaac, in another to Jacob, in another to Noah, Daniel, David, Solomon, Isaiah, and to each of the holy prophets. Still in another way to Elias and again differently to Moses . . . To each of the saints, likewise, God appeared as he wished so as to refresh them, to save and lead them into a knowledge of God. (St Macarius the Great, *Homilies* 4.13, in Maloney, *Intoxicated with God: The Fifty Spiritual Homilies of Macarius*)

UNION WITH GOD

Θεία ἕνωσις

"Even as thou, Father, art in me, and I
in thee, that they also may be in us."
(Jn 17.21)

"But he who is united to the Lord
becomes one spirit with him."
(1 Cor 6.17)

U NION WITH GOD, or *theia henosis* (Θεία ἕνωσις), is a concise theological term describing a state that Christ petitioned the Father to grant on our behalf: "that they also may be [one] in us" (Jn 17.21). This petition has been answered for us in the death and resurrection of Christ. We have thus become, according to the apostle Peter, "partakers of the divine nature" (2 Pet 1.4).

The Church sets this aim before its children the moment they enter the baptismal font. According to St Irenaeus, "Through the Holy Spirit, we are raised up to Christ, and through Christ, we are raised up to the Father" (*Against Heresies* 5.36.2, ANF 1.567). Union here is manifested at three levels—Father, Son, and Holy Spirit. According to St Athanasius, "We were made sons in Him" (*Discourses* 2.76, NPNF, 2nd series, 4.389). And union here signifies a firm establishment in an immortal and eternal sonship to God.

The writings of the great church fathers throw into sharp relief the new potentials that human nature as a whole has gained through the incarnation of Christ. There has occurred a change, which the Fathers term as deification, through the mediation of Christ. Human nature has undergone a heavenly re-creation from water and from the Spirit. It has achieved a state of union with God through grace: "For the Son of God became man that we may become God" (*On the Incarnation* 54, NPNF, 2nd series, 4.65).

Owing to the importance of this theological doctrine, which claims the possibility of man's deification, we refer briefly to some of the places where it is met with in the early Fathers:

1. St Justin, *Dialogue with Trypho* 124 (PG 6.765, ANF 1.262): "All men are deemed worthy of becoming "gods," and of having power to become sons of the Highest."

2. Irenaeus, *Against Heresies* 5.1.1 (ANF 1.526).

3. Clement of Alexandria, *The Protreptique* 9.88; 11.114 (ANF 2.203).

4. St Athanasius, *On the Incarnation* 54.3 (NPNF, 2nd series, 4.65): "For he was made man that we might be made God."

5. St Basil the Great, *On the Holy Spirit* 9.23 (PG 32.109BC): "highest of all [gifts], the being made God" (NPNF, 2nd series, 8.16).

6. St Gregory of Nyssa, *Catechetical Discourses* 37 (PG 45.93–97): "The God who was manifested infused himself into perishable humanity for this purpose, viz. that by this communion with Deity mankind might at the same time be deified." (NPNF, 2nd series, 5.506).

The following are some theological excerpts from the Fathers that deal with this major Orthodox doctrine:

93. I pray for a union both of the flesh and spirit of Jesus Christ, the constant source of our life, and of faith and love, to which nothing is to be preferred, but especially of Jesus and the Father. (St Ignatius of Antioch, *Letter to the Magnesians* 1.2, ANF 1.59)

94. For in no other way could we have learned the things of God, unless our Master, existing as the Word, had become man. For no other being had the power of revealing to us the things of the Father, except his own proper Word. What other person "knew the mind of the Lord," or who else "has become his counselor" (Rom 11.34)? Again, we could have learned in no other way than by seeing our Teacher and hearing his voice with our own ears, that, having become imitators of his works as well as doers of his words, we may have communion with him, receiving increase from the perfect one . . . who, redeeming us by his own blood in a manner consonant to reason, gave himself as a redemption for those who had been led into captivity . . . and redeemed them as his own property . . . giving his soul for our souls, and his flesh for our flesh. [Our Lord] has also poured out the Spirit of the Father for the union and communion of God and man, imparting indeed God to men by means of the Spirit, and, on the other hand, attaching man to God by his own incarnation, and bestowing upon us at his coming immortality, durably and truly, by means of communion with God. (St Irenaeus, *Against Heresies* 5.1.1, ANF 1.526)

95. Hail, O light! For in us, buried in darkness, shut up in the shadow of death, light has shone forth from heaven, purer than the sun, sweeter than life here below. That light is eternal life, and whatever partakes of it lives, for this is the meaning of the new creation. . . . He has changed sunset into sunrise, and through the cross brought death to life; and having wrenched man from destruction, he has raised him to the skies, . . . having bestowed on us the truly great, divine, and inalienable inheritance of the Father, deifying man by heavenly teaching, putting his laws into our minds, and writing them on our hearts. (St Clement of Alexandria, *Exhortation to the Heathen* 11.114, ANF 2.203)

96. For he was made man that we might be made God; and he manifested himself by a body that we might receive the idea of the unseen Father; and he endured the insolence of men that we might inherit immortality. (St Athanasius of Alexandria, *On the Incarnation* 54.3, NPNF, 2nd series, 4.65)

97. For by partaking of him, we partake of the Father; because that the Word is the Father's own. Whence, if he was himself too from participation, and not from the Father his essential Godhead and Image, he would not deify, being deified himself. For it is not possible that he, who merely possesses from participation, should impart of that

partaking to others, since what he has is not his own, but the Giver's.
(St Athanasius of Alexandria, *De Synodis* 51, NPNF, 2nd series, 4.477)

98. For man would have not been deified if joined to a creature, or
if the Son were not very God; nor would man have been brought
into the Father's presence, if he had not been his natural and true
Word who had put on the body . . . so also man would not have been
deified if the Word who became flesh had not been by nature from
the Father and true and proper to him. For therefore the union was of
this kind, that he might unite what is man by nature to him who is in
the nature of the godhead, and that his salvation and deification might
be sure. (St Athanasius of Alexandria, *Discourse II Against the Arians* 70,
NPNF, 2nd series, 4.386)

99. Therefore he was not man, and then became God, but he was God,
and then became man, and that to deify us . . .
     . . . all that are called sons and gods, whether in earth or in heaven,
were adopted and deified through the Word. (St Athanasius of Alexandria, *Discourse I Against the Arians* 39, NPNF, 2nd series, 4.329)

100. Who will not admire this? Or who will not agree that such a thing
is truly divine? For if the works of the Word's godhead had not taken
place through the body, man would not have been deified; and again,
if the properties of the flesh (like death, for example) had not been
ascribed to the Word, man would not have been thoroughly delivered
from them. (St Athanasius of Alexandria, *Discourse III Against the
Arians* 33, NPNF, 2nd series, 4.411)

101. For as the Lord, putting on the body, became man, so we men are
deified by the Word as being taken to him through his flesh, and hence-
forward inherit life everlasting. (St Athanasius of Alexandria, *Discourse III Against the Arians* 34, NPNF, 2nd series, 4.413)

102. For he has become man, that he might deify us in himself, and he
has been born of a woman, and begotten of a virgin, in order to trans-
fer to himself our erring generation and in order that we may become
henceforth a holy race, and "partakers of the divine nature," as blessed

Peter wrote. (St Athanasius of Alexandria, *Letter to Adelphos* 4, NPNF, 2nd series, 4.576)

103. And we are deified not by partaking of the body of some man, but by receiving the body of the Word himself. (St Athanasius of Alexandria, *Letter 61 to Maximus* 2, NPNF, 2nd series, 4.578–79)

We find that of all the church fathers, St Athanasius of Alexandria is the one who uses this theological term "deification" most frequently. He explains and highlights at every occasion the essential link between the incarnation of God and the deification of man.

But the deification (θεοποίησις) that the Fathers had in mind does not mean the change of the human nature into a divine one. Rather, it means qualifying human nature for life with God in a communion of love. This is accomplished by lifting the serious barrier that severs the life of man from that of God—namely, sin. This takes place through our ablution and sanctification by the blood of Christ and our partaking of his Body. For this reason, deification—or union in its perfect sense as a life with God—cannot be fulfilled except at the resurrection from the dead. But we have been granted means of grace, commandments, and a divine power by which to conquer sin, the world, and the life of this age. We have thus a new door opened before us. Through this door we can have—here and now—a foretaste of the union with God in communion of love and in obedience.

Therefore, the union of man with God, or deification, is a legitimate aim to seek. This is due to the preexisting union between divinity and humanity in the incarnation. It is Christ, then, who has set it before us as an aim. Union here includes all the gratuitous means of grace—baptism, Holy Communion, and perpetual repentance. Union also includes struggles such as fasting, chastity, bridling of tongue and mind. It involves constant prayer as well as acts of love and humility. It certainly includes as well God's invisible succor to those who strive to reach him.

It is true that union with God is an ultimate aim that cannot be perfected except in the resurrection from the dead. But it is also the outcome of faith and works that must be completed here in this life.

In brief, union with God in the context of this life means a perpetual change from a life according to the flesh into a life according to the Spirit. This change we undergo every day and every hour in faith, effort, and tears. We

have to conform to the will of God. We have to fulfill the demands of his kingdom as declared by the gospel.

What we have to bear always in mind about the potentiality of union with
God is the person of Jesus Christ himself. It is through obedience and love to
Christ that union with God is perfected. It is he who has first completed the
union of divinity and humanity in himself to deliver it to us in a mystery of
transcendent love.

In Christianity, union is a practical reality that we experience in our worship and love for Christ but cannot understand or grasp with our minds.
According to human logic it is inconceivable. But according to the mystery of
the incarnation and the experience of love and faith, it is the truth and a pal-
pable reality.

Union with God is not a subsidiary issue in faith or doctrine. It is the basis
of all faith and doctrine. It is the ultimate aim of God for sending his only Son
to the world to become man: "For he has made known to us in all wisdom and
insight the mystery of his will, according to his purpose which he set forth in
Christ as a plan for the fulness of time, to unite all things in Christ, things in
heaven and things on earth" (Eph 1.9–10).

So the mystery of union between mankind and Christ is the ultimate aim
of the incarnation, the crucifixion, the resurrection—nay, of creation in full.

Let us read what St Macarius the Great says in this respect:

> **104.** Indeed, a great and divine work and wonderful is the soul . . . And
> in one word he created it such as to be his bride and enter into union
> with him so that he may inter-penetrate it and be "one spirit" with it.
> (St Macarius the Great, *Homilies* 46.5–6, in Maloney, *Intoxicated with
> God: The Fifty Spiritual Homilies of Macarius*)

We can thus see that union with God is the foundation of the Church and the
mystery of the gospel. The work of the Church or the aim of the gospel is but
calling mankind to faith in the person of the Lord Jesus. The action of faith in
Christ and its ultimate aim are union of humankind in the mystical body of
Christ. This union aims at manifesting the kingdom of Christ. It also aims at
revealing the kingdom of saints. The kingdom of saints will reign in Christ,
and Christ will reign in it. About this mutual reign or mutual inheritance,
which expresses most strongly the union with God, St Macarius the Great says:

105. This also is what God, the lover of mankind, does to the person who comes to him and ardently desires him. But there is even much more. Impelled by love, he himself, by the goodness which is inherent in him and is all his own, enters with that person "into one spirit" (1 Cor 6.17), according to the apostolic saying.

When a person clings to the Lord and the Lord has pity and loves him in his coming and clinging to him, and when a person has the intention thereafter to remain constantly in the grace of the Lord, they become one spirit and one temperament and one mind, the person and the Lord. And though his body is prostrate on the earth, his mind has its complete conversation with the heavenly Jerusalem, rising up to the third [spiritual] heaven and clinging to the Lord and serving him there.

And he, while sitting on the throne of majesty in the heights, in the heavenly city, is totally turned toward him in his bodily existence. He has indeed placed his image above in Jerusalem, the heavenly city of the saints and he has placed his own image of the ineffable light of his godhead in his body. He ministers to such a person in the city of his body, while he serves him in the heavenly city.

He has inherited him in heaven and he has inherited him on earth. The Lord becomes his inheritance and he becomes the inheritance of the Lord. (St Macarius the Great, *Homilies* 46.3–4, in *Spiritual Homilies*)

From our Church heritage, we can infer that all the facts of theology revealed to the great theologian fathers, who were filled with the Holy Spirit, were actually proved by the simple ascetic fathers. This took place at the level of daily life, conduct, and personal experience in a most vivid and articulate manner. Through the example of these ascetic fathers, we are encouraged to believe and to trust that the Holy Spirit invites us as well to share in this holy and blessed communion with the Father, the Son, and the Holy Spirit.

SAYINGS OF THE FATHERS ON UNION WITH GOD

St Macarius described this spiritual union with God as the holy matrimony of
the soul and God: the soul as the bride and Christ as the heavenly Bridegroom.
But this is not merely a simile. It is a real sacrament, which takes place between
the devout soul and God, making them one spirit. Here are his words in
this respect:

106. He is wounded with love for the heavenly Spirit, and through the grace
that dwells within him, he burns with desire for the Heavenly Bridegroom.
This stirs him to the perfect longing, the longing to be deemed worthy to enter
into the mystical and awe-filled communion with him, in the sanctification of
the Spirit.

The face of the soul is unveiled, its eyes fix upon the Heavenly Bridegroom:
face to face in that ineffable light. Clasping him with full certitude of faith, he
becomes conformed to his death. He yearns always to die for Christ. (St
Macarius the Great, *Homilies* 10.4, in *Spiritual Homilies*)

107. The soul whom Christ, the Heavenly Spouse, has asked to be his bride
in a mystical and divine fellowship has tasted the riches of heaven. This soul
ought to strive diligently, sincerely to please the Bridegroom, Christ . . . it
should display the serenest modesty and love toward him, should behave
becomingly in the house of the Heavenly King. (St Macarius the Great, *Homilies* 15.2, in *Spiritual Homilies*)

108. Do you not understand that heaven and earth will pass away, but
you have been called to immortality, to sonship; a brother and a spouse of
the King?

In the life around us, all that belongs to the spouse, belongs to the bride as
well, and so it is with all things that belong to the Lord, no matter how much
they be, He entrusts to you. (St Macarius the Great, *Homilies* 16.13, in *Spiritual
Homilies*)

In these words, St Macarius tells of the highest gift a Christian may receive.
He who is sanctified by truth is counted worthy for this wonderful mystical
union with Christ, a holy matrimony in the Spirit. The blessed communion
with the Bridegroom and the heritage reserved in Christ's glory are both his.

Here are some other meditations on this union by another saint:

109. Out of the mist of that light, where the Lord is said to dwell, the beams of mercy dazzle onto the mind deserving. The soul beholds the face of its Lord. It is delighted at the taste of his sweetness. It inhales his pure savor . . . It enters in and clasps him, not knowing how to depart except he thrust it away from union with him.

This is an imprisonment in a mountain of light, an engulfing in light. This is what the assumption will be, which is described as the vision of God's glory. (St John of Dalyatha, *Homily on the Visitations of the Spirit* 3, "The degree of perfection," in "Spiritual Elder")

110. The union with your eternity is like the union of the members of the body with their head. But it is the grace of union with your glory and not with your eternal person or essence. It is for the sake of our joy, for we yearn to be changed into a glory such as yours. (St John of Dalyatha, *Homily on the Mystery of the New World*, in "Spiritual Elder")

111. "Even as thou Father art in me and I in thee, that they also may be in us" (Jn 17.21). Blessed is he who has tasted this beatitude . . . Blessed is he whose soul, flesh and bones commingle with this delight. (St John of Dalyatha, *Homily on the Warm Pleasure which Commingles with Those Who Love God when They See His Glory*, in "Spiritual Elder")

112. Each one beholds you inwardly and rejoices at your beauty and marvels and thinks that you dwell in him alone. But in fact, in your perfection, you dwell in everyone . . . Each beholds you in his mind as perfectly present therein, while you are perfectly dwelling in all. (St John of Dalyatha, *Homily on the Revelations of Christ*, in "Spiritual Elder")

113. At that time they will become not clothed in light but they themselves will turn into light: "Then the righteous will shine like the sun in the kingdom of their Father" (Mt. 13.43). There they will no longer see the likeness of God, but the glory of his Godhead. (St John of Dalyatha, *Homily on the Love of God*, in "Spiritual Elder")

114. Their union with God is like the union of fire and iron. The iron retains its properties but it turns into fire, its nature becomes like that of fire. So do the righteous become like God in their nature. This is no lie: I truly assert, by reason of my intimacy with God, that oftentimes those who have attained a love for God see greater and more excellent things. (St John of Dalyatha, *Homily on the Love of God*, in "Spiritual Elder")

115. Once divine light dawns upon the soul, once it unites with it, the soul mentally traverses the whole [physical] creation, in heaven or on earth, be they mountains or oceans or people or solid bodies. It beholds them as they *really* are. It becomes one with them in mental vision . . . From this *theoria* it ascends to the *theoria* of spiritual beings [which have no material substance], and then rises to the sphere of the Holy Light and this vision swallows up the soul. Everything other than that Light then disappears from its sight as if it never existed. The soul then forgets itself in its union with the glory of that Light. (St John of Dalyatha, *Homily on the Theoria which Severs the Mind from the World*, in "Spiritual Elder")

116. Who can understand the mystery of union between the mind and God? The mind becomes confined within God, it shares the likeness of its Creator. It unites with his presence, the divine presence which, pervading all, is greater than all, is beyond all comprehension. What words can ever explain the manner of such union which engulfs the mind and so rids it of all thoughts of distraction, all earthly motion. (St John of Dalyatha, *Homily on the Theoria which Severs the Mind from the World*, in "Spiritual Elder")

Union with God is the aim of the life of prayer and worship. It is a fore-taste of the glory Christians will enjoy in the age to come. This St Macarius describes as "the mystical communion between the soul and the heavenly Bridegroom" and St John of Dalyatha describes as "the strong union which fastens the mind to God." All these expressions articulate the powerful union of the soul and God into one spirit. This is the kingdom of God into which the gospel guides us. It is within us. Once we reach this state we will know what the meaning of perfect love is—love of God with all the heart, soul, and mind and love of neighbor as ourselves.

By union with God we transcend the limits of matter and reach beyond this visible world. This is what the Lord Jesus meant in his prayer to the Father when he said: "I am not praying for the world . . . I am no more in the world . . . I am not of the world . . . I do not pray that thou shouldst take them out of

the world . . . Holy Father, keep them in thy name which thou hast given me
. . . that they may be one even as we are one . . . even as thou, Father, art in me
and I in thee" (Jn 17).

Prayer is the journey to the kingdom: the arrival is union with God. The
kingdom is not far from us, but is within us. The union with God that the
saintly fathers experienced is the end of all endeavors: corporal acts of mercy,
the labor of the soul, or perseverance in spiritual contemplation. "I have fought
the good fight, I have finished the race, I have kept the faith. Henceforth there
is laid for me the crown of righteousness" (2 Tim 4.7).

Those who are redeemed by the blood of the heavenly Bridegroom have
an essential right of their own: the right to strive to reach a vital intimacy with
God—an intimacy that transcends the present world.

Spiritual gifts are dispensed to us. What is needed is all our strength, will,
and mind: the struggle to gain such gifts. Grace, always present with and
within us, aids us in this struggle: "Make love your aim, and earnestly desire
the spiritual gifts . . . So with yourselves; since you are eager for manifestations
of the Spirit, strive to excel in building up the church" (1 Cor 14.1, 12).

A spiritual gift is not to perform signs and wonders. It is to live for the
Spirit and experience and taste his fruits. It is called a "gift" because it transcends the present world. But it does not transcend the afterlife; it is the very
nature of the age to come. If then we are truly not of this world, as Christ
wishes us to be, our conduct has to be identical with the life of the age to come.
We should be bent on proceeding according to the standards of the Spirit and
not those of this world. Our longing should always be for reaching God, for
unity with him.

His divine power has granted to us all things that pertain to life and
godliness, through the knowledge of him who called us to his own
glory and excellence, by which he has granted to us his precious and
very great promises, that through these you may escape from the corruption that is in the world because of passion, and become partakers
of the divine nature. For this very reason make every effort to supple-
ment your faith with virtue, and virtue with knowledge, and knowledge with self-control, and self-control with steadfastness, and
steadfastness with godliness, and godliness with brotherly affection,
and brotherly affection with love. For if these things are yours and
abound, they keep you from being ineffective or unfruitful in the

knowledge of our Lord Jesus Christ. For whoever lacks these things is blind and shortsighted and has forgotten that he was cleansed from his old sins. Therefore, brethren, be the more zealous to confirm your call and election, for if you do this you will never fall; so there will be richly provided for you an entrance into the eternal kingdom of our Lord and Savior Jesus Christ (2 Pet 3–11).

This partaking of the divine nature to which the apostle Peter invites us is the same mystery that the apostle John unveils to us as the "marriage of the Lamb": " 'Let us rejoice and exult and give him the glory, for the marriage of the Lamb has come, and his Bride has made herself ready; it was granted her to be clothed with fine linen, bright and pure'—for the fine linen is the righteous deeds of the saints" (Rev 19.7–8). What is the marriage? Who is the bride clothed with fine linen bright and pure? " 'Come, I will show you the Bride, the wife of the Lamb.' And in the Spirit he carried me away . . . and showed me the holy city Jerusalem . . . having the glory of God" (Rev 21.9, 10, 11).

What is Jerusalem which has "the glory of God" but the Church? What is the Church but the congregation of saints? What is the glory which surrounds them but the power of their union with Christ? It is thus that the Christian church adopted in its earliest period this tradition describing the mystical relationship that binds the chaste soul to Christ: the soul is the redeemed bride adorned with sanctity. The Bridegroom is the Lamb slain for the souls he has betrothed for himself: "I will betroth you for me forever" (Hos 2.19); "For I betrothed you to Christ to present you as a pure bride to her one husband" (2 Cor 11.2). As for the marriage, it is the union that exists between the soul and Christ.

117. He who truly loves God and Christ, though he may perform a thousand good works, considers himself as one who has done nothing because of his insatiable longing for the Lord. Let him tear down the body with fasts and vigils: in his own eyes he has never even yet begun to develop virtues. Let the various gifts of the Spirit, let even revelations and heavenly mysteries be given to him: he believes that he has acquired nothing because of his immense and insatiable love for the Lord.

Hungry, thirsty for faith and love, he daily perseveres in prayer. He has an insatiable desire for the mysteries of grace and for every virtue. He is wounded with love for the heavenly Spirit, and through the grace which dwells within him he burns with desire for the Heavenly Bridegroom. This stirs him to the perfect longing, the longing to be deemed worthy to enter into the mystical and awe-filled communion with him, in the sanctification of the Spirit.

The face of the soul is unveiled, its eyes fix upon the Heavenly Bridegroom: face to face in that ineffable light. Clasping him with full certitude of faith, he becomes conformed to his death. He yearns always to die for Christ. He certainly and completely believes that he will obtain liberation from his sins and his dark passions through the Spirit—so that, soul and body purified by the Spirit, he may become a pure vessel to receive the heavenly unction and become a worthy habitation for Christ, the noble heavenly King. (St Macarius the Great, *Homilies* 10.4, in *Spiritual Homilies*)

118. A maiden, espoused to a wealthy man, may receive any number of gifts before the consummation: ornaments, clothing, or precious vessels. But she is not satisfied until the time of the marriage comes and she arrives at full communion. So also the soul, betrothed to the Heavenly Bridegroom, receives as pledge from the Spirit gifts of healing or of knowledge or of revelation. But it is not satisfied with these until it reaches the perfect communion, that is, of love unchangeable and unfailing. It frees from passion and agitation those who have desired it.

So also, an infant might be decked out with pearls and costly clothing. When it is hungry, it thinks nothing of the things it wears, it cares only for the breast of its nurse—how it may receive milk. So also consider it to be with the spiritual gifts of God to whom be glory forever. Amen. (St Macarius the Great, *Homilies* 45.7, in *Spiritual Homilies*)

Behold the Bridegroom is coming,
See, O my soul, that you sleep not . . .
But watch that you may meet the Lord Christ with the oil of fatness
    and that he may grant thee the true wedding of his divine glory.
           (Midnight Office, First Watch, *Coptic Canonical Hours*)

Aspects of the Interior Activity of Prayer

"Those who have their faculties trained
by practice to distinguish good from
evil." (Heb 5.14)

"In toil and hardship, through many a
sleepless night, in hunger and thirst,
often without food, in cold and
exposure." (2 Cor 11.27)

I N PART ONE WE LOOKED AT everything that is distinctive about prayer. In Part Two, we will look at the attributes of the person who prays. We will be concerned mainly with the factors that contribute to success in prayer and those that impede it. During our discussion, we may deal with matters that relate to the practice of certain virtues—for example, asceticism. However, we will only deal with disciplines that are indispensable: the quintessence of the qualities needed for prayer. Such practices are kinds of interior activity, which are to prayer what burning charcoal is to incense.

The various kinds of asceticism, such as fasting, silence, and constant vigilance, are vital for a life of prayer. They mortify the lust of the Adamic life and the will to sin, which are embedded within our members. We have already gained the right to die to the life of this world—in baptism. We died to our Adamism to receive our Christian life. It comes to us as a free gift of redemption, since Christ has died in our place.

So if we practice a life of asceticism and austerity, it is only as an extension of the death-to-the-world process begun at baptism. Nevertheless, important as this mortification is, it has to be handled with some care. For this reason, we will note down at the outset a few guidelines for the practice of asceticism. This we will do to safeguard our asceticism from any distortion that might lure us away from the right path.

1. We should not see austerity, or asceticism, as an end in itself. Neither should we delight in practicing it to the exclusion of everything else. By doing so we are only allowing it to distract us from progressing toward God and completing our union with him in mature love.

2. Ascetic disciplines are nothing more than the means to mortify the old Adam and crucify our will, our passions, and the desires that work in us for iniquity. Ascesis is only a way of showing our love and tender feelings toward God.

3. Perseverance in practicing the kinds of austerities after being renewed and filled with grace serves only to counter the tendency to hanker after what the world offers. It helps to restrain the will from inclining toward sin.

4. If we make progress in such a discipline, this should not become a matter of pride. If it does, we will open ourselves up to the spirit of self-righteousness. This will immediately arrest our spiritual growth.

5. The most austere asceticism can never erase even a single sin. It cannot atone for the slightest transgression we may have committed. Such is the case if that austerity is devoid of love toward God or of the intercession of free grace. For this is only attainable by the blood of Christ.

6. Our asceticism should not be so severe as to be cruel to our own body. It should not prevent us from performing the daily tasks of life actively.

7. Our attention should be inwardly focused upon the will, which drives us to lust and sin. This perverse will of ours craves for what belongs to it. All its aims terminate at one point: the ego. The ego is our enemy. We have to struggle against it with our fasts and vigils until it dies completely. It is only then that we will possess the new will, which carries out the will of God alone.

8. Asceticism should not assume the form of a bodily suppression or repression. For once the practice of ascesis disappears, the result is an acute reaction. Man returns to his former state or even to a more depraved one. Asceticism should be soberly and wisely practiced, not out of grief or pain but in joy and happiness. The limits of the ascetic life should be set by the guidance of a prudent spiritual father. Those who practice it should not underreach or overreach the limits of their abilities. Otherwise, the practice may cease altogether, in which case the ascetic life will lose its desired fruit. Ascetic discipline should begin below the level of one's ability. It should then ascend and grow until it turns into a natural personal quality that forms a major part of one's way of life.

9. If ascetic discipline is devoid of love and joy in the Lord, it turns into a source of depression, sullenness, and perturbation. It may also be a cause of pride and self-righteousness.

10. Many are those who have struggled and freed themselves from the world by the most severe austerities. However, since they did not submit themselves to the hand of God and the work of grace in lowliness and humility, they have gone astray. If we are freed from the world, we must also be freed from ourselves, so that God can take us and shape us freely.

CHAPTER FOUR

The Freeing of the Soul

"Desiring nothing, fearing nothing in
this world, I seemed to myself to stand,
as it were, on the summit of things."
(St Gregory the Great, *Epistles* 1.5, "To
Theoctista," NPNF, 2nd series, 12B.75)

T HE HUMAN SOUL IS CREATED light and pure. It is quickly responsive to
the call of God. It has a strong desire to abide with him and cleave to
him. It has the freedom to soar up high. It also has a loving disposition toward
its own kind, that is, toward every other human soul. It is open to the feelings
of others without reserve. It is thus extremely loving and openhearted by
nature. By such nature it can form one perfect entity of love and intimacy and
live in harmony with God and man.

In a human soul that is true to God, the elements of power, quickness, freedom, and pure love are unlimited. They have a limitless capacity for growth,
increase, and integrity. For the human soul draws continually upon God to
gain these properties. What is it then that shackles the airiness of the soul,
checks its movement, and takes away its freedom? The answer to this question is most crucial. It is the prime issue in the spiritual life.

There is an element that weighs down heavily upon the soul. It pulls
it down to the earth and brings its motion to a halt. It deprives it of its freedom and hampers its expansion and growth. Once we discover this element,
we will be able to focus our attention, struggle, and prayers upon it until we
are set free. As for this dangerous and hostile power, it is nothing but the
human ego.

The human ego (or self) can will what God does not will. It can desire and
covet what is against God's will. It can move against his orders, paying no heed
to his call or warning. It can reject his counsel and despise his love. It can slight
his kindness and long-suffering. Last of all, it can bring about man's own
destruction.

But is the human ego (or self) something other than the human soul? In fact, the ego is nothing other than the soul. Here, two states are possible. First, the soul might be totally subject to God, and the human ego would then not be independent, that is, it would not have an existence independent of God—the ego's will would then be God's will and its desire his desire. In this case, the human ego would be well prepared for perpetual existence with God and in God. It would be dead to itself and alive to God.

Or, the soul might not be subject to God, choosing freely to be independent of his will, following its own passions and desires. In this case the human ego would be alive to itself and dead to God. It becomes a being independent of him, but in fact, it cannot exist except in evil, based on materialistic delusion. This independence from God, this existence in sin, is only transient. So the ego that is independent of God becomes a perishable ego.

However, departure of the ego from God's will is only induced by the deception of the devil, like the deception of the serpent to Eve in paradise: "But I am afraid that as the serpent deceived Eve by his cunning, your thoughts will be led astray from a sincere and pure devotion to Christ" (2 Cor 11:3).

Is there any means, then, by which we can mortify the human ego to itself that it may live to God? Yes. But the only means is total submission to the will of God. For in total submission, any independence on the part of the human ego is done away with. Submission here means total surrender to God's will, whether as to what has happened or what is actually happening or what will be happening, without anxiety, grumbling, or despair. Not that man should stop his efforts to solve problems, avoid damage, or make decisions with a watchful spiritual will drawn from God. But he should surrender himself to the will of God in total contentment with the final results after he has spent his utmost efforts. Man has always to make sure that his will is the same as the will of God. He should not do anything in pride, folly, or rashness prompted by his own private will.

But how can the submission of the human ego to God be effected in such a manner as to release the soul and let it live in total surrender to the will of God? The following are guidelines for those who choose to submit to God.

1. Never rely on your own wisdom or might or on human strength in any of your works. Otherwise, your mind will become dim and your insight blurred, thus blocking the way for grace to enter you and show you the way of God. You will thus be led astray from truth and fall into the enemy's trap. At the end, you will be enslaved to your own ego and to the desires of other

people. "Woe to those who are wise in their own eyes, and shrewd in their own sight!" (Is 5.21).

2. Beware of thinking highly of yourself. Never feel that without you the world would stop. For your self would seem great and grand in your own eyes. Know instead that God can use another to do work better than you. He can make the weak mighty and the mighty weak, the wise foolish and the foolish wise. Everything good and useful in you is from God and not from you. If you do not hand it over to God and with conviction attribute it to him, he will tear it away from you. If you boast of your intelligence or virtue, God will leave them to you as merely human gifts. They will then turn into corruption, loss, and damage.

3. Your ego might hate submitting to God. It might escape surrendering to him. In the meantime, you would be making much of your own power—attributing your intelligence, virtue, and success to yourself. In this case, God will deliver you to continual discipline; discipline after discipline, tribulation after tribulation, until you succumb and surrender in brokenness. But if you reject discipline and cannot stand tribulation, God will forsake you forever.

4. Take heed then and open your ears: Either count yourself as nothing in word and deed and make up your mind to surrender yourself to God with all your might—and you will then gladly be released from your ego by the grace of God; or, you will be delivered to discipline until you are set free from your ego in spite of yourself. So if you wish to opt for the easier way, take that of voluntary submission. Count yourself from now on as nothing, and follow the path of grace wherever the Spirit may wish to lead you.

5. Know for certain that submission to God and total surrender to his will and divine plan are a free gift of grace. It thus demands, besides prayer and supplication, a trusting faith to receive this gift. This should be coupled with a longing springing from one's heart that God may not deliver us to discipline for our folly, nor abandon us to our own wisdom. For this reason, we should have an extremely resolute will to renounce our own self at all times and in all works. This should not be done ostentatiously before people but within our conscience. Blessed is the man who can discover his own weakness and ignorance and confess them before God to the last day of his life.

6. If you fall under discipline, know for sure that this is a great profit, for God chastises the soul that has forgotten its weakness and has been puffed up by its talents and success. This is carried on until it realizes its weakness, especially when God does not provide in tribulation a way of escape. He besieges

the soul from all sides and embitters it with inward and outward humiliation, whether by sin or by scandal, until it abhors itself, curses its own intelligence, and disowns its counsel. Finally, it surrenders itself to God, feeling crushed and lowly. At such a time, it becomes easy for man to hate himself. He even wishes it to be hated by everybody. This is the way of true humility. It leads to total surrender to divine plan. It ends up with freeing one's soul from the tyranny of the ego, with its deception, its stubbornness, and its vanity.

7. If you wish to free your soul by the shortest and simplest way, sit down every day under the discipline of grace. Examine your thoughts, movements, intentions, purposes, words, and deeds in the light of God's word. It is then that you shall discover the corruption of the ego, its imposture, slyness, deception, vanity, and lack of chastity. If you persist in doing this regularly in contrition, you will manage to sever yourself from your false and devilish ego. You will then be able to overpower it bit by bit until you can deny it altogether, hate it, and break jail from its tyranny. You will at last discover the catastrophe into which your ego has led you for obeying it, finding peace in its shelter, boasting of it, and seeking its respect.

The moment you realize at the bottom of your heart that you are nothing and that God is everything, then the truth shall have set you free.

There also exist hidden factors that intermingle with the spiritual motion of the soul. They hamper its movement and throw it headlong on the ground at the end. First among these is ignorance—ignorance of the will of God; ignorance of the narrow way that leads to eternal life; ignorance of the wiles of Satan, who never stops beguiling us that we may fall into pride and then into covetousness and thus disobey God; ignorance of the nonsense of this world and the transience of its glory; ignorance of the meanness of sensual pleasure.

As for ignorance of God's will, its remedy is Bible reading and constant prayer.

As for ignorance of the narrow way, its remedy is courage and striking out fearlessly from this moment onward.

As for ignorance of the wiles of Satan and his guile, its remedy is to stand humbly before God and watch over one's soul.

As for ignorance of the triviality of this world and the transience of its glory, its remedy is an outing to a graveyard!

But there still exists another dangerous factor that sneaks into the life of prayer and confines its scope. It holds sway over its motion and puts out its flame. This consists in the bodily and mental habits and the unchristian conduct and manners that a man may learn from his family. Examples of bodily habits are the pleasure of excessive eating, laziness, and love of much sleep and sexual pleasures (all of which lead to escape from work, struggle, and prayer) as well as the distaste for spiritual reading of intellectual depth or contemplating spiritual matters. Instead, pleasure is found in intellectual sloth, trivial talk, being absorbed in television, reading newspapers, magazines, and worthless books, consigning oneself all day long to all sorts of distractions that have no valuable aim, or staying awake all night long to engage in trivial chatter.

Breaking loose from these bonds cannot be gained except by cutting them off as if with a sharp knife of spiritual verve and putting on the spirit of manhood. For the way of God demands champions in faith and works.

These mental habits are either symptoms of weakness—such as lying, pretension, slander, criticism, hesitation, cowardliness, flattering others, sympathy for one's ego, weeping over hurt pride—or, they might be forms of self-aggrandizement—such as being self-opinionated, stubbornness of thought and mental pride, allowing the use of power, oppression, calumny, and the lust for dominance, despotism, and pontificating. But of whichever fault these habits are symptoms, they are a direct result of the perversion of the self. This is due to its remoteness from God and the lack of total submission to his will and plan. Breaking loose from these bonds is not possible without sincere and contrite repentance under God's hand.

As for unchristian ethics, they consist in habits such as cruel and despotic treatment of servants, making fun of weak or deformed people, despising poor classes, lack of faithfulness in carrying out duties, despising laws and rulers, claiming an eye for an eye, and making little of the rights of others and their dignity. These base morals reveal the gulf that severs the soul from Christ. The remedy consists in nothing other than returning to the meaning of the cross of Christ.

If we tie a bird with a string he will not be able to fly. If he tries to fly while he is tied, his wing will certainly be broken and his body will be bruised. If we afterwards untie him, he will not be able to fly.

How great the number of souls that could fly toward God were they not fastened to the things of this world! It is in vain that man should try to ascend toward God while he is bound with the cords of this earth. Even if he manages to release himself from all of them except one (however little or trivial that one is), he cannot live for God. The peril is even greater because of this last bond. For he will try to take off while weighed down heavily by this thing to which he is still bound. The result is that after becoming airborne for a little while and having the illusion that he is heading for God, he is surprised to find that this thing still weighs him down as before. He thus falls from his spiritual height, and his soul is broken with despair. After repeating this trial, he gives up his passion and enthusiasm for a breakthrough in the spiritual life.

Many are those who, while trying to grow in the life of prayer and worship, suddenly find their progress arrested and apathy overtaking them. They then fall back and recoil. The reason behind this lamentable backsliding may be a hidden cord. It may be a sin or some addiction to a drug or a certain habit. It may be lusting after a worldly pleasure; it may be a hidden quest for fame, honor, and vainglory, or a sensual love for someone or something in this world. Only one of these impediments is enough to shackle the soul and fetter its movement. It thus cannot enjoy perpetual release in the heaven of prayer or the life of contemplation.

There is an important piece of advice, which we recommend every honest seeker of eternal life to follow: Do not be beguiled if you feel you have been released from your previous sins and fetters. For many are those who confided in their own selves when God vouchsafed to relieve them from the load of their sins and evils. They thus felt able to free others through their own abilities. Believing themselves to be so enabled, they plunged into the circles of ministry and action before their spirits had attained the maturity that makes their freedom divine and not human. They got involved in this before they were capable of working for the glory of God and not for the fame of self or their own name. The result was often that their previous sins leapt out at them once more. New and horrid forms of wickedness assumed power over their souls. They then fell prey to an inner schism and a hypocritical showing of piety. Thus, their last state became worse than their first.

Freeing of the soul, then, should not be confined to a single aspect but should include the whole inner life. Man should not soft-pedal his struggle with the world. He should never succumb to a counsel that fetters his freedom in Christ, whatever that counsel may be. It is better for him to live as good as dead in people's eyes and be saved than to ascend to the highest ranks but lose his freedom or his eternal life. He might be spoken of as ignorant or weak and be despised, but in reality be striding in the way of truth and life. This is much better than to find his only pleasure in receiving praise in public meetings as one who is powerful and great, while his inner life is an empty ruin, harassed by darkness.

If there is a final piece of advice concerning the freeing of the soul that we would recommend for the man or woman who loves God, it is this: Beware of adding new sins to your former ones by your dissoluteness, recklessness, and uncontrolled passions. For if the old sins need copious tears and much restraint for man to rid himself of their unhealthy effects, how much harder then is it to cure him who adds every day new sins to his old ones.

As for the initial practical step by which we enter upon true freedom and its power, it is to surrender totally and absolutely to God's will and his guidance in relation to ourselves without any resistance on our part. This qualifies us for bearing in our hearts a kind of freedom or liberation from our ego and our passions. For we would then be within the sphere of the action of grace and its influence. The man who lives in the sphere of God's will, obstinately and unrelentingly clinging to it in submission, thankfulness, and total surrender, gains a kind of immunity against every attempt to submit him to sin, evil, or any sort of perversion.

Whenever the process of the soul's submission to God reaches its full stride, man will never be able to bear any pleasure, comfort, or corruptive seduction that draws him away from his state of submission to God and his enjoyment of his obedience to him. This is freedom, absolute freedom.

SAYINGS OF THE FATHERS ON THE FREEING OF THE SOUL

119. No one can offer prayer of a proper intensity and sincerity, unless he is seeking to live in the following way. First of all, there must be no anxiety about the bodily needs. Not even the recollection of a piece of business, let alone any worry about it. There must be no detraction, no gossip: above all, no anger nor wrongful sorrow, for these cannot but disturb the spirit: no lust of the flesh: no love of money.

Therefore, before we begin to pray, we ought to try to be the kind of people whom we wish God to find when we pray. Whatever we do not want to creep into our time of prayer, we must try to keep out of the heart when we are not praying. (Abba Isaac, *Conferences of John Cassian* 9.3, in Butler, *Western Asceticism: The Teachings of SS Augustine, Gregory and Bernard on Contemplation and the Contemplative Life,* p 215)

120. A good comparison can be made between the soul and a feather, small and delicate. If a feather has not been touched by damp, it is so light that the slightest breath of wind can puff it high into the air. But if even a little moisture has weighed it down, it cannot float, and falls straight to the ground. In the same way the mind, if not burdened by sin and the care of daily life and evil passion, has a natural purity which lifts it from earth to heaven at the least breath of meditation upon the invisible things of the spirit . . .

So if we want our prayers to reach the sky and beyond the sky, we must make sure that the mind is so unburdened by the weights of sin and passion as to be restored to its natural buoyancy. Then the prayer will rise to God. (Abba Isaac, *Conferences of John Cassian* 9.4, in Butler, *Western Asceticism,* pp 215, 216)

121. You who are abandoned in blindness [that is, the material affairs and darkness of this world], raise your heads that the light may shine upon your faces. Give up the passions of this world . . . that the Light proceeding from the Father may find you. He will bid his servants to unbind you and let you go to the light where his Father is. Would that our bands were torn that we might see our God! (St John of Dalyatha, *Homily on Caution and Precaution*, in "Spiritual Elder")

122. He who retains any relationship with the world or its lust cannot enter the city of spiritual beings. Nobody is allowed there except he who hates the familiarity of people and the vanity of this life. Anyone whose flesh and bones have been infused with the love of Christ cannot bear the dirt of hateful lust. He who has become a friend of the angels can never bear the company of this world or its intrigues. He who has bound his mind to God and occupied it with heavenly things cannot bind it to the world or occupy it with earthly things. (St John of Dalyatha, *Homily on the Greatness of the Rank of Spiritual Beings*, in "Spiritual Elder")

123. If your lust is earthly, then you share it with dogs and swine—I mean gluttony and fornication. But if it is for God, then you share it with the angels. (St John of Dalyatha, *Homily on the Gifts of the Spirit*, in "Spiritual Elder")

124. First loose yourself from all external bonds and then you may strive to bind your heart to God, because unification with God is preceded by loosing from matter. (St Isaac the Syrian, *Homilies* 4, in *The Ascetical Homilies of Saint Isaac the Syrian*, p 29)

125. Have no care which might hinder you from the divine vision of the Lord. The more, my beloved brethren, the mind takes leave of care for the visible and is concerned with the hope of future things (according to the measure of its elevation above care for the body and all deliberation with respect to such care), the more it is refined and becomes translucent in prayer . . . For if a man is not liberated from all these and from their causes, as we have said, his mind will not look upon secret things. Therefore the Lord gave as a commandment that before all else a man should hold fast to nonpossessiveness and should withdraw from the turmoil of the world and release himself from the cares common to all men. He said, "Whosoever forsaketh not his entire human state and all that belongeth to him, and renounceth not himself, cannot be My disciple" (cf Lk 14.33). (St Isaac the Syrian, *Homilies* 63, in *Ascetical Homilies,* pp 302, 303)

126. Do not imagine that merely the possession of gold and silver is possessiveness; rather, it is the acquisition of anything whatsoever that your will clings to. (St Isaac the Syrian, *Homilies* 4, in *Ascetical Homilies,* p 30)

127. To the degree that a man despises this world in his ardent concern for the fear of God, to that degree does divine providence draw nigh to him; he secretly perceives its assistance, and is given limpid thoughts to understand it. (St Isaac the Syrian, *Homilies* 56, in *Ascetical Homilies,* p 276)

128. When illness, and want, and bodily exhaustion, and fear of bodily harm perturb your mind so as to sway it from the joy of your hope and from your unsullied care to please the Lord, then know that the flesh and not Christ lives within you. (St Isaac the Syrian, *Homilies* 56, in *Ascetical Homilies,* p 277)

129. Let us pray, therefore, to God that he give us "the wings of a dove" (Ps 55.7) of the Holy Spirit so we may fly to him and find rest. Let us pray that he may take away from our soul and body the evil wind: sin itself, inhabiting the members of our soul and body. For this he alone is able to do. For it says: "Behold, the Lamb of God who takes away the sins of the world" (Jn 1.29). (St Macarius the Great, *Homilies* 2.2, 3, in Maloney, *Intoxicated with God: The Fifty Spiritual Homilies of Macarius*)

130. For the Lord demands of you that you be angry with yourself and engage in battle with your mind, neither consenting to nor taking pleasure in wicked thoughts.

The uprooting of sin and the evil that is so embedded in our sinning can be done only by divine power. For it is impossible and outside man's competence to uproot sin. To struggle, yes, to continue to fight, to inflict blows and to receive setbacks is in your power. To uproot, however, belongs to God alone. If, indeed, you could have done it on your own, what would have been the need for the coming of the Lord? For just as an eye cannot see without light, just as one cannot speak without a tongue, nor hear without ears, nor walk without feet, nor carry out one's works without hands, so you cannot be saved, nor enter into the kingdom of heaven without Jesus. (St Macarius the Great, *Homilies* 3.3, 4, in *Spiritual Homilies*)

131. For the soul that has been considered worthy through its consuming desire, expectation, faith, and love to receive from on high that power, the heavenly love of the Spirit and has obtained the heavenly fire of eternal life, is one that is being stripped of every worldly affection and freed from every bond of evil. (St Macarius the Great, *Homilies* 4.13, in *Spiritual Homilies*)

132. "For this reason, let a man leave his father and mother and adhere to his wife and they will be two in one flesh" (Gen 2.24). If, therefore, I say, earthly love can detach one from all other loves, how much more in the case of those who have been made worthy to enter into a true fellowship with that Holy Spirit, the heavenly and loving Spirit, shall be freed from all worldly love? (St Macarius the Great, *Homilies* 4.15, in *Spiritual Homilies*)

133. In the same way those who are burning with a holy and venerable longing for the heavenly Spirit are wounded in their soul with love for the love of

God. They burn with a divine and heavenly fire which the Lord came on this earth to enkindle, and how he wishes that it be quickly accomplished (Lk 12.49). They are inflamed with a heavenly longing for Christ so that everything, as was said, that is of this world, considered outstanding and precious is repulsive and despised on account of the fire of their love for Christ who binds them, burns them, and inflames them with a passion for God . . . From such a love nothing of the earth or underworld will separate them, as the apostle Paul testified, namely: "Who will separate us from the love of Christ?" (Rom 8.35). (St Macarius the Great, *Homilies* 9.9, in *Spiritual Homilies*)

134. I say that there are other movings within the soul that belong to it and different passions from those of the flesh that I wish to tell you. Such are: vanity, offensiveness toward others, anger, cowardice, lack of self-control, as well as the rest of the passions. If the soul surrenders itself to the Lord with all its might, the righteous God will grant it true repentance, and expose to it these passions one after the other that it might avoid them, so the movements of the enemy will not overcome it. (St Antony the Great, *Letters* 1.4, in "The Letters of St Antony the Great," Manuscript 23, Arabic version)

135. Truly I tell you, my beloved sons, my soul is stupefied and my spirit astonished: while we are all given the freedom to do the deeds of the saints, we instead get drunk with passions like people drunk with the pleasure of wine. (St Antony the Great, *Letters* 5.4, in "The Letters," Arabic version)

136. Whoever wishes to become perfect in the ascetic way should not be enslaved to any of the evils. For he who worships one form of evil is far away from the border of perfection. As it was said, I have freed myself from everything (cf 1 Cor 9.19). (St Antony the Great, *Letters* 17.1, in "The Letters," Arabic version)

137. I beseech you, my beloved children, know for sure that we have been created with an authority over ourselves. For this reason we are assailed by the vicious spirits that surround us. But note what is written in the psalm, "The angel of the Lord encamps around those who fear him, and delivers them" (Ps 34.7). (St Antony the Great, *Letters* 6.10, in "The Letters," Arabic version)

CHAPTER FIVE

Purification of the Heart

"Keep your heart with all vigilance; for
from it flow the springs of life." (Prov 4.23)

"For from within, out of the heart of man,
come evil thoughts." (Mk 7.21)

"So shun youthful passions and aim at
righteousness, faith, love, and peace, along
with those who call upon the Lord from a
pure heart." (2 Tim 2.22)

I N ITS BIBLICAL CONCEPT, the heart is the source of all the potentiality of the
spiritual and physical life: "Keep your heart with all vigilance; for from
it flow the springs of life" (Prov 4.23). This applies not only to good potential-
ities but to evil ones as well: "For out of the heart come evil thoughts, murder,
adultery, fornication, theft, false witness, slander" (Mt 15.19).

So the heart has become the expression of the final condition of man,
whether he be good or evil: "The good man out of the good treasure of
his heart produces good, and the evil man out of his evil treasure produces
evil" (Lk 6.45). This means that the inclinations of the inmost heart set the
tone of the whole man—they color his thoughts, his words, and his deeds.
Man's speech thus inevitably betrays the nature of his heart: "For out of
the abundance of the heart, his mouth speaks" (Lk 6.45). So man's words
usually testify to the state of his heart. They can justify him or condemn him:
"For by your words you will be justified, and by your words you will be
condemned" (Mt 12.37).

The relationship between one's heart and one's lips is defined by St Paul as
follows: "For man believes with his heart and so is justified, and he confesses
with his lips and so is saved" (Rom 10.10). So when the heart believes, the lips
must confess what kind of faith is in the heart.

However, the Bible tells us that it is possible for two kinds of heart to exist side by side in man, one expressing his true nature and another falsifying his thoughts, words, and deeds. In the latter case, a person talks of good deeds and actually does them to give people the false impression that he is virtuous, while in fact he is wicked: "You brood of vipers! How can you speak good, when you are evil? For out of the abundance of the heart the mouth speaks" (Mt 12.34).

From the words of the Lord, we learn that it is impossible for man to speak good words out of himself while being wicked. Good words coming from an evil source could only occur with the help of an auxiliary power—or of another heart implanted by the devil to mimic good deeds. We can infer this from the way our Lord describes those who counterfeit good deeds as a "brood of vipers." The viper is a symbolical expression of the devil. Here the intention behind showing off virtue is to safeguard evil and guarantee its lasting effect— which is the very work of the devil. The devil's work, with regard to the heart, is not merely confined to contaminating it with evil desires. It is not just that he makes the evil treasured up in the heart produce evil. He even adds to this the possibility of giving man another heart from which he can speak gilded words. This he does to keep the evil intent secret and make sure that it is carried out.

As for God's work concerning the heart, it is the complete removal of the evil heart and the creation of a new one that he implants into man. Thus, when man's heart is transformed into a new heart, man of necessity is turned into another man: "Then the spirit of the Lord will come mightily upon you, and you shall prophesy with them and be turned into another man . . . When he turned his back to leave Samuel, God gave him another heart" (1 Sam 10.6, 9).

In the Bible, the reality of creating a new heart for man goes hand in hand with three basic actions: (1) contrition of the sinner's heart; (2) man's complete cleansing or purging from within; and (3) the indwelling of the Holy Spirit. These three actions we find most clearly expressed in Psalm 51 of the prophet David:

> Have mercy on me, O God, according to thy steadfast love;
> According to thy abundant mercy blot out my transgressions.
> Wash me thoroughly from my iniquity . . .
> Purge me with hyssop, and I shall be clean; wash me, and I shall be
>   whiter than snow . . .

Create in me a clean heart, O God, and put a new and right spirit
within me.
Cast me not away from thy presence, and take not thy Holy Spirit
from me . . .
A broken and contrite heart, O God, thou wilt not despise.

However, the creation of a new heart for a person in the Old Testament
was an exceptional and individual case. In the New Testament, the act became
universal, not merely to create a new heart, but for creating a whole new man.

We find these three actions implied in the sacrament of baptism. We find
within it the image of cleansing and inward purging: "[He] cleansed their
hearts by faith" (Acts 15.9). This takes place during burial in water in the name
of Christ. However, cleansing and purging cannot happen except through contrition of heart. It calls for genuine repentance: a complete U-turn from sin. It
is on account of this that forgiveness is granted: "Repent, and be baptized every
one of you in the name of Jesus Christ for the forgiveness of your sins; and you
shall receive the gift of the Holy Spirit" (Acts 2.38). That is, by thorough cleansing and purging through faith and repentance, the Holy Spirit comes to dwell
in us. It has thus become possible for every man to obtain the new creation and
the new heart—by water and the Spirit, through faith and repentance.

However, purification of the heart through faith and repentance is one
thing, but the acceptance of a heart newly created and purified by the Holy
Spirit is another. There is a crucial distinction between the two. Purification of
the heart is a necessary and vital activity in which we should be intimately
involved. But the creation of a new and pure heart is an action that transcends
our nature and belongs to God alone. God's work should be adjoined to our
own. To the extent that we purify our own hearts from evil by faith and repentance, we become able to embrace the new heart created within us in God's
image. In other words, insofar as we hate wickedness, are distressed by evil
passions and thoughts, and abhor acts of sin, we become able to embrace the
power of holiness. This power dwells in us as a new nature, with the activity
of divine love and the promptings, or intimations, of righteousness. Not only
that, but as we strive to purify our hearts from the darkness of sin, which
blinds our spiritual sight, we become able to face the truth, letting it live within
us and penetrate to the very roots of our being. In other words, the more we
can put off of the old man with its evils and abominations, the more we can
emerge in the power of the new, divine man: "Seeing that you have put off the

old nature with its practices and have put on the new nature, which is being
renewed in knowledge after the image of its creator" (Col 3.9, 10).

We thus enter the sphere of ascetical theology. Ascetical theology makes
out of man's labor and struggle, which are sustained by grace, an essential basis
for the gifts of God. Such gifts, however, transcend human action and nature.
The ascetic fathers in general set purification of the heart as a vital basis for
salvation. It qualifies us for the revealing of the new man, that we may live in
the newness of life as spiritual men in Christ.

In its patristic concept, the heart, ἡ καρδία, is identical with its biblical concept. The Fathers consider the "heart" the quintessence or real basis of human
nature in general. "The heart" in its spiritual and patristic sense corresponds
to what medical jargon calls the brain. This is true both of its characteristics
and its activity. It may even be more than that. It is the center of faculties, talents, intelligence, insight, volition, wisdom, vision—all of which emanate
from it and pour into it:

> **138.** In the same way the heart has a captain in the mind, the con-
> science, which tests the thoughts that accuse and defend. (St Macarius
> the Great, *Homilies* 15.33, in Maloney, *Intoxicated with God: The Fifty
> Spiritual Homilies of Macarius*)

In the same homily, St Macarius describes the heart as "a workshop of justice, injustice, righteousness, unrighteousness." He also says that though the
heart may be the meeting place of all evils, it may also be a meeting place for
God and his angels:

> **139.** There likewise is God; there also the angels; there the life and the
> kingdom; there the light and the apostles; there the treasures of grace;
> there all things. (St Macarius the Great, *Homilies* 43.7, in *Spiritual
> Homilies*)

> **140.** And when grace gives pasture to the heart, it rules over all the
> members and the thoughts. For there in the heart, the mind abides as
> well as all the thoughts of the soul and all its hopes. This is how grace
> penetrates throughout all parts of the body. (St Macarius the Great,
> *Homilies* 15.20, in *Spiritual Homilies*)

From this, we infer that the Fathers see grace pervading all our faculties:
the mind, the will, the conscience, and the physical members of the body. But

all this depends on grace reigning first and foremost over the heart. In other words, if grace reigns over a person's heart, it changes its very nature: the result is a new, spiritual nature. This is where the value of the purification of the heart is clearly shown: it is a preparation for the indwelling of grace.

St Macarius the Great insists that the evil heart contaminates the will. It corrupts the natural inclinations and instincts of a man. Without his knowing it, everything that such a person sees and touches becomes impure for him:

> **141.** So, on the contrary, as many as are sons of darkness, sin has control over their heart and infiltrates into all the members. "For out of the heart proceed evil thoughts" (Mt 15.19). And thus diffused throughout, sin covers man with darkness . . . Just as water runs through a pipe, so also sin runs through the heart and the thoughts. All those who deny these statements are refuted and ridiculed by sin itself, which is always intent on victory. For evil tries to hide itself and remain undetected in man's mind. (St Macarius the Great, *Homilies* 15.21, in *Spiritual Homilies*)

Hence, first among man's struggles and concerns is to purify his heart. His endeavor is to overcome the deviations of the will and to correct the inclinations and instincts that have been subjected to the rule of evil. This means that he has to confront the tendency of his heart toward evil activity. He has to bridle it, curb it, and finally destroy this tendency.

In his fifteenth homily, St Macarius describes the heart as "the palace of Christ in which he retires." He also describes it as "the captain [who] rules and directs all the sailors." Also, "it is like a chariot. The reins, horses, and the whole apparatus are under one driver. When he wishes, he drives the chariot at high speed. When he wants, he stops it. Wherever he wishes to steer the chariot, there it goes. For the whole chariot is under the power of the driver. So also the heart."

St Macarius thus expresses the crucial role of the heart as a captain of the ship of our life. It is the driver of the chariot that our bodies pull. If the captain is ignorant or foolish, what will become of the ship? Or, if the driver is careless or crazy, what will the end of the chariot and its horses be? If the house is impure how can the King dwell or rest in it?

> **142.** How much more the house of the soul, in which the Lord finds his rest, needs ordering so that he may be able to enter and there rest,

he who is without any reproach, spot or blemish! In such a heart both
God and the whole heavenly church find rest. (St Macarius the Great,
Homilies 15.45, in *Spiritual Homilies*)

The rebuilding of a city begins by pulling down the ruins, the cultivation
of a land by burning the thorns. In the same way, St Macarius believes, we start
out on the road to life by purifying the heart:

> **143.** Let us take the example of someone who wishes to rebuild a
> city that has been totally destroyed. He must first get rid of the ruins
> and knock down whatever is a menace . . . Likewise, for one who
> wishes to develop a garden in barren or swampy, dirty places, he must
> first begin to clean up the place . . . In a similar manner, the intentions
> of men, after the fall, are barren, devastated and thorny . . . Therefore,
> there is need of much labor and sweat so as to seek and lay down a foun-
> dation until fire comes into men's hearts. (St Macarius the Great, *Hom-
> ilies* 15.53, in *Spiritual Homilies*)

But why did God especially choose the heart of man to set apart exclusively
for himself and not any other part? "My son, give me your heart, and let your
eyes observe my ways" (Prov 23.26). Also, the first commandment is: "You
shall love the Lord your God with all your heart" (Deut 6.5).

In fact, man has nothing deeper than the heart as far as compassion, tenderness, mercy, and love are concerned. The heart expresses the center of the
most tender and sincere of man's emotions. Yet, it is not for this that God seeks
the heart of man. For there exists another characteristic of the heart that transcends kindness, tenderness, mercy, or love. This consists in its being the well-
spring of man's personality, from which all its main characteristics flow. The
heart is man's holy of holies. It is exclusively this feature that makes it fit for
the indwelling of God. For if man loves God with all his heart, it means that
he loves him with all his being. He has given himself unreservedly to God.

St Macarius says that the heart includes the mind, conscience, and thoughts
among its constituents. He has thus put his finger on the decisive factor that
urged God to seek man's heart and be interested in his love. God is not interested in emotional love however intense or sweeping, for it is a love that is
inevitably extinguished once emotions are wounded or insulted. God is interested in the love of man's heart, which means that man has renounced his ego

along with all his being. This is the love that wounds incite, sufferings hone, and death perfects all the more.

Hence, the purification of the heart is to those who love God a matter of overriding importance. For God never seeks nor is he ever satisfied with half-hearted or partial love. The whole heart must be dedicated to him. The word *whole-hearted* means clearing the heart completely from the impurities of human emotions, for such emotions stem from the bonds of flesh and blood or sensual inclinations and affections. It also means cleansing it entirely from all secret idols and gods, for the holy of holies should be consecrated and adorned for God alone.

SAYINGS OF THE FATHERS ON THE PURITY OF HEART

144. It is necessary to "guard thine heart with the utmost care" (Prov 4.23), so as on no account to lose the thought of God, and not to obscure the remembrance of his wonders with vain imaginations, but to bear everywhere with oneself an indelible seal, a constant and pure remembrance; the holy thought of God printed on our souls. For in this way we acquire love for God, which constrains us to fulfill the Lord's commandments. And love is in turn guarded by the law, making it unceasing and unwavering. (St Basil the Great, *Long Rules* 5, PG 31.921)

145. What, succinctly, is purity? It is a heart that shows mercy to all created nature . . . And what is a merciful heart? It is the heart's burning for the sake of the entire creation, for men, for birds, for animals, for demons, and for every created thing; and by the recollection and the sight of them the eyes of a merciful man pour forth abundant tears. From the strong and vehement mercy which grips his heart and from his great compassion, his heart is humbled and he cannot bear to hear or to see any injury or the slightest sorrow in creation. For this reason he offers up tearful prayer continually even for irrational beasts, for the enemies of the truth, and for those who harm him, that they be protected and receive mercy. (St Isaac the Syrian, *Homilies* 71, in *The Ascetical Homilies of Saint Isaac the Syrian*, pp 344–45)

146. Lo, heaven is within you (if indeed you are pure), and within it you will see both the angels in their light and their Master with them and in them. (St Isaac the Syrian, *Homilies* 15, in *Ascetical Homilies,* p 84)

147. God is fire which warms and inflames the heart and womb. And so, if we feel in our hearts coldness, which is from the devil, for he is cold, then let us pray to the Lord for he came to warm our hearts with perfect love, not only of him but of our neighbor too. And in the face of his warmth the cold of the hater-of-good will flee away. (St Seraphim of Sarov, "The Exhortation of Our God-Bearing Father St Seraphim of Sarov the Miracle Worker," *The Journal of the Moscow Patriarchate* 8 [1991], p 40)

148. Question: What is the sign that a man has attained to purity of heart, and when does a man know that his heart has entered into purity?

Answer: When he sees all men as good and none appears to him to be unclean and defiled, then in very truth his heart is pure. For how could anyone fulfill the word of the Apostle, that "A man should esteem all better than himself" (Phil 2.3) with a sincere heart, if he does not attain to the saying, "A good eye will not see evil" (Hab 1.13)?

Question: What is purity and where is its boundary?

Answer: Purity is the forgetting of the contranatural modes of knowledge which in the world are invented by [human] nature. And its boundary is when a man is liberated from, and found outside of, these modes of knowledge and he enters into the primordial simplicity and guilelessness of his nature and he becomes like an infant without, however, the deficiencies of an infant. (St Isaac the Syrian, *Homilies* 37, in *Ascetical Homilies,* p 177)

149. Christians, therefore, should strive in all things and ought not to pass judgment of any kind on anyone, not on the prostitute nor on sinners nor on disorderly persons. But they should look upon all persons with a single mind and a pure eye so that it may be for such a person almost a natural and fixed attitude never to despise or judge or abhor anyone or to divide people and place them into boxes.

If you see a man with one eye, do not make any judgment in your heart but regard him as though he were whole. If someone has a maimed hand, see him as not maimed. See the crippled as straight, the paralytic as healthy. For this is purity of heart, that, when you see the sinners and the weak, you have compassion and show mercy toward them. (St Macarius the Great, *Homilies* 5.8)

150. If you are really born from Christ, then every other man born from Christ is your brother. But if you love yourself more than your brother, then this increase is not from Christ. (St John of Dalyatha, *Homily on the Gifts of the Spirit*, in "Spiritual Elder")

151. Beware of judging your neighbor secretly while sitting [in your cell], for this roots out all your works and virtues even if you have reached perfection. (St Isaac the Syrian, *Homily on the Discernment of Spiritual Stages,* in "The Four Books of St Isaac the Syrian, Bishop of Nineveh," 2, Arabic version)

152. Every inordinate desire in which the heart may have been entangled can only be got rid of by a thousand stratagems, struggles, works, prayers, and tears. (St Isaac the Syrian, *Homily on the Discernment of Spiritual Stages,* in "The Four Books," 2, Arabic version)

153. If you are yearning for purity of heart and peace of mind, root out from your heart the tree of knowledge of good and evil, which God commanded our first ancestor not to eat from, lest he should die. (St Isaac the Syrian, *Homily On the Solitary Life,* in "The Four Books," 2, Arabic version)

154. If you sit judging the behavior of the brothers and their way of life, you will inevitably lose much. For you will condemn others and, without knowing, blame the Author of creation and justify yourself, and so fall into pride. (St Isaac the Syrian, *Homily On the Solitary Life,* in "The Four Books," 2, Arabic version)

155. Few people are able to renounce the abundance of scholarship they have acquired, few prefer to live in simplicity of heart. Such as these are diadems in the crown of the King. (St Isaac the Syrian, in "The Four Books," 4.2, Arabic version)

156. God's pleasure lies in our being pure in the purity of our first creation. We make him sad when we alter the image in which we were created, for the soul was created in the pure image of God. We have exchanged this purity for its opposite, for when the soul was first created it was able to look upon God in intimacy, but we have now strayed away from him and have worshiped the lusts of the world and the flesh. (St Isaac the Syrian, *Homily on the Solitary Life,* in "The Four Books," 2, Arabic version)

157. Nothing can bring the heart so near to God as almsgiving, and nothing brings such serenity to the mind as voluntary poverty. To be called an ignoramus by the many because of the generosity of your hands, the measureless liberality which springs from your fear of God: that is better for you than to be called wise and sound of mind by reason of your niggardliness. (St Isaac the Syrian, *Homilies* 4, in *Ascetical Homilies,* p 37)

158. Love the poor, that through them you may also find mercy. (St Isaac the Syrian, *Homilies* 5, in *Ascetical Homilies,* p 51)

159. Bear the noisome smells of the sick without disgust, and especially of the poor, since you too are wrapped about with a body. (St Isaac the Syrian, *Homilies* 5, in *Ascetical Homilies,* p 51)

160. Love sinners, but hate their works; and do not despise them for their faults, lest you be tempted by the same. (St Isaac the Syrian, *Homilies* 5, in *Ascetical Homilies,* p 51)

161. Remember that you share the earthly nature of Adam and that you are clothed with his infirmity. (St Isaac the Syrian, *Homilies* 5, in *Ascetical Homilies,* p 51)

162. If you are truly merciful, do not grieve inwardly when you are unjustly deprived of something you possess, and do not tell others of your loss. Nay rather, let the loss you suffer from others be swallowed up by your own mercy, as the sharp edge of wine is swallowed up by much water. (St Isaac the Syrian, *Homilies* 6, in *Ascetical Homilies,* p 55)

163. Show the fullness of your mercy by the good with which you repay those who have done you injustice. (St Isaac the Syrian, *Homilies* 6, in *Ascetical Homilies,* p 55)

164. A man who is truly humble is not troubled when he is wronged and he says nothing to justify himself against the injustice, but he accepts slander as truth; he does not attempt to persuade men that he is calumniated, but he begs forgiveness. (St Isaac the Syrian, *Homilies* 6, in *Ascetical Homilies,* p 55)

165. Spread your cloak over the man who is falling and cover him. And if you cannot take upon yourself his sins and receive his chastisement in his stead, then at least patiently suffer his shame and do not disgrace him. (St Isaac the Syrian, *Homilies* 51, in *Ascetical Homilies,* p 247)

166. As for those who do not come to him with all their hearts, but are double-hearted, and all that they do they do outwardly only to win glory from people (Mt 6.2), God never gives an ear to any of their petitions, but his wrath is even greater toward them. (St Antony the Great, *Letters* 10.1, in "The Letters," Arabic version)

167. Know that without purity of body and heart no one can be perfect before God, as it is written in the holy gospel: "Blessed are the pure in heart, for they shall see God" (Mt 5.8) . . . Make every effort not to be found spiteful one against another when you leave this world and therefore be counted among murderers, as it is written: "Any one who hates his brother is a murderer" (1 Jn 3.15) . . . And if any of you is wronged, let him accept it with joy and surrender the matter to the Lord, for he is the just Ruler to whom retribution belongs. And if any of you wrongs his neighbor, let him hurry to humble himself before the Lord and implore his neighbor, that the Lord may forgive him. Do not let the sun go down on your anger, as the scriptures teach us (Eph 4.26). (St Antony the Great, *Letters* 20.3, 12, 13, in "The Letters," Arabic version)

CHAPTER SIX

Contrition of the Spirit

"But this is the man to whom I will look,
he that is humble and contrite in spirit
and trembles at my word." (Is 66.2)

"I was not rebellious, I turned not
backward. I gave my back to the smiters
and my cheeks to those who pulled out the
beard; I hid not my face from shame and
spitting. For the Lord God helps me;
therefore I have not been confounded."
(Is 50.5–7)

"He was oppressed, and he was afflicted,
yet he opened not his mouth." (Is 53.7)

"Learn from me; for I am gentle and lowly
in heart, and you will find rest for your
souls." (Mt 11.29)

IF WE WERE TO GRASP, even for a single moment, the reality of God and our relationship to him, our own reality would at once be unveiled to us. We would then realize that we are nothing when compared to the infinite greatness of God.

This unveiling of the self is what actually occurred in the lives of the saints. The intensity of the saints' humility, their contrition, and their incessant self-reproach was only a realization of their nothingness before God's glory. But the fruits of this unveiling of the self we cannot extort for ourselves; sanctity cannot be copied slavishly. First, we have to advance properly in the life of grace and know who we really are. Otherwise, we are false and may even lead ourselves to negate the very virtues we wish to attain.

The saints were not attracted to the virtues of humility and contrition because of the intrinsic beauties of these qualities. They were not seeking to treasure them up or to adorn themselves with them. No, it was the finding of their lost selves in God's light that led them to humble contrition.

Humility is not to claim that we are sinners without feeling this reality in the depths of our hearts. Such a claim, on the contrary, leads us astray from knowing our true selves and knowing what true humility is. Contrition should be a result of our conviction that we have provoked God to anger. We would have conquered; we would have progressed in the life of grace and grown closer to God. However, we have instead freely chosen the lust of this world and this fleeting life.

The "natural man" of this world loves the "natural" things that belong to it: he can never love God of his own accord without the mediation of grace. He may feel from time to time a besetting need or an obscure longing for God. This mute call is only a cry of the divine nature that dwells in him. This divine nature can be renewed and strengthened by the Holy Spirit to overcome the earthly nature, if the soul is totally submissive and contrite; that is, if one is sorry for one's previous sins. Penitence happens in the light of God's love and in longing for him. Were it not for the sin that has invaded our nature, we would be living with God in the clear light of love. Sin has dwelt in us, and for this reason, our worship is now mingled with sorrow and our love with contrition. Our wickedness stands stripped and naked before God. Who then can ever mock him? Says St Paul, "Do not be deceived; God cannot be mocked" (Gal 6.7). Our relationship with God should have its roots in humility and absolute contrition. It is only then that it may be described as a realistic relationship that springs from a factual reality.

One fact should shame us all. While we persist in sinning against God and in defying his rights and commandments, he still looks upon us with compassion without ever diminishing his love for us. How can we not feel contrite when pondering the great love of God who humbled himself and even underwent contrition for us on the cross! And at whose hands? Was it not at the hands of mankind, of which you and I are members? The thought of the sufferings of the crucified God is enough to occasion contrition upon contrition.

Contrition cannot be grasped in a day or be taught from a book. It is life that flows between the soul and God. At first glance, it looks arduous, being a struggle against self-regard and a humiliation of one's pride. But after awhile, when the soul is cleansed from its false majesty and conceit, the life of contrition becomes a poignant, sweet melody that makes shorter the soul's long journey to God. It invites the soul to make its approach to God's dwelling place until it finds its complete rest in him.

A contrite soul is full of peace. As it grows in grace and perfection, contrition and humility flow out. Any perversion toward pride or vainglory makes it shudder as a musician shudders at a discordant note in a beautiful symphony.

In biblical language, contrition does not mean crushing (ἔθραυσα), in the sense of breaking down an object to demolish its height and make it lowly and powerless. Rather, it means a combination of humility, meekness, self-denial, and mortification of the will. The biblical idea of contrition by no means implies damaging or humiliating the human spirit that was created in God's image. If there is a breaking and destruction involved here, they are aimed against the parts of the self that are false and conceited. In this way, the soul can return to its authentic and simple bounds. Within such limits, man does not aspire to what is higher than his stature. He does not covet what does not suit the measure of his faith or his personal struggle. As St Paul says, "For by the grace given to me I bid every one among you not to think of himself more highly than he ought to think, but to think with sober judgment, each according to the measure of faith which God has assigned him" (Rom 12.3).

Contrition of the spirit in this sense is a positive thing, part of the rebuilding of an authentic soul, a soul without narcissism, cocky ambition, or self-importance. This rebuilding would return it to its original image. It would be a preparation for reaching its ultimate aim in Christ, which is union with the divine nature.

Contrition of the soul takes place at two levels: a negative, voluntary level and a positive, involuntary level. Man is responsible for honing down the false parts of his self manifested in his character, conduct, and false ambitions, for they obstruct his spiritual growth. This is what is meant by negative, voluntary honing of the soul. At the same time, he is asked to accept all the honing that comes about from God, for it is meant to humble his soul and bring it back to its original littleness and authenticity. This is what is meant by positive, involuntary honing. This kind of honing of the soul is a great gift from God, for man, left alone, is often unable to humble himself and hone down his soul properly. Without God honing our souls, we inevitably remain wanting in humility and meekness.

Honing one's soul is a delicate and serious operation that requires faithful discernment. In practicing lowliness, man should learn how to stop at the level that is proper to his soul. He should not lower himself below that level. Otherwise, he would assume another form of pretense, which is false humility—pretending to be foolish while actually not feeling foolish; pretending to be naive beyond his actual simplicity; pretending to be weak while not actually being so weak. In this way, man is transformed into something other than himself and engages in hypocrisy under the pretense of humility. Such is the danger of the virtue of contrition.

In a life of contrition, man strives to shatter all pride, ambition, self-importance, or sense of superiority. This is carried on until he reaches the reality of his authentic, powerless, and pitiable self. He should stop at these limits, never trying to trespass them and so to negate the grace that dwells in him. In self-denial, he should not deny the work of God in him. This is what St Paul meant when he so briefly and clearly said that we should not stretch our spiritual sight beyond what belongs to us. Neither should we stretch it higher than what our inward life may allow. Instead, we should confine it, with discernment and balance, within the limits of the gifts that Christ has apportioned to us.

If someone is urged by egotistical zeal and ambitious virtue to proceed unreasonably in contrition and self-denial, he shows himself to be below the level of his gift and faith. We find that self-denial trespasses its prescribed limits, denying faith and the grace of God. The inevitable result will then be the end of contact between God and man. Faith will then shrink, and grace will withdraw from managing the affairs of such a man.

But if that same man conducts himself authentically in his contrition and humility until he reaches his true, simple level, his soul will then be opened wide toward God. His soul will employ its full potential in God's service. It will then be qualified for true contact with God. It will grow more and more in its humble authenticity, which will in turn qualify it for further communication and further growth. So, the cycle of growth continues. "But this is the man to whom I will look, he that is humble and contrite in spirit, and trembles at my word" (Is 66.2). We can thus see that true and authentic contrition leads to true contact with God and to the fullness of grace. Conversely, exaggerated contrition breaks up our true relation with God and slowly empties us of grace.

All the fathers, without exception, consider contrition of the soul for the sake of true humility as the foundation of all virtues. It is the outset of every spiritual action, and the aim of all knowledge. To this effect St Augustine says, "Humility of the soul is the very purport of the Christian religion." This is true and applicable to contrition if it is practiced voluntarily by self-control. Therein one can subject his own self to the truth and subdue it in the fear of God to live within the limits of faith and purity. But it is also true of contrition if it is practiced involuntarily by total submission to the chastisement of God, however hard or humiliating. Therein one happily surrenders himself to God's will and without reservation, complaint, or condition.

Superficially, words about contrition look bitter and harsh. They seem to imply a hard struggle against the tyranny of one's ego, the pride of one's self, and the false ambition of one's spirit. They also foreshadow difficulties, chastisements, and insults, which we must accept from God's hand.

However, the truth of the matter is exactly the opposite, for the experience of contrition within proper limits is exceedingly sweet. It can hardly be described in words, for words can never make us truly relish anything. Is it possible to describe the sweetness of honey? The mind may delight in words but the spirit delights only in living reality. Contrition of the soul is a reality to be lived out. Words about it are as bitter as gall, but its taste is sweeter than honey. What we think ourselves obliged to inform the reader of in words is only to describe where this heavenly honeycomb is to be found, and how it is to be harvested and eaten secretly.

The vale of humility is indeed dark and gloomy in appearance. But no sooner do you step into that holy vale than you are met by the guards of the heavenly watchtower. They come running to your aid to wash the wounds that have torn your soul or body when you ventured suddenly from the false mountains of this world down the dreadful scarp of humility. They take you to have a little rest, after which they invite you to tour the watchtower. This watchtower stands at the top of the long vale. You can survey all the details of this holy vale through a telescope given by the guards. On its slopes are honeycombs for passers-by to eat. Meanwhile, Grace watches them all the time to rest assured that their wounds are healed. Her bandages absorb pain and turn wounds into brilliant marks.

Wonder fills you: How does this valley look so dark and depressing without the heavenly telescope, as if death and ruin fill every corner of it? At close inspection it is full of honeycomb and of merciful healing. There is in this vale a hidden light, which illumines the interior before the exterior of man. You marvel at the mystery of this vale!

The guards ask you to lift the telescope a bit. You see what lies beyond the vale and what awaits you there at the end of the journey. When you raise the telescope you see the Mount of Transfiguration far off with its transcendent light. There the Lord opens his arms to embrace those who reach the end of the vale. On his hands, the blood shines with a resplendent light that illuminates the whole mount. Its light is mystically reflected upon the dark vale, and when that light falls upon the wounds of those walking along, they also shine as the moon reflects the rays of the sun across the darkness of space.

Now joy and peace overtake you. Now you burn with desire to storm the darkness of this holy vale. The secret of this joyful contrition, the brilliant wounds and the bitterness that hides the honeycomb have all been unveiled to you.

The truth is that the location of this holy vale—the vale of contrition, wounds, and bitterness—is nowhere else than in the heart of man. The guards of the watchtower that stands at the beginning of the vale are none other than the fathers. They have experienced contrition with its bitterness. They have described its ruggedness as well as its worth. The telescope is nothing other than the proper, practical discipline of humility offered in love and honor for the Crucified. The honeycomb is the pleasure gleaned from partaking of the Lord's sufferings. The bleeding wounds are hurt feelings of dignity, and these fall into three types: the superficial, which man enacts upon himself; the deeper wounds and bruises caused by other people; and the deadly fissures in the walls of the heart caused by the chastisement of God. These fissures are made to bleed out all the selfish, earthly blood that superficial or deep wounds cannot draw out of us.

As for the divine rays shining from the wounds of the Lord and reflected upon the wounds and fractures of humility, they are the partial communion in the glory of God that is promised in surety. They shall reach their highest brilliance when our Lord appears "as he is" (1 Jn 3.2).

SAYINGS OF THE FATHERS ON CONTRITION OF THE SPIRIT

168. God, for your sake, humbled himself, and you will not be humbled for your own sake, but you remain proud and inflated. He came to take upon himself your afflictions and burdens and to bestow his rest on you. But you refuse to bear any difficulties and to suffer in order that in this way you may obtain the healing of your wounds. (St Macarius the Great, *Homilies* 26.26, in Maloney, *Intoxicated with God: The Fifty Spiritual Homilies of Macarius*)

169. As Christ, having taken on "the form of a servant" (Phil 2.7), through humility conquered the devil, so at the beginning through pride and vainglory the serpent overthrew Adam. And now the same serpent, hiding in human hearts, through vainglory destroys and dissolves the race of Christians. (St Macarius the Great, *Homilies* 27.5, in *Spiritual Homilies*)

170. Take the example of a certain free and well-born man, according to the world, who has much wealth and continues to prosper and bring forth much fruit. He loses his balance and puts his confidence in himself. He becomes intolerable, kicking and beating everybody. So it is with certain persons lacking discretion who, as soon as they begin to experience some bit of quiet and peace in prayer, begin to be puffed up spiritually. They lose their balance and begin to criticize others. And so they fall to the lowest parts of the earth.

That very serpent, who threw Adam out of the garden through pride, saying, "you shall be as gods" (Gen 3.5), now also suggests pride in human hearts, saying: "You are perfect, you are sufficient unto yourself, you are rich, you need nothing, you are blessed." (St Macarius the Great, *Homilies* 27.6, in *Spiritual Homilies*)

171. But if anyone is not confirmed in great humility, he is handed over to Satan and is stripped of all divine grace bestowed on him. And he is tempted by many afflictions. Then his idea of himself is manifested because he is naked and despicable. Therefore, he who is rich in the grace of God ought to be grounded in great humility and possess a contrite heart. (St Macarius the Great, *Homilies* 41.3, in *Spiritual Homilies*)

172. Humility, even without works, gains forgiveness for many offenses; but without her, works are of no profit to us. (St Isaac the Syrian, *Homilies* 69, in *The Ascetical Homilies of Saint Isaac the Syrian*, p 338)

173. For a man who for God's sake humbles himself, and thinks meanly of himself, is glorified by God. (St Isaac the Syrian, *Homilies* 5, in *Ascetical Homilies,* p 50)

174. Humility always receives mercy from God; but hardness of heart and littleness of faith contend with fearful encounters. (St Isaac the Syrian, *Homilies* 5, in *Ascetical Homilies,* p 50)

175. One of the saints wrote that, "If a man does not count himself a sinner, his prayer is not accepted by the Lord." (St Isaac the Syrian, *Epistle to Abba Symeon,* in *Ascetical Homilies,* p 435)

176. When you fall down before God in prayer, become in your thought like an ant, like the creeping things of the earth, like a leech, and like a tiny lisping child. Do not say anything before him with knowledge, but with a child's manner of thought draw near God and walk before him, that you may be counted worthy of that paternal providence which fathers have for their small children. It has been said, "The Lord preserveth the infants" . . . And not only those who are tiny of body, but also those, who being wise in the world, abandon their knowledge, and applying themselves entirely to that other, all-sufficing wisdom, and becoming like babes of their own free will, learn that other wisdom, which is not learned through study's labors. Well did Paul say, who was wise in things divine, "He that seemeth to be wise in this world, let him become a fool, that he may be wise" (1 Cor 3.18). Ask God, however, to grant that you attain the measure of faith. (St Isaac the Syrian, *Homilies* 72, in *Ascetical Homilies,* p 351)

177. Through the toil of prayer and the anguish of your heart commune with those who are grieved at heart, and the Source of mercy will be opened up to your petitions. (St Isaac the Syrian, *Homilies* 2, in *Ascetical Homilies,* p 12)

178. The recompense is not given for labor but for humility . . . From mourning humility is born, and a gift is bestowed upon humility. Therefore the recompense is not for virtue, nor for toil on account of virtue, but for humility that is born of both. (St Isaac the Syrian, *Homilies* 57, in *Ascetical Homilies,* p 282)

179. In this monastery to which I have been referring, there was a man named Isidore, from Alexandria. He had belonged to the ruling class but had become a monk. I met him there. The most holy shepherd, after having let him join, discovered that he was a troublemaker: cruel, sly, and haughty. But he shrewdly managed to outwit the cunning of the devils in him. "If you have decided to accept the yoke of Christ," he told Isidore, "I want you first of all to learn obedience."

"Most holy Father, I submit to you like iron to the blacksmith," Isidore replied.

The superior, availing himself of this metaphor, immediately gave exercise to the iron Isidore and said to him: "Brother, this is what I want you to do. You are to stand at the gate of the monastery, and before everyone passing in or out you are to bend the knee and say, 'Pray for me, Father, because I am an epileptic.'" And Isidore obeyed, like an angel obeying the Lord.

He spent seven years at the gate. He found compunction and achieved a deep humility.

After the statutory seven years, and after the wonderful steadfastness of the man, the superior deemed him fully worthy to be admitted to the ranks of the brethren and wanted to ordain him. Through others and also through my feeble intercession, Isidore begged the superior many times to let him perfect his course. (St John Climacus, *Ladder of Divine Ascent* 4.26, pp 97–98)

180. Men of high spirit endure offense nobly and willingly. But only the holy and the saintly can pass unscathed through praise. (St John Climacus, *Ladder of Divine Ascent* 22.12, p 202)

181. It is not the self-critical who reveals his humility (for does not everyone somehow have to put up with himself?). Rather it is the man who continues to love the person who has criticized him. (St John Climacus, *Ladder of Divine Ascent* 22.17, p 203)

182. If ever we seek glory, if it comes our way uninvited, or if we plan some course of action because of our vainglory, we should think of our mourning and of the blessed fear on us as we stood alone in prayer before God. If we do this we will assuredly outflank shameless vainglory. (St John Climacus, *Ladder of Divine Ascent* 22.41, p 205)

183. An admirable man said once to me: "Think of a dozen shameful passions. Love one of them, I mean pride, and it will take up the space of all the other eleven." (St John Climacus, *Ladder of Divine Ascent* 23.5, pp 207, 208)

184. A proud monk argues bitterly with others. The humble monk is loath to contradict them. (St John Climacus, *Ladder of Divine Ascent* 23.6, p 208)

185. An old man, very experienced in these matters, once spiritually admonished a proud brother who said in his blindness: "Forgive me, father, but I am not proud." "My son," said the wise old man, "what better proof of your pride could you have given than to claim that you were not proud?"

A help to the proud is submissiveness. (St John Climacus, *Ladder of Divine Ascent* 23.14, 15, p 208)

186. Pride makes us forget our sins, for the remembrance of them leads to humility. (St John Climacus, *Ladder of Divine Ascent* 23.22, p 209)

187. He who loves praise imagines causes for praise [that is, to be praised for them]. As for the humble, he feels ill at ease if he is praised. (St Isaac the Syrian, in "The Four Books of St Isaac the Syrian, Bishop of Nineveh," 1.4, Arabic version)

188. He who is governed by the affairs of this transient world, or bound to anything that belongs to it, cannot be humble or pure in heart. For the humble is dead to the world and the world dead to him, and therefore it cannot incline his heart to any of its belongings. So if you wish to be humble you must first of all detach yourself from worldly matters and follow God in hope, faith, and love: instead of the world which you have left you will receive a life which never passes away. (St Isaac the Syrian, in "The Four Books," 1.4, Arabic version)

189. If you are weak or unable to perform any good deed because of an illness or for any casual reason, then you should, like the publican, use humility and offer a lowly prayer to be justified before God without works. (St Isaac the Syrian, in "The Four Books," 1.4, Arabic version)

190. If your self is scorned in your eyes, the hosts of demons will succumb to you, and the fountain of knowledge will be opened within you. (St Isaac the Syrian, in "The Four Books," 1.4, Arabic version)

191. So long as you are in this life, scorn your self by the constant remembrance of your sins. Confess them before the merciful God in contrition and you will gain intimacy with him. (St Isaac the Syrian, in "The Four Books," 1.4, Arabic version)

192. God can never leave a contrite heart without solace. (St Isaac the Syrian, in "The Four Books," 1.4, Arabic version)

193. The sacrifice acceptable to God is a contrite spirit and a broken heart. He who is alien to these two is alien to God's mercy. (St Isaac the Syrian, in "The Four Books," 1.4, Arabic version)

194. If your heart is brazenly confident of your works and knowledge, then know that this foreshadows impending tribulations. (St Isaac the Syrian, in "The Four Books," 1.4, Arabic version)

195. God permits tribulations and adversities to befall people—even the saintly—so that they may persist in humility. But if we harden our hearts against adversities and tribulations, he also hardens these tribulations against us. On the other hand, if we accept them in humility and with a contrite heart, God will mingle tribulation with mercy. (St Isaac the Syrian, in "The Four Books," 1.4, Arabic version)

196. As soon as grace sees that a little self-esteem has begun to steal into a man's thoughts, and that he has begun to think great things of himself, she immediately permits the temptations opposing him to gain in strength and prevail, until he learns his weakness, and takes to flight, and clings to God in humility. (St Isaac the Syrian, *Homilies* 72, in *Ascetical Homilies,* p 355)

197. We advance toward humility by means of trials. He who rests on his virtue without suffering tribulation has the door of pride open before him. (St Isaac the Syrian, *Homilies* 57, in *Ascetical Homilies,* p 283)

198. The grace of God always stands at a distance from man watching him during prayer. If a thought of humility stirs within him, it immediately approaches him with its immense powers of aid. This happens particularly during prayer rather than at other times. (St Isaac the Syrian, "Four Books," 1.5, Arabic version)

199. If you practice an excellent virtue without tasting its succor, do not marvel; for until a man becomes humble, he will not receive the reward of his labor. (St Isaac the Syrian, *Homilies* 57, in *Ascetical Homilies,* p 282)

200. "Before ruin cometh pride," says the wise man (Prov 18.12); and before a gift comes humility. (St Isaac the Syrian, *Homilies* 57, in *Ascetical Homilies,* p 283)

201. Know with certainty, therefore, that to stand is not within your power, nor does it pertain to your virtue, but it belongs to grace herself which carries you upon the palm of her hand, that you be not alarmed. (St Isaac the Syrian, *Homilies* 61, in *Ascetical Homilies,* p 338)

202. Not everyone who is naturally gentle, or quiet, or prudent, or meek, has attained to the stature of humility. But he is truly humble of mind who secretly possesses something worthy of pride, and does not pride himself, but in his thought reckons it as dust, earth, and ashes. (St Isaac the Syrian, *Homilies* 77, in *Ascetical Homilies,* p 383)

203. And neither do we call the man humble who humbles himself through remembrance of his sins and transgressions . . . although this is a laudable thing . . . But the man of perfect humility is he who has no need of devising reasons with his mind in order to be humble, but who has come to possess humility in all these matters perfectly, naturally and without labor, like a man who has received in himself some great gift, more excellent than the whole of creation and nature. Yet with his own eyes he sees himself as a sinner, vile, and contemptible. (St Isaac the Syrian, *Homilies* 77, in *Ascetical Homilies,* pp 383, 384)

204. If you treat yourself with contempt so as to be honored, God will expose you publicly; yet if you disparage yourself for the sake of the truth, God will move all his creatures to hymn your praise. (St Isaac the Syrian, *Homilies* 5, in *Ascetical Homilies,* p 50)

205. Truly, O Lord, if we do not humble ourselves, Thou dost not cease to humble us. (St Isaac the Syrian, Homilies 36, in *Ascetical Homilies,* p 162)

206. Beloved Sons, what is it that forced our Lord Jesus Christ to gird his waist with a towel, remove his garments, pour water into a basin and wash the feet of his inferiors? (Jn 13.4,5). He wanted to teach us to be humble, being an example to us by what he did. So all those who like to return to their previous status [before the fall] have no alternative other than humility. (St Antony the Great, *Letters* 6.11, in "The Letters of St Antony the Great," Arabic version)

CHAPTER SEVEN

Faith and Perseverance

> "[One] should always pray and not give up." (Lk 18.1)

> "And whatever you ask in prayer, you will receive, if you have faith." (Mt 21.22)

> "And without faith it is impossible to please him. For whoever would draw near to God must believe that he exists and that he rewards those who seek him." (Heb 11.6)

> "In your struggle against sin, you have not yet resisted to the point of shedding your blood." (Heb 12.4)

FAITH IS THE VITAL BOND that binds us to God: "Without faith it is impossible to please him. For whoever would draw near to God must believe that he exists and that he rewards those who seek him" (Heb 11.6). Faith is the highest gift offered to mankind, for through faith we are granted salvation from our bondage to sin and death: "He who believes and is baptized will be saved; but he who does not believe will be condemned" (Mk 16.16).

Everything can be done by him who believes. This applies equally to the possible and the impossible: "You will say to this mountain, 'Move from here to there,' and it will move; and nothing will be impossible to you" (Mt 17.20); "All things are possible to him who believes" (Mk 9.23).

The Lord Jesus has granted those who believe in him the authority to do the same works that he did and even greater ones: "Truly, truly, I say to you, he who believes in me will also do the works that I do; and greater works than these will he do" (Jn 14.12).

What Is Faith?

—Faith is not a feeling or an emotion.

—Neither is it an obscure blind call to mystery.

—Nor is it forcing one's soul to feel the existence of God and the invisible world.

—Nor is it deceiving the mind to convince it of salvation, justification, redemption, or the like.

—Nor is it contriving an artificial feeling of complacency about things imperceptible to the senses.

—Nor is it repressing the doubts clouding issues not easily acceptable to a materialistic mind.

—Nor is it embezzling for oneself a personal property, whose secrets cannot be shared with everyone.

—Nor is it a private opinion.

—Nor is it a mental conviction resulting from analysis, deduction, or comparison.

—Nor is it the fruit of scientific evidence.

Faith Is the Mental Affirming of the Truths of Christianity Readily and Gladly

It is imperative here for the mind to accept these truths and submit itself to faith without resistance or investigation. It should yield all its imagination and intellect to faith, giving up all its powers of analogical or comparative reasoning gladly. Once the mind has declared its resignation and offered total surrender to all the facts of faith in God in such loving obedience, the Holy Spirit starts to reveal to the devoted mind all that relates to these facts of faith: "The Holy Spirit . . . will teach you all things" (Jn 14.26); "Then he opened their minds to understand the Scriptures" (Lk 24.45). The Holy Spirit leads the mind in the light of this newly gained spiritual knowledge until it reaches the truth, which is nothing other than God: "Did I not tell you that if you believe you will see the glory of God?" (Jn 11.40). "Blessed are you Simon Bar-Jona! For flesh and blood has not revealed this to you, but my Father who is in heaven" (Mt 16.17).

Therefore, the mind should first accept the facts of faith with all submission and surrender. It will become illumined with spiritual knowledge. It will find that all its previously eminent imaginative and intellectual powers, all its analogies and comparisons, now serve only to increase the lucidity of these facts. The mind will even find that with the facts of faith it is filled with a widened and renewed perception.

What brings us into submission and surrender to the doctrines of faith is their divine inspiration. No one can ever declare them, reveal them, or explain them to us except God. No philosophical process or physical perceptions can ever lead us to apprehend these facts, for they are not of this world.

Faith in God Is the Acceptance of His Knowledge on the Grounds of the Facts That He Has Revealed about Himself in His Very Words and in His Own Idiom

God knew the impotence of the human mind and its absolute disability to perceive any of the facts about him unaided. Hence, God has undertaken to reveal himself to us and all that concerns his relationship to us. To accept these truths is to accept him in person and believe in him: "If a man loves me, he will keep my word" (Jn 14.23). If we believe in him and keep his commandments, he will then make up for the imperfection of our faith by manifesting himself to us: "He who has my commandments and keeps them, he it is who loves me; and he who loves me will be loved by my Father, and I will love him and manifest myself to him" (Jn 14.21).

Faith and confidence in his promises is faith in him.

Our Knowledge of God Will Remain Wanting until We Know Him As He Is

This knowledge "God has revealed to us through the Spirit. For the Spirit searches everything, even the depths of God" (1 Cor 2.10). This is living faith: perceiving God in himself and in ourselves through the Holy Spirit. "Have I been with you so long, and yet you do not know me, Philip? He who has seen me has seen the Father; how can you say, 'Show us the Father'" (Jn 14.9)?

Philip's question is nothing other than a cry for perfection of faith. This is what engages the heart of each one of us. Jesus answered his disciples, "I am in the Father and the Father [is] in me" (Jn 14.10). How then can we see Christ, how can we know him and thus know the Father as well?

Christ has answered this question: "I do not pray for these [that is, his disciples] only, but also for those who believe in me through their word, that they may all be one; even as thou, Father, art in me, and I in thee, that they also may be in us" (Jn 17.20, 21).

The Enemies of Faith

Faith has three enemies: reliance on natural reason, fear, and skepticism.

1. *Reliance on Empirical Reason.* Reliance on empirical reason hampers the work of faith and frustrates the acceptance of its effectiveness, for it is well known in nature that man cannot walk on the sea or move mountains or rebuke the wind and waves or raise the dead. As for faith, it pays no regard to nature and its laws. Faith can do all this and even more. For this reason, if man depends entirely on his empirical reasoning, his faith will be paralyzed: "Jesus said, 'Take away the stone.' Martha, the sister of the dead man, said to him, 'Lord, by this time there will be an odor, for he has been dead four days.' Jesus said to her, 'Did I not tell you that if you would believe you would see the glory of God' " (Jn 11.39, 40)?

Natural reason and calculation foster fear, and fear leaves no room for faith. It is common knowledge, for example, that vipers and scorpions are noxious. The look of them strikes terror into the heart. But faith has a transcendent vision and can look upon them as blessed creatures created by God. Faith stands fearless before them: "Behold, I have given you authority to tread upon serpents and scorpions, and over all the power of the enemy; and nothing shall hurt you" (Lk 10.19). Science proves that poison is deadly, but faith does not know this: "They will pick up serpents, and if they drink any deadly thing, it will not hurt them" (Mk 16.18).

We can thus see that scientific reason constrains the work of faith and hinders its consummation.

2. *Fear.* Fear is a proof that man still longs to defend his own ego and pities himself. It is a symptom of self-love and stands in opposition to faith. Fear weakens faith and deprives man of its fruits.

Faith in itself is an exodus from man's ego and a denial of self, an exodus urged by man's love for God and for other people. A true believer is one who has surrendered his soul and body to God. Fearing nothing at all, he puts all his trust in God's faithful promises: "He who believes in me, though he die, yet shall he live" (Jn 11.25). It is in this spirit that Abraham offered his son: "He considered that God was able to raise men even from the dead" (Heb 11.19). In this spirit also did the three young men, undaunted, enter into the fiery furnace. They were sure that God would save them from its flames:

"O Nebuchadnezzar, we have no need to answer you in this matter. If it be so, our God whom we serve is able to deliver us from the burning fiery furnace; and he will deliver us out of your hand, O king" (Dan 3.16, 17). When thrown into the den of lions, Daniel trusted in his God: "So Daniel was taken up out of the den, and no kind of hurt was found upon him, because he had trusted in his God" (Dan 6.23).

In order to grasp the danger of fear and the harm it inflicts on our spiritual life, we should ponder this verse: "But as for the cowardly, the faithless, the polluted, as for murderers, fornicators, sorcerers, idolaters, and all liars, their lot shall be in the lake that burns with fire and sulphur, which is the second death" (Rev 21.8).

You might be surprised to see the cowardly placed at the head of this sinister list. The reason for this is that fear is the element that causes our fall into the rest of all these sins.

3. *Skepticism.* It may seem that doubt is a mild form of fear. However, the converse is true. Fear is but a symptom of an imperfect knowledge, while doubt is a sin directly aimed against God: doubt is disbelief in God's promises. Doubt fosters fear. Doubt is the first weakening of trust in God, but it gives rise to fear, the farthest point away from God. When Peter saw how violent the wind was, he employed his powers of assessment and concluded that he could go no further. He surrendered to fear and began to sink. He doubted the Lord's command. This is what the Lord disclosed to him in clear terms. "'Lord, if it is you, bid me come to you on the water.' He said, 'Come.' So Peter got out of the boat and walked on the water and came to Jesus; but when he saw the wind, he was afraid, and beginning to sink he cried out, 'Lord, save me.' Jesus immediately reached out his hand and caught him, saying to him, 'O man of little faith, why did you doubt'" (Mt 14.28–31)? In the same way, St James the Apostle says in clear terms that if doubt tarnishes our petitions, we cannot reap any fruit from our struggle: "But let him ask in faith, with no doubting, for he who doubts is like a wave of the sea that is driven and tossed by the wind. For that person must not suppose that a double-minded man, unstable in all his ways, will receive anything from the Lord" (Jas 1.6, 7). "Truly, I say to you, whoever says to this mountain, 'Be taken up and cast into the sea,' and does not doubt in his heart, but believes that what he says will come to pass, it will be done for him. Therefore I tell you, whatever you ask in prayer, believe that you have received it and it will be yours" (Mk 11.23, 24).

Signs of Faith

Persistence in prayer and worship is one of the signs of effective faith. If faith represents the columns on which the temple of spiritual life stands, perseverance represents the stones by which the whole edifice is constructed. But to assess the value of the spirit of persistence in prayer, we should first consider the spirit of despondency.

Despondency is the folly of pride and stiffness of neck. The desperate man follows his own stubborn counsel and chooses the torment of everlasting hell. He does not wish to yield to God or accept from his hand the sweetness and the bitterness of this life. By doing so, he refuses the crown of eternal life.

The spirit of perseverance, on the other hand, is a sign of humility and surrender. The man who persists in prayer and worship does not think himself worthy of anything; his self is not dear to him. He persists in submission and obedience because he cannot cease from persistence and submission. On what else can he rely if his self is powerless and worthless in his eyes? "Jesus said to the twelve, 'Do you also wish to go away?' Simon Peter answered him, 'Lord, to whom shall we go? You have the words of eternal life'" (Jn 6.67, 68).

The spirit of persistence springs from an inward conviction that life is but one single way that leads to the kingdom of heaven. Persistence in walking along that way is then the only means of arrival, the only means of overcoming difficulties. Those who stop on the way, for whatever reason, have fallen into Satan's snares: "Walk while you have the light, lest the darkness overtake you" (Jn 12.35). That is, so long as you walk the light attends you and leads you, but if you stop, darkness—that is, the enemy—will overtake you at once. Regression is a kind of miscarriage of the soul, a failure, and a fall into its deadly pride and its strange desire for perdition: "No one who puts his hand to the plough and looks back is fit for the kingdom of God" (Lk 9.62).

It is really amazing that for those traveling along the way of prayer and worship, rest lies only in doubling their pace and increasing their struggle!

The word *faith* (πίστις) is used in Orthodox terminology to denote two specific meanings. The first is strictly objective. It concerns the facts of faith and its creeds as they are expressed in the Bible and literally recorded by the canons of the Church. Here, faith is stated in fixed, unalterable expressions and technical terms set by the authority of the church councils and the opinions of distinguished theologians. In this objective sense of faith, divine truth and reason cannot cohere except by the intervention of grace.

The second sense of faith is totally subjective. It concerns the ability of one's heart to respond directly to God in person, but only in conformity with the creeds of faith. In this subjective meaning of faith, man submits his whole being to God, and therefore to all his commandments. This is to be done in love and obedience and not by reason or logic. Reason and logic may enter afterward as servants to love and obedience but not as initiators or authorities: "Faith work[s] through love" (Gal 5.6).

From these two definitions of faith we can infer that objective faith needs the riches of man's thought, reason, logic, and study. However, he can never reach the stage of belief except by grace. As for subjective faith, it needs love, obedience, and personal intimacy. A profound relationship with God is composed of fidelity and absolute confidence in God in all affairs, conditions, or situations. This will result in total reliance on him and absolute surrender to his will, no matter how such fidelity may collide with so-called reality or reason.

Hence, the Orthodox Church maintains that in both its objective and subjective senses, faith is a gift of grace. Objective faith depends on the incarnation and the resurrection, both of which are supernatural works. Equally, the demands of subjective faith also require a supernatural bent of mind. For he who believes in God is required neither to covet nor to fear anything, and both of these proscriptions are requirements that surpass the laws of nature: "Apart from me you can do nothing" (Jn 15.5).

What makes faith a virtue besides being a gift is its dependence on man's will. Man can never accept faith unless he wants to believe, and this desire must be accompanied by a submissive will—a will that complies from the first moment. This makes man's reason ready to accept facts that transcend reason. A compliant and submissive will makes man's mind ready to accept the "new thing." In submission, the mind, ready and open, becomes a vessel fit to hold grace and divine truth. It is then that the unreasonable will become reasonable, and the preternatural, natural. For this reason, St Augustine defines faith as "thought attended by compliance."

This compliant and conforming will is the main factor that makes faith a work for which one is to be rewarded. Thus, faith is a gift and a virtue at the same time. It is a work of grace and a work of man together. Man responds to the intimations and the entreaties of grace, and grace, most graciously, responds to this enterprise of man. Here are reconciled the two principles of faith and works (as conceived by the apostles Paul and James, respectively).

From this discussion it becomes clear to us that man's will is free not to respond to God and not to believe and also free to respond and to believe. St Paul says: "Faith is not given to everyone" (2 Thess 3.2). Man's will is an essential element to faith; its submission is considered as a work by itself. By faith man is justified.

Faith and will are intimately related, distinct but indivisible. In meeting the paralytic (Jn 5.6: "Do you want to be healed?") Christ stressed the primacy of will or desire in faith. It is only when we will something that we can be counted worthy of God's response.

On other occasions, our Lord underlines the contrary: the importance of faith in the will. An example of this may be the blind man who kept crying aloud behind him or the two blind men who followed him asking to be healed. These three men had faith in profusion. But here we find Christ probing the element of faith in will: "Do you believe that I am able to do this?" (Mt 9.28). In both of these examples, we can see that will led to faith and faith effected miracles. The will to believe, intermeshing with the action of grace, results in a miracle. This is how faith works. The greatest miracles of faith are but total surrender to God through which man actually enters into the communion of eternal life with him.

We have considered here the submission of the will in faith, the general sense of faith in God. But what if we introduce here the element of redemption and faith in the person of the redeemer? In this case, we find that faith has a new direction, namely, the direction of love. For faith in the redemption means faith in the fatherly love springing from God toward us graciously, persistently, and with so costly a sacrifice. When the heart apprehends this redemptive love, faith in God becomes a sweeping passion. The heart yearns to offer one's entire being to God, for the redemption, which God has perfected for us by the blood of his Son, has become, as it were, a scorching fire that devours the coldness of man. His faith is fervent, his passion is fiery, and he almost longs to die for his God.

The introduction of the element of redemption into the notion of faith has important repercussions for the keeping of God's moral laws as well. Before Christ, faith only represented a reconciliation of the conflict between the will of God and the will of man. Faith was a series of demands, without redemption. Man had to reconcile his will to the will of God, and this was done by keeping the law, the written commandments. Keeping the commandments had been a heavy, or even an impossible, task, which, as St Peter the Apostle described it, "neither we nor our fathers have been able to bear" (Acts 15.10). It could even incur death as a penalty for failure.

With the introduction of redemption through Christ, however, faith has changed into something new. Faith no longer just seeks reconciliation, a cessation of the hostility of man's will. It seeks union, the unity of the will of man with the will of God in the embrace of love through the blood of Jesus. In this new context of redemption, of "faith working through love," what were formerly "commandments and laws" have become "spirit and life." Commandments and laws are no longer chiseled letters on stone, condemning man. They are now written by the Holy Spirit on the loving heart as an anointment of power for life and renewal. And thus the very commandment that had brought death has now become the power of inner life for the man who believes in Christ. Bearing the yoke of the law in written letter was very burdensome: we are now able to bear the law with the help of grace. Grace has made obedience bearable. Not only bearable, it is an easy yoke now, a yoke we can love. All this is brought about by faith made effective through the mystery of Christ's love. Let us read what St Macarius the Great has to say:

> **207.** It is like this in Christianity for anyone who tastes the grace of God. For it says: "Taste and see how sweet the Lord is" (Ps 34.8). The taste is this power of the Spirit working in the heart to effect full certainty in faith. For as many are sons of light and in the service of the New Covenant through the Holy Spirit, these learn nothing from men. For they are taught by God. His very grace writes in their hearts the laws of the Spirit. They, therefore, should not put all their trusting hope solely in the scriptures written in ink. For, indeed, divine grace writes on the "tables of the heart" (2 Cor 3.3) the laws of the Spirit and the heavenly mysteries.
>
> For the heart directs and governs all the other organs of the body. And when grace pastures the heart, it rules over all the members and the thoughts. (*Homilies* 15.20, in Maloney, *Intoxicated with God: The Fifty Spiritual Homilies of Macarius*)

We can thus see that with the introduction of the factor of redemption, faith has been turned into a reciprocated love for God. Piety is no longer one-sided, a burden borne by man in fear of punishment and death. Man is now endowed with faith in Christ in mutual love with God in which he is freely beloved by the Father: "For the Father himself loves you, because you have loved me and have believed that I came from the Father" (Jn 16.27).

Moreover, by reason of God's love, which is poured into our hearts by the Holy Spirit, faith has come to possess new amazing powers, which transcend nature. Man is no longer the old Adam. He has become another being united to a divine force that pervades him through and through. St Macarius also says:

> **208.** If, then, anyone loves God, God also shares his love with him. Once man believes in him, God bestows on him a heavenly faith and so man becomes twofold. As you, therefore, offer (or consecrate) to God any part of yourself, he himself shares with your soul similar parts of his own being, so that all you do you may do sincerely and purely, loving and praying in this same way. (*Homilies* 15.22, in *Spiritual Homilies*)

The Fathers teach us the value of faith in ascetical theology, that is, in the spiritual life in general, which includes prayer. But we have not found anyone who has given better expression to this relationship than St Isaac the Syrian, bishop of Nineveh. The material in which this great saint has dwelt on the subject of faith is extensive and profuse. We will thus summarize here the main tenets to focus the reader's attention and thereby perhaps help him increase his faith.

SAYINGS OF THE FATHERS ON FAITH AND PERSEVERANCE

209. Certainty of faith in God is not the soundness of a man's confession (although this is the mother of faith), but a soul that beholds the truth of God by the power of her disciplines. When you find faith united to disciplines in the Holy Scriptures, do not suppose the sense of it to refer to right confession. The faith that gives the confidence of trust is never attained by the unbaptized or those whose mind is perverted from the truth. The certainty of faith reveals itself in the soul in proportion to the lofty mode of life of those who pay heed to the practice of the Lord's commandments.

Continual reflection on the Scriptures is light for the soul, because they imprint on the intellect recollections helpful for guarding against the passions and for continuance with God through love and the purity of prayer. (St Isaac the Syrian, *Homilies* 54, in *The Ascetical Homilies of Saint Isaac the Syrian,* p 266)

210. Faith in God is the wings of prayer. (St Isaac the Syrian, in "The Four Books of St. Isaac the Syrian, Bishop of Nineveh," 1.1, Arabic version)

211. Negligence and sloth impede God's help to man, and therefore shake man's faith in God. (St Isaac the Syrian, in "The Four Books," 1.4)

212. Everything is possible to faith if man fixes his sight on God and not on the thing desired. (St Isaac the Syrian, in "The Four Books," 1.4)

213. If you truly have faith in the omnipotence of God and believe that he manages all your affairs, do not then employ human craftiness. (St Isaac the Syrian, in "The Four Books," 1.4)

214. Until the soul becomes drunk with faith in God by receiving a perception of faith's power, she can neither heal the malady of the senses, nor be able forcefully to tread visible matter underfoot, which is the barrier to things that are within and unperceived. (St Isaac the Syrian, *Homilies* 1, in *Ascetical Homilies,* p 4)

215. By the experience of many interventions of divine assistance in temptations, a man also acquires firm faith. Henceforth he has no fear, and he gains stout-heartedness in temptations from the training he has acquired. (St Isaac the Syrian, *Homilies* 61, in *Ascetical Homilies,* p 296)

216. Simplicity is attended by faith. (St Isaac the Syrian, *Homilies* 72, in *Ascetical Homilies,* p 351)

217. Those upon whom the light of faith has dawned are no longer so audacious as to pray on behalf of themselves; nor do they entreat God, saying, "Give this to us," or "Take that from us"; nor do they in any wise take care for themselves. For at every moment, by the noetic eyes of faith, they see the fatherly providence which comes of the true Father to shelter them: he who in his great and immeasurable love surpasses all in paternal affection and who, more than all, has the power and might to help us in a measure superabundantly greater than anything we might ask, think, or conceive. (St Isaac the Syrian, *Homilies* 52, in *Ascetical Homilies,* pp 253–54)

218. But faith requires a mode of thinking that is single, limpidly pure and simple, far removed from any deviousness or invention of methods. (St Isaac the Syrian, *Homilies* 52, in *Ascetical Homilies,* p 254)

219. For knowledge is opposed to faith; but faith, in all that pertains to it, demolishes the laws of knowledge . . . For such is the definition of knowledge, that without investigation and examination it has no authority to do anything . . . Knowledge is not so bold as to attempt anything that has not been given to nature. How so? The liquid nature of water cannot support upon its back the footsteps of a body; the man who comes too close to fire burns himself . . . Knowledge watchfully guards itself from such things and will in no wise be persuaded to overstep their boundaries. But faith transgresses them with authority, saying: "If thou go through fire, thou shalt not be burned, and the rivers shall not overflow thee" (Is 43.2) . . . For it is by faith that men have entered into flames . . . and they have trodden upon the back of the sea as upon dry land. All these are above nature and opposed to the modes of knowledge. (St Isaac the Syrian, *Homilies* 52, in *Ascetical Homilies,* pp 254, 255)

220. There is no knowledge that is not impoverished, however rich it should be; but heaven and earth cannot contain the treasures of faith. The man whose heart is upheld by the confidence of faith will never be in want; and when he has nothing, by faith he possesses all, as it is written: "All things whatsoever ye shall ask in prayer, ye shall receive" (Mt 21.22); and again, "The Lord is at hand, have care for nothing" (Phil 4.5, 6).

Knowledge always seeks means to safeguard those who have acquired it . . . The man who takes refuge in faith never employs, or is engaged in, ways and means. For knowledge everywhere sings the praises of fear . . . But what says faith? "He was afraid and began to sink" (Mt 14.30) . . . and again, "Fear them not nor flee from their face." (St Isaac the Syrian, *Homilies* 52, in *Ascetical Homilies,* p 255)

221. Knowledge enjoins all those who journey in its path to investigate according to its laws the end of anything before making a beginning, and thus to commence, lest the end of the thing prove unachievable by the limit of human ability and labor be spent in vain, and lest the thing prove difficult and impossible to realize. But what says faith? "All things are possible to him that believeth" (Mk 9.23) for to God nothing is impossible. (St Isaac the Syrian, *Homilies* 52, in *Ascetical Homilies,* p 256)

222. O unspeakable wealth, O ocean rich in its billows and its marvelous treasures which abundantly spill forth by the power of faith! How filled with boldness, how replete with sweetness and hope is the journey accompanied by faith! How light are faith's burdens, how sweet its labors! (St Isaac the Syrian, *Homilies* 52, in *Ascetical Homilies,* p 256)

223. Whom does the man resemble that has been deemed worthy to taste the sweetness of faith and who afterwards turns again to unspiritual knowledge? He resembles the man who has found a pearl of great price and exchanges it for a copper obol. (St Isaac the Syrian, *Homilies* 52, in *Ascetical Homilies,* p 256)

224. I say not that knowledge is blameworthy, but that faith is higher . . . Knowledge is a step whereby a man can climb up to the lofty height of faith. (St Isaac the Syrian, *Homilies* 52, in *Ascetical Homilies,* pp 256, 257)

225. By faith we mean not that wherewith a man believes in the distinctions of the Divine and worshipful Hypostases, in the singular and unique nature of the very Godhead, and in the wondrous dispensation to mankind through the assumption of our nature, although this faith is also very lofty. But we call faith that light which by grace dawns in the soul and which fortifies the heart by the testimony of the mind, making it undoubting through the assurance of hope that is remote from all conceit. This faith manifests itself not by aural tradition . . . The Comforter shows a man the holy power that dwells within him at every moment.

. . . This power is the Comforter Himself Who, in the strength of faith, consumes the parts of the soul, as it were by fire. The soul then rushes forward, despising every danger because of her trust in God. (St Isaac the Syrian, *Homilies* 52, in *Ascetical Homilies,* pp 262, 263)

226. Ask God, however, to grant that you attain the measure of faith . . . Pray for this diligently, and entreat for it with fervor, and with great earnestness make supplication until you receive it. Then you will weary yourself no longer. You will be counted worthy of these things if with faith you first compel yourself to cast your care upon God, and exchange your own providing for his providence. When he sees your volition, that with complete limpid purity of thought you have set your faith in God alone, rather than in yourself, and that you compel yourself to hope in God more than in your own soul, then power which is unknown to you will come to dwell upon you, and you will sensibly perceive this very power which is most certainly with you. (St Isaac the Syrian, *Homilies* 72, in *Ascetical Homilies,* p 352)

227. But if you are caught fast in the noose of human knowledge, it is not improper for me to say that it would be easier for you to be loosed from fetters of iron than from this. You will never be far from the snares and bonds of delusion, nor will you ever be able to have boldness and confidence before the Lord; at every moment you will walk the edge of a sword, and by no means will you be able to escape sorrow. Take refuge in weakness and simplicity, that you may live acceptably before God and be without care. For just as a shadow follows a body, so also does mercy follow humility. If, then, you wish to pass your life in these things, by no means encourage your feeble deliberations. Even if all ills and evils and dangers should surround and frighten you, give no heed to them, neither take them into account.

If once you have set your faith in the Lord who is himself sufficient for your protection and your care, and if you are following after him, take no thought again for any such thing, but say to your soul: "He suffices me for all, to Whom I have altogether committed myself. I am not here [i.e., absent to all earthly concerns]; he knows this." And then you will see in reality the wonders of God, how on every occasion he is at hand to deliver those who fear him, and how his providence encompasses them and is not observed. (St Isaac the Syrian, *Homilies* 72, in *Ascetical Homilies,* pp 353–54)

228. Toil for God's sake and sweat in his husbandry precede hope in him. If you believe in God, you do well, but faith has need of labors also, and confidence in God is the good witness of the conscience born of undergoing hardship for the virtues. (St Isaac the Syrian, *Homilies* 7, in *Ascetical Homilies,* pp 64–65)

229. A cowardly man shows that he suffers from two diseases: love of his flesh and lack of faith. (St Isaac the Syrian, *Homilies* 40, in *Ascetical Homilies,* p 202)

230. A courageous heart and scorn of perils comes from one of two causes: either from hardness of heart or from great faith in God. Pride accompanies hardness of heart, but humility accompanies faith. (St Isaac the Syrian, *Homilies* 40, in *Ascetical Homilies,* pp 202–3)

231. Faith is the wing of prayer, and without it my prayer will return to my bosom. Faith is the unshaken stance of the soul and is unmoved by any adversity. The believing man is not one who thinks that God can do all things, but one who trusts that he will obtain everything. Faith is the agent of things unhoped for, as the thief proved (cf Lk 23.42–43). (St John Climacus, *Ladder of Divine Ascent,* 27.69–72, p 271)

232. In asking God for that which is virtuous, do not cease to ask until you have received. The Lord drew our thoughts to this when he related the parable about the man who obtained bread at midnight from a friend by his persistence (cf Luke 11.5). (St Basil the Great, *Short Rules* 261; PG 31.1257)

233. After a long spell of prayer, do not say that nothing has been gained, for you have already achieved something. For after all, what higher good is there than to cling to the Lord, to persevere in unceasing union with him? (St John Climacus, *Ladder of Divine Ascent,* 28.32, p 278)

234. Faith is the key of God's treasury, she dwells in simple, kind, loving hearts: "All things are possible to him what believeth" (Mk 9.23). (Fr John of Kronstadt, in Moore, "Some Aspects of Orthodox Prayer," p 37)

235. As often as I have prayed with faith, God has always heard me and fulfilled my prayers. (Fr John of Kronstadt, in Moore, "Some Aspects of Orthodox Prayer," p 43)

236. Prayer, as conversation with God, is in itself the highest blessing, often much greater than what the person is asking for. The merciful God does not fulfill the request, leaving the supplicant at his prayer, lest he should lose it, lest he should leave this highest blessing when he receives the much smaller blessing asked for. (Bishop Ignatius Brianchaninov, in Moore, "Orthodox Prayer," p 43)

237. If you lack the virtue of perseverance, do not expect to have true consolation in your prayer. For perseverance means labor. (St Isaac the Syrian, in "The Four Books," 1.3, Arabic version)

238. Without perseverance no discipline, whether prayer, fasting or vigil, ever bears fruit. The end of your labor will be just the same as its beginning. (St Isaac the Syrian, in "The Four Books," 1.3, Arabic version)

239. For this reason our Lord fortified our infirmity by prayer, saying, "Awake, watch, and pray that ye enter not into temptation" (cf Mt 26.41). Pray and be not slothful, being watchful and praying always. "Ask, and ye shall receive; seek, and ye shall find; knock, and it shall be opened unto you: for everyone that asketh receiveth; and he that seeketh findeth; and to him that knocketh it shall be opened" (Mt 7.7) . . . O the ineffable encouragement! The Giver incites us to entreat him to the end that he might give us his divine gifts. And although the Lord, as he himself knows, provides us with everything that will profit us, nonetheless what he here says is filled with great power to give us courage and to make us confident. (St Isaac the Syrian, *Homilies* 70, in *Ascetical Homilies,* p 340)

240. My Sons . . . I never get tired of pleading with the Lord on your behalf, that you may know the grace that has become your own. For God in his mercy stimulates every one by the various means of his grace. So never lose heart or be slothful, my Sons, in crying to the Lord day and night. By this you will forcefully cause God's righteousness to grant you power from on high. (St Antony the Great, *Letters* 5.1, Arabic version)

241. He who does not immediately receive, because of God's delay and patient longing, is inkindled much more . . . But, indeed, as long as the Lord, by his delaying the gift, is patiently loving him by testing his faith and love of his will, the person himself should all the more keenly and with greater diligence, without becoming remiss, ought to seek the gift of God, having once for all believed and assured himself that God is without deceit and is truthful, who has promised that he would give his grace to those who faithfully ask in all patience until the end. (St Macarius the Great, *Homilies* 29.3, in *Spiritual Homilies*)

CHAPTER EIGHT

Struggle and Constraint

"The kingdom of heaven has been coming
violently, and men of violence take it by
force." (Mt 11.12)

"For we are not contending against flesh and
blood, but against the principalities, against
the powers, against the world rulers of this
present darkness, against the spiritual hosts
of wickedness in the heavenly places . . .
Stand therefore . . . Pray at all times in the
Spirit, with all prayer and supplication."
(Eph 6.12, 14, 18)

T HE BLESSINGS OF THE CONTEMPLATIVE LIFE do not burst in on our lives
like a flash of lightning. They do not arrest our attention the moment
we open our eyes to look for them. Rather, they permeate our lives impercep-
tibly. They are like the light of the rising sun. The first faint light of dawn penetrates the veil of darkness—slowly but surely. Although it is difficult to trace
the inception of this light, it spreads until it pervades everything. It dispels the
darkness before the sun rises into view.

In order to attain a fruitful life of prayer, we should not expect blessings to
fall upon us suddenly. Rather, we should make our way through with slow but
sure steps. We need a long, disciplined struggle. We need patience and constraint. It is enough to make progress however slow that progress may seem or
however pitch-dark the world around us and around our faith may appear.
Mere progress in the life of prayer and intimacy with God is a sure sign that
we will reach our goal. It is proof positive that the light must appear, however
long it may be hidden from us. Once it appears, the fruit of our laborious struggle and our faith and patience will materialize. When we constrain ourselves

in our struggle, when we expend our sweat and our tears, when we contend with our doubts and whispers—walking on in spite of the darkness that shrouds everything in us, our own eyes may not see in ourselves anything but weakness. The eyes of God, however, see precious and valuable signs of growth: "Blessed are those who have not seen and yet believe" (Jn 20.29); "For God is not so unjust as to overlook your work and the love which you showed for his sake" (Heb 6.10).

But while waiting in patience for progress, we must also avoid another misconception about growth in the contemplative life. It is conceived by some that the way of worship, contemplation, and solitude is strewn with flowers and roses—by no means. For the way is an arid wilderness. It has no comeliness that we might desire it in itself. Let it suffice to know that Christ described it as a narrow gate and a tough, rugged path. After you cover some distance, you are overtaken by fear and shot through with doubt. You will then ask, "Am I truly heading for God? But where is he?" This is only the beginning of the ordeal that your soul will undergo on the way. It will find itself destitute of any help from any human being. It will feel devoid of any spiritual comfort or sign whatsoever—even of one word of promise or encouragement. Common sense will become your adversary. Thus, your faith will be tested and vision will be denied you.

At the onset of this spiritual dryness, many can no longer bear the sight of the rugged path ahead. They turn back. They speak with the perplexity of a Nathaniel: "Can anything good come out of Nazareth?" (Jn 1.46). As for those who carry on in faith in such conditions, they are truly blessed. "If you would believe you would see the glory of God" (Jn 11.40).

However, if you intend to follow this path, you must also be forewarned that even faith will not sustain you with the same strength throughout the whole journey. It will fail you from time to time, for on the way you will seek your former pleasures. Your heart shall crave once more for Egypt with its leeks and onions. Your self will come out and blame you: Why have you led me out to the wilderness, to kill me? Both your soul and mine are poverty stricken and well nigh incorrigible. We shall hanker after meat in the wilderness. We shall ask for a sign on the way but none shall be given us.

Many are those who have stood bewildered, asking: Where are we? What is the purpose behind our journey? What were we doing coming this way in the first place? But these are questions of doubt, a cry of retreat. Many have turned back before reaching the end because they preferred to live by sight.

They asked for a sign for themselves, thus proving their lack of faith. Their wish being rejected, they gave up the trail and flung themselves with a vengeance into the arms of the madding crowd. They plunged with all their might into the countless crazes of this world and have become obsessed with them. This they have done not because they see any real benefit in these activities, but because they want to escape the truth that confronted them. For fear seized them when they were forced to face the fact that they had to walk by faith alone and not by sight.

Had it not been for Moses, Israel would not have journeyed for a single day in the desert. Yet Moses journeyed forty years in the hope of reaching the promised land. His only resource throughout this long struggle was faith. By means of his towering faith, he managed to lead an obstinate people forty years in a most arid wilderness. We need the leadership of Moses for ourselves so that we can walk by faith. By faith we can push ourselves to go on even though we can see nothing. However long our struggle may last, we should keep on going along the way of God, for we are certain that at the end of the trail lies the heavenly Jerusalem prepared like a bride for her bridegroom. But so long as the journey goes on, we should be satisfied with God's faithfulness to his promises, the secret encouragements that he gives us, and his voice speaking to us out of eternity.

The discussion in this chapter revolves around man's will. In ascetical theology, speaking about man's will is a most subtle and crucial task. In this single word, *will,* man's lawful struggle may change from a struggle according to the rules into a subverted, erroneous one that hurls him headlong into the world of delusion and mania.

There is a lawful and healthy kind of struggle or constraint. We would like to make clear to the reader from the first of what such a struggle, which leads to Christ and eternal life, consists. In brief, it consists of guiding one's will to absolute surrender to God. Constraint of the will is here aimed at subduing the self to the guidance of grace in untiring faith, whatever the conditions. This should be done in such a way as to leave no room for private aspirations, unless they are kept compliant to the voice and commandments of God.

We should beware here of the waywardness of the ego. During the warmth of worship, the signs of success begin to appear, followed by joy and happiness. The ego in such moments inclines to have a greater share in this success and happiness. It thus resorts to an autonomous effort to create more success and more joy. Here lies the crucial point. Struggle and constraint change here from their lawful, healthy course into a subversive, egotistic one. Struggle is no longer aimed at subjection to God. Neither is voluntary constraint practiced for obedience any longer. Instead, struggle becomes dependent on the ego, and constraint is practiced for developing personal abilities.

We would like to make clear to the reader that success and spiritual joy by themselves are not the work of man in the least. They are the work of God alone. It is God who increases them whenever he likes and in whatever portion he chooses, whether man is the reason or without reason at all.

Struggle and constraint, therefore, should not have any motive whatsoever other than loving God, in the person of Jesus Christ, with all one's heart. The expression of this love consists of nothing but constraining one's ego to obey God's commandments however great the price. It also consists in constraining one's will and intention to surrender to God's dispensation, whatever the damage to one's ego. Moreover, struggle and constraint should not depend on earthly supports such as self-esteem or people's praise. Neither should they waver in the face of criticism or condemnation.

As for the aim we have to set before us in our struggle and constraint, it is total submission to God and absolute surrender to his good and perfect will. Let these words be illuminated signposts along the way of struggle and constraint:

1. Beware of a will that is taut like a tightrope, for it may hurl you down into a whirlpool of egotistic struggle. When your will becomes active and ardent, bind it at once to obedience to Christ. This should be done to safeguard you from doing anything of your own accord.

2. Reject any feeling of your own responsibility for success or failure. Turn it at once into a sense of responsibility for the discharge of your duty in simple, straightforward honesty.

3. Do not feel that you must resort to the unseen powers as an extra guarantee of protection. For Christ has left you destitute of nothing. He has taken upon himself all the demands of your journey. Therefore, be contented with the power of Christ, which is with you. Strive with this reality as your benchmark. If ever succor and solace come from above, rejoice then and be happy. But never make them a foundation for your struggle. Otherwise your progress will be hampered and blocked.

4. Never practice struggle or constraint to gain something for yourself, such as strength for your willpower or courage to face your enemy. On the

contrary, struggle and constraint help you abdicate your self, renounce your willpower, relinquish your courage, and take shelter in Christ so that you do not attempt to face your enemy in your own strength.

5. Inasmuch as you rely on your own will, your sense of God's succor is weakened. Conversely, the more you confine your struggle to surrendering your own will, the more you feel the reality of God at work, managing your life and providing for you. Through calm submission and perseverance in self-restraint, you learn to accept God's dispensation in full.

6. In your obedience to God's commandments, never give up your struggle or constraint however you fail or whatever your temptations. For behind your vanquished soul stands Christ and in his hand the crown for your struggle. You are then responsible not for your success, but for your effort.

7. The struggle and constraint we undertake, even if correctly performed, do not qualify us for justification. Neither do they move us closer to God. They only remove us a long distance from our ego and sever us from the life of sin and transgression. As for justification, it is freely given by God, and as for growing close to God, it is for Christ to bring this about.

The fact that should not be overlooked by the reader is that the person who is relying on himself and his own will to struggle does not feel that his struggle is egotistic. Neither does he feel that his reliance is not on God. So he goes his own way, keeping to himself. Jolting and stumbling along, he drags himself out of one pit only to fall into another, cursing himself and blaming his own will. He pulls himself together again—for more jolts, stumbling along in dejection, still convinced that he is trusting in God alone.

But the truth of the matter is quite to the contrary. The way of surrendering one's will to God never blames the will as if it were responsible for stumbling or falling. Stumbling and falling arise not from the weakness of one's will but from its power to interfere. This becomes clear when we know that victory, salvation, and blessing do not result from the strength of one's will but from its concealment behind grace. For when the will hides behind grace, man grows stronger. He prevails, staying alert, successful, and growing. But when the will wakes up, storms the scene, rebels, and becomes rigid and unbending, there is no way to avoid the stumbling blocks. So falling reveals the obstructive force of man's will, its activist nature, and its tendency to take pride of place over grace. Therefore, if after stumbling and falling we blame and curse our will, this only goes to show that we admit to walking according to the dictates of our own will. We are not in reality submissive to God. If after falling we rally our will once again and reinforce it, we are, in fact, preparing ourselves for another fall of greater violence. In this way, we insist on making our will responsible for spiritual progress.

But if we really wish to avoid stumbling blocks, sins, and falls, we have to refrain from blaming our will and spurring it on for further activity and ardor. Nay, we must abdicate our will and lose all hope in it completely. We must subdue it and offer it, with all integrity, definitively to God. This can only be carried out by overwhelming the voice of the ego with the voice of God. The will must be coerced to fulfill God's commandments, whatever the cost or insult. It should then be constrained to put up with tedium and toil, with standing in prayer and keeping the night vigil in obedience to all the directions and rules of the Fathers. In this way, the will may succumb and its authority buckle under the power of the Holy Spirit. Afterward, it begins to conceal itself behind grace. It is only then that man can manage to overcome obstacles to spiritual growth.

In this context, any compassion on the self is a devilish attempt to revive its private will and desire. As for all the stumbling blocks we suffer from on the way, they only betray our tendency to draw back from absolute surrender of our will to God and, consequently, our lack of confidence in him. Stumbling on the way should therefore prompt us to ask ourselves whether we have actually surrendered our will to God and whether our confidence in him is growing or not. It should also inspire us with the need for disavowing our private will, which drags us into gratifying our own lusts. Our having stumbled should then urge us to resume our penitence with calm tenacity.

However, the excessive dejection to which man may surrender after falling into a sin is actually a sign of pride and self-esteem. Man here regards his will with more respect than it really deserves. He thinks it outrageous that he should fall at all. He thinks his will is too great to stumble. So he keeps seeking comfort and solace in false encouragement from people or from a confessor to bind his wounds with the pride of his injured self.

As for the correct attitude toward falling into any sin, it lies in confessing the sin and resorting at once to repentance. After this, man should take up the thread of his struggle with self-restraint, surrender his will again, and recommit his soul to God.

SAYINGS OF THE FATHERS ON STRUGGLE AND CONSTRAINT

242. People say that if you feel no inclination to pray, it is better not to pray; but this is crafty, carnal sophistry. If you only pray when you are inclined to, you will completely cease praying; this is what the flesh desires. "The Kingdom of Heaven suffereth violence" (Mt 11.12). You will not be able to work out your salvation without forcing yourself. (Fr John of Kronstadt, in Moore, "Some Aspects of Orthodox Prayer," p 45)

243. Why is long continued prayer necessary? In order that by prolonged, fervent prayer we may warm our cold hearts, hardened in prolonged vanity. For it is strange to think, and still more so to require, that the heart, hardened in worldly vanity, could be speedily penetrated during prayer by the warmth of faith and the love of God. No; labor and labor, time and time are needed to attain this. "The Kingdom of heaven suffereth violence, and the violent take it by force" (Mt 11.12). The Kingdom of Heaven does not hastily come into the heart, when men themselves so assiduously flee from it. The Lord himself expresses his will that our prayers should not be short, by giving us for an example the importunate widow who often came to the Judge and troubled him with her requests (Lk 18.2–6).

Our Lord, our Heavenly Father knows, even before we ask him, what things we have need of (Mt 6.8), and what we want; but we do not know him as we ought, for we give ourselves up to worldly vanity, instead of committing ourselves into the hands of our Heavenly Father. Therefore in his wisdom and mercy he turns our needs into a pretext for our turning to him. "Turn ye, my wandering children, even now unto Me, to your Father, with your whole hearts. If before you were far from Me, now at least warm your cold hearts by faith and love for Me." (Fr John of Kronstadt, in Moore, "Some Aspects of Orthodox Prayer," p 47)

244. The person that wishes to come to the Lord and to be deemed worthy of eternal life and to become the dwelling place of Christ and to be filled with the Holy Spirit so that he may be able to bring forth the fruits of the Spirit and perform the commandments of Christ purely and blamelessly, ought to begin first by believing firmly in the Lord and giving himself completely to the words of his commands and renouncing the world in all things so that his whole mind may be taken up with nothing ephemeral.

And he ought to persevere constantly in prayer, always waiting in faith that expects his coming and his help, keeping the goal of his mind ever fixed upon this. Then he ought to push himself to every good work and to doing all the commandments of the Lord because there is sin dwelling within him.

Thus let him strive to show humility before every person and to consider himself the least and the worst . . . Let him continue incessantly in prayers, always beseeching and believing that the Lord may come to dwell in him and may perfect and give him power to accomplish all his commands and that the Lord himself may become the dwelling place for his soul.

And thus, the things he now does with effort of a reluctant heart, he may perform one day willingly, accustoming himself always to the good and remembering the Lord and waiting for him always in great love.

Then the Lord, seeing such an intention and his good diligence, seeing how he strives to remember the Lord and always seeks to do good, and is humble and meek and loving, how he guides his heart, willing or not, to the best, has mercy on him and frees him from his enemies and from indwelling sin. He fills him with the Holy Spirit. And gradually, without force or struggle he keeps all the Lord's commandments in truth. Or, rather, it is the Lord who keeps in him his very own commandments and then he brings forth the fruits of the Spirit purely. (St Macarius the Great, *Homilies* 19.1, 2, in *Spiritual Homilies*)

245. It is, however, necessary at first for one coming to the Lord to force himself thus to do good, and even if he should not in his heart be so inclined, he must constantly await his mercy with unshakened faith and push himself to love even if he has none, to mercy and to have a merciful heart. He must force himself to be disregarded, and when he is looked down by others, let him rejoice. When he is made light of or dishonored, let him not become angry according to the saying: "Beloved, do not avenge yourselves" (Rom 12.19). Let him push himself to prayer even when he does not possess the prayer of the Spirit.

And so, God, seeing him striving so and pushing himself by determination, even if the heart is unwilling, gives him the authentic prayer of the Spirit, gives him true charity, true meekness, "the bowels of mercies" (Col 3.12), true kindness, and, simply put, fills him with the fruits of the Spirit. (St Macarius the Great, *Homilies* 19.3, in *Spiritual Homilies*)

246. In all of these matters a person must push himself if he desires to gain the approval of and be pleasing to Christ so that the Lord, seeing his determination and purpose in forcing himself to all goodness and simplicity and kindness and humility and charity and prayer with full determination, may give himself completely to him. The Lord himself does all of these things in truth in him without labor and force, which before he could not perform, even by his own determination because of sin that indwelled in him. And now all the practice of virtues come to him as though they are a part of his nature. The reason is really that the Lord comes and dwells in him and he is in the Lord. (St Macarius the Great, *Homilies* 19.6, in *Spiritual Homilies*)

247. Since certain persons insist that once they have accepted grace, they need no further solicitude. But God demands even in those perfect a will of the soul to cooperate in the service of the Spirit, namely, that they freely consent. For the Apostle says: "Do not quench the Spirit" (1 Thess 5.19). (St Macarius the Great, *Homilies* 17.8, in *Spiritual Homilies*)

248. Those who have not been honored by the Word of God nor instructed in the divine law are "vainly puffed up" (Col 2.18). They believe that by their own free will they can abolish the sources of sin, which is condemned only by the mystery found in the cross. For that free deliberation lies in the power of man to resist the devil, but this power is not absolute control over the passions. "Unless the Lord build the house" (Ps 127.1). (St Macarius the Great, *Homilies* 25.1, in *Spiritual Homilies*)

249. In the material world of things around us, the farmer works the earth. So also in the spiritual world there are two elements to be considered. It is necessary for man to work the soil of his heart by a free deliberation and hard work. For God looks to man's hard work and toil and labor. But if the heavenly clouds from above do not appear and the showers of grace, the farmer for all his labor avails nothing. (St Macarius the Great, *Homilies* 26.10, in *Spiritual Homilies*)

250. We have already often spoken about the parable of the farmer . . . Now apply this to the spiritual world. If a man relies only on his own efforts and does not receive something beyond what is due to his own nature, he cannot produce fruits worthy of the Lord. What is the working of man? To renounce, to leave the world, to remain persevering in prayer, to make night vigil, to love God and the brothers.

This is up to him to labor perseveringly. But if he endures in his own doing and does not hope to receive something else and the winds of the Holy Spirit

do not blow upon his soul and if clouds from the heavens do not appear and
rain from the heavens does not fall and moisten the soul, man cannot give to
the Lord fruits that are worthy of Him. (St Macarius the Great, *Homilies* 26.19,
in *Spiritual Homilies*)

251. But whatever does not bring forth fruit, he uproots and gives to be
burned. Indeed, this is becoming man, that, if he fasts or keeps the night vigil
or prays or does anything of good, he should attribute it all to the Lord, and
say: "If God had not empowered me, I could never have fasted or prayed or
left the world."

In this way, God sees your good intention, that you ascribe to God all the
things that by your nature you accomplish and he gifts you with the things that
are of him, namely, the spiritual things, the divine and the heavenly. (St Macarius the Great, *Homilies* 26.20, in *Spiritual Homilies*)

252. Note how tedium hits you when you are standing, and if you sit down,
it suggests that it would be a good thing to lean back. It suggests that you prop
yourself up against the walls of your cell. It produces noise and footsteps—and
there you go peeping out of the window. (St John Climacus, *Ladder of Divine
Ascent,* 13.7, 14, p 163)

253. At the third hour, the devil of tedium causes shivering, headache, and
vertigo. By the ninth hour, the patient has recovered his strength, and when
dinner is ready, he jumps out of bed. But now when the time for prayer comes,
his body begins to languish once more. He begins his prayers, but the tedium
makes him sleepy and the verses of the psalms are snatched from his mouth by
untimely yawns . . .

. . . When the psalms do not have to be sung, tedium does not arise, and the
office is hardly over when the eyes are ready to open again. (St John Climacus,
Ladder of Divine Ascent, 13.7, 14, p 163)

254. Before anything else, rest assured that no one will be crowned unless
he competes according to the rules, as the Apostle Paul says (2 Tim 2.5). If
anyone then does not compete according to the rules of the career he has chosen for himself, he will not be crowned. Therefore, it behooves him who has
stepped forward to take up the spiritual way to coerce himself in every rule he
fulfills before God, whether that be fasting, prayer, or any other virtue.

Know also, you who have taken up your discipleship to the Truth, that you cannot hold out in divine virtues unless you coerce yourself every time. (St Isaac the Syrian, in "The Four Books of St Isaac the Syrian, Bishop of Nineveh," 1.2.3–8, Arabic version)

255. Insofar as man spends effort, struggles and constrains himself for God's sake, divine succor thereupon aids him, surrounds him, makes his struggle easy and paves the way before him. (St Isaac the Syrian, in "The Four Books," 1.2.10)

256. If you ask: to what extent should I constrain myself, I would tell you: to the point of death for God's sake. (St Isaac the Syrian, in "The Four Books," 1.2.15)

Constrain yourself in the midnight office and add more psalms to it, even just one psalm more, and more prostrations than the usual rule; for your soul will then be revived and the aid of God will approach you, and you will be qualified for the safeguarding of the angels. (St Isaac the Syrian, in "The Four Books," 1.2.17–22)

Constrain yourself in prostrations, for they incite sorrow [for one's sins] in prayer.

Constrain yourself in meditating on the psalms (that is, pondering over them after recitation).

If time for prayer comes, constrain yourself and stand up to share in the office, and thrust away the laziness of the flesh, which wishes to be absolved from worship.

Constrain yourself to pray before prayer times, that the duty of prayer may become lighter to you.

Pray the psalms patiently, unhurriedly, with long-suffering and without boredom, and do not recite them as if under pressure.

Compel yourself to rise and worship at night before the cross, although sleep may be pressing and the flesh pulling you back. This is the accepted time. This is the time of succor. (St Isaac the Syrian, in "The Four Books," 1.2.23–28)

257. Beware of skipping any of the canonical hours. Wear your body out with prayer that you might be qualified for the guardship of the angels and that your bed may be sanctified with the sweat of prayer. Without the fatigue of prayer do not ever sleep. (St Isaac the Syrian, in "The Four Books," 1.2.115–16)

258. Believe me, brother, that boredom, accidie, sluggishness, irritation, mental fatigue and the other causes of distress that the enemy of righteousness inflicts upon ascetics, are all with divine permission. If man puts up with them patiently and without buckling, they will be rendered to him as a pure oblation and a holy accomplishment—provided he is free from pride and vanity. (St Isaac the Syrian, in "The Four Books," 1.5.92–94)

259. The spirit of the devil, not the Spirit of God, dwells in those who pass their life in ease. (St Isaac the Syrian, *Homilies* 60, in *The Ascetical Homilies of Saint Isaac the Syrian,* p 293)

260. It is better for us to die in our struggle, than to live in our fall. (St Isaac the Syrian, *Homilies* 73, in *Ascetical Homilies,* p 359)

261. This world is the course of the contest and the arena of the courses . . . each is examined whether he persevered in the contest and refused to admit defeat, or he turned his back. For many times it happens that a man who is altogether useless, who, because of his lack of training, is constantly pierced and thrown down, who is feeble at all times, suddenly seizes the banner from the hands of the mighty warriors, the sons of the giants, and makes his name famous . . . for this reason no man should despair; only, let us not be negligent in prayer, nor be slothful to beseech the Lord for succor. (St Isaac the Syrian, *Homilies* 70, in *Ascetical Homilies,* pp 342, 343)

262. *Question:* What should we do with our body when pain and heaviness encompass it, for together with the body, the will is enfeebled in its aspiration for the good and loses its first strength?

Answer: It is often the case with some that one half of their soul goes out in pursuit of the Lord and one half remains in the world. Their heart is not severed from things here, but they are divided within themselves, and sometimes they look ahead, sometimes backward. I am of the opinion that the sage exhorted such divided men as these, who draw near to the way of God, with the words: "Come not unto the Lord with double hearts," but come unto his way as one who sows and as one who reaps. And our Lord also, saw that among those who wish to make a total renunciation there are some whose wills are prepared to do so, but whose thoughts turn back by reason of the fear of tribulations and because they have not yet cast away the love of the flesh from themselves. Seeing this, he uttered this definitive word to them, wishing to disperse the sluggishness of their minds: "If any man will come after Me, let him deny himself," and so on. (St Isaac the Syrian, *Homilies* 37, in *Ascetical Homilies,* pp 167, 168)

263. And the Godbearing Basil, the lover of wisdom, writes, "Do not expect the man to be eminent in great things who is slothful in small ones." Do not be disheartened in the works through which you wish to find life, nor shrink from dying for them. (St Isaac the Syrian, *Homilies* 40, in *Ascetical Homilies,* p 202)

264. Whatever virtues we may gain by labor will be lost little by little if we become negligent in practicing them. (St Isaac the Syrian, in "The Four Books," 4.1, Arabic version)

265. When St Seraphim of Sarov was asked if the Christians of his own day lacked any of the conditions necessary to produce the same fruits of sanctity which had been so abundant in the past, he replied: there is one condition only lacking—a firm resolve. (Lossky, *The Mystical Theology of the Eastern Church*, p 216)

CHAPTER NINE

Bridling the Mind

"And take every thought captive to obey
Christ." (2 Cor 10.5)

"Speak, for thy servant hears."
(1 Sam 3.10)

"—Where are your hearts?
—They are with God." (*Coptic Liturgy*)

O NE OF THE GIFTS THAT God has granted to man is a broad imagination. Its scope can expand even beyond the limits of this material world. So human thought can not only encompass all that exists on earth, but also reach beyond it to imagine what exists in heaven as well.

With this lively imagination God has given us, we may imagine incidents of the past: live in them, share in their blessings, and take care to avoid the errors inherent in them. We can draw on the life of Christ and the lives of the prophets and saints: "Learn from me," Christ says (Mt 11.29), and "consider the outcome of their life" (Heb 13.7). When the past is impressed on our memory in the form of vivid images, we can connect it with the present in which we live. Then we can stretch our imagination forward to visualize a better future.

So imagination is a cord that binds together facts of the past, events of the present, and hopes for the future. Breadth of imagination, however, varies from one person to another. A person may be gifted with a gigantic, limitless imagination with which he can picture things as they really are—without ever setting eyes on them! As his gaze falls upon things that seem quite ordinary to others, he senses their hidden beauty and significance, their refinement and perfection. Another person may imagine incidents only in their transient, simple form. In this case, images are exposed to his imagination only fleetingly. No sooner do they arouse the mildest interest than they fade away without leaving a lasting impression on his soul. Still another person may imagine incidents with a profound sensory perception. His senses can be totally immersed in the setting of a narrative, for example. He actually feels as if he is truly living in that narrative. People who have such a powerful imagination are especially touched at a deep level by spiritual biographies: they can easily receive images of previously living persons and impress them on their own lives. They can turn memories of the past into facts of the present.

Like all the natural gifts granted by God to man, imagination is liable to distortion. Instead of being a means for growing in virtue, it may sometimes subvert a person and cause him to drift away. It may prey on his mind with evil images of lust, trivia, or fanciful incidents divorced from reality. In this way, a person may get obsessed with deceptive daydreams. We must be alert to this sort of subversion and resist it with unremitting determination. If we fail to bridle our thoughts and get a grip on our imagination, these images will become a snare to us, especially during times of prayer.

But we should know what imagination springs from. Imagination may appear to move freely, but it doesn't just exist in isolation. It is, rather, the out-working of a range of forces: ambition, disability, repressed passion, bitter jealousy, anger, fear—all of which are decisive factors that propel one's thinking out of the world of factual reality. By so doing, the ego can attain in fantasy what it could not fulfill in reality.

The remedy of the mind that often drifts into daydreaming and preoccupation with things outside the world of reality consists in tracing the path of our wandering thoughts. This type of analysis is not difficult and can be carried out by the distracted person. But to guarantee a sure result, the diagnosis of such thoughts is better done by a spiritual father.

It is no use trying to control one's thoughts by coercion. This is absolutely impossible. The mind must be occupied with one thing or another. Thought must expand so long as there is breath in man's nostrils—whether he is awake or asleep. The remedy then lies in first knowing why thought wanders into vain things. The next step is to demolish the causes of repression. We should also provide a benevolent sphere of expansion for one's mind to satisfy its love for imagination and contemplation—which is a human instinct. This could be carried out by training oneself to recall and reflect on incidents in the Bible and the lives of the saints as a daily discipline or drill.

However much can be said or done to bridle one's mind, especially during prayer, no way has proved more effective for reaching inward repose and mental quietude than love: love that springs from faith in God. Voluntary means of bridling the mind may succeed in getting partial control over thoughts and images. However, they cannot succeed in linking one's thought to God. But when love bursts out of one's heart Godward, it besieges not only the mind but also even all the other senses. A person then becomes an ear that listens and a mouth that speaks. No power will ever be able to dislodge him from such a stance of love—that is, listening and speaking to God.

When the love of God warms the heart, it holds sway not merely over the mind or senses, but the whole person. We are ushered into a repose and quietude, which are nothing other than paradise. This is due to the degree of security and infinite tranquility that a person feels when living in the presence of the almighty, omnipotent God. Neither the past, with its tragedies and depressing images, nor the present, with its demands, will any longer be seen on the horizons of the prayerful mind. Neither will there be anxiety over what surprises the future may hold, for the soul of man will be lying in the bosom of God. In him it confides without limits, like a child lying on the breast of his mother.

The love the soul bears for God is able to persuade it to surrender its will, its longings, and its weaknesses into the hands of its Lover—all at once and without effort. This mysterious power is the strongest effect that love has on the human soul. A person stands up to pray, feeling not only mentally sober and in control of his thoughts, but also knowing acceptance, tranquility, and repose. He is free from anxiety under the most stressful conditions and in situations of danger or violence. The all-conquering power of love is vividly evoked in the image of the martyr stepping forward to face the sword. In all calmness and quietude, he raises his hands and eyes towards heaven in prayer. The readiness of the loving person sacrificially to deny himself is the strongest shield that he has. It protects him against unwelcome threats, alarms, or sources of anxiety: against everything that would undermine his mental concentration during prayer and ministry.

SAYINGS OF THE FATHERS ON BRIDLING THE MIND

266. How can we attain to recollection? Be convinced without doubt that God is before your eyes. If anyone sees his chief or superior before him and converses with him, he does not turn his gaze from him. How much more should he who prays to God (with obvious conviction) not turn his mind from him who tries the heart and mind. How much more should he seek to fulfill what is written: "Lifting up holy hands without wrath and contention" (1 Tim 2.8). (St Basil the Great, *Short Rules* 201; PG 31.1216C)

267. Can recollection be attained in everything and at all times? And how can it be attained? That the attainment is possible is shown by him who said: "My eyes are ever toward the Lord" (Ps 24.15), and: "I behold the Lord always before me; for he is on my right hand, therefore I shall not be moved" (Ps 15.8). And as to how this perpetual recollection is possible, that is said above—namely, that no time should be given to the soul to be idle of thought about God and the works and gifts of God, and from confessing and thanking him for everything. (St Basil the Great, *Short Rules* 202; PG 31.1216CD)

268. At the time when your mind is scattered, persevere in reading rather than in prayer. Not all books, however, are profitable for the concentration of the mind . . . Love stillness far more than labors. Give more honor to reading, if possible, than to standing, for it is a source of pure prayer. (St Isaac the Syrian, *Homilies* 64, in *The Ascetical Homilies of Saint Isaac the Syrian,* p 307)

269. Fight constantly with your thoughts and call them back when they wander away. God does not demand of those under obedience that their thoughts be totally undistracted when they pray. And do not lose heart when your thoughts are stolen away. Just remain calm, and constantly call your mind back. (St John Climacus, *Ladder of Divine Ascent* 4.101, p 112)

270. Those unclean and unspeakable thoughts (of blasphemy) come at us when we are praying, but, if we continue to pray to the end, they will retreat, for they do not struggle against those who resist them.

Anyone disturbed by the spirit of blasphemy and wishing to be rid of it should bear in mind that thoughts of this type do not originate in his own soul but are caused by that unclean devil who once said to Lord: "I will give you all this if only you fall down and adore me" (Mt 4.9). So let us make light of him and pay no regard whatever to his promptings. Let us say: "Get behind me, Satan! I will worship the Lord my God and I will serve only him" (Mt 4.10). (St John Climacus, *Ladder of Divine Ascent,* 23.6, 9, pp 211–12)

271. Brave and determined thinking is a friend of stillness. It is always on the watch at the doors of the heart, killing or driving off invading notions. What I mean by this will be well understood by the man who practices stillness in the deep places of the heart . . . He says, "I sleep, but my heart is awake" (Song 5.2). (St John Climacus, *Ladder of Divine Ascent,* 27.3, 18, pp 262, 263)

272. Those with a mind accustomed to true prayer talk directly to the Lord, as if to the ear of the emperor. Those praying aloud fall down in front of the Lord as if before the entire senate. Those who live in the world make their pleas to the emperor in the midst of bustling crowds. (St John Climacus, *Ladder of Divine Ascent,* 27.22, p 263)

273. Light and recollection come to mind by way of reading the scriptures. The words are those of the Holy Spirit, and they provide guidance to the readers. Let your reading be a preliminary to action, since you are a doer. (St John Climacus, *Ladder of Divine Ascent,* 27.93, p 272)

274. Try not to talk excessively in your prayer, in case your mind is distracted by the search for words. One word from the publican sufficed to placate God, and a single utterance saved the thief. Talkative prayer frequently distracts the mind and deludes it, whereas brevity makes for concentration.

If it happens that, as you pray, some word evokes delight or remorse within you, linger over it; for at that moment our guardian angel is praying with us. (St John Climacus, *Ladder of Divine Ascent,* 28.10, 11, pp 275, 276)

275. Make the effort to raise up, or rather, to enclose your mind within the words of your prayer; and if, like a child, it gets tired and falters, raise it up again. The mind, after all, is naturally unstable, but the God who can do everything can also give it firm endurance. (St John Climacus, *Ladder of Divine Ascent,* 28.17, p 276)

276. A man stands before an earthly monarch. But he turns his face away and talks to the enemies of the king—the king will be offended. In the same way, the Lord will be offended by someone who at time of prayer turns away toward unclean thoughts. (St John Climacus, *Ladder of Divine Ascent,* 28.57, p 280)

277. Do not seek, while still a beginner, to pray without distraction and so stop praying to cleanse your thoughts first. Rather, persevere in prayer, and out of perseverance and labor thoughts will be cleansed and distractions will withdraw. (St Isaac the Syrian, in "The Four Books of St Isaac the Syrian, Bishop of Nineveh," 1.2, Arabic version)

278. If you insist on not praying until you are freed from distraction, you will never pray; for distracting thoughts decline and disappear when we persist in prayer itself. He who seeks perfection before action and labor will achieve nothing. (St Isaac the Syrian, in "The Four Books," 1.2, Arabic version)

279. If you wish to calm down your thoughts and find chance for pure prayer, stop hankering after material things. Renounce the obsession with the affairs of this world and the ambition for attaining them. For insofar as the motion of the world subsides in you and you renounce it, prayer will find a place to dwell in you. (St Isaac the Syrian, in "The Four Books," 1.2, Arabic version)

280. We will not be condemned for the motion of [sinful] thoughts within our minds. On the contrary, we will be rewarded if we hold out without conforming to them and resist them with all our might. But if we relish evil thoughts and allow them time and consent to them in our mind, we will be condemned for them. (St Isaac the Syrian, in "The Four Books," 1.2, Arabic version)

281. Do what I tell you: Whenever the demons start stirring thoughts of lust, anger or vainglory within your heart, do not respond to them neither in thought nor in action . . . Constrain yourself to flee from the pleasure of sin, crossing over instead to the passion for loving God, asking him for help and victory. Once God finds that you refuse to relish these thoughts, even with your mind, for the sake of your love and fear of him, he will nod to your guarding angel to expel from your mind all the fighting demons. They will fly away like dust before a tempest. (St Isaac the Syrian, in "The Four Books," 1.3, Arabic version)

282. God does not demand of man not to have thoughts at all passing through his mind while praying. Rather he demands that man pays no attention to them or relish them. And you, brother, do not aspire not to have your thought distracted at all, but transform it from an evil to a righteous thought. So if your mind is occupied with divine matters, this is a higher degree of prayer, but the mind cannot always be occupied with contemplating God except by frequent prayer. (St Isaac the Syrian, in "The Four Books," 1.7.8–11, Arabic version)

283. Turn this body in which you are clothed into a censer in which you burn all your evil thoughts and musings. Raise them before the Lord that he might raise your hearts to him. Ask him with all the might you possess in your minds to bring down his immaterial fire from on high to consume all that is found in that censer and purify it . . . You will then see [the new] man coming out as water from the divine font . . . (St Antony the Great, *Letters* 6.8, in "The Letters," Arabic version)

284. [Man] must enter into the lists and do battle against his thoughts. For the Lord demands of you that you be angry with yourself and engage in battle with your mind, neither consenting to nor taking pleasure in wicked thoughts. Still to uproot sin and the evil that is so imbedded in our sinning can be done only by divine power. (St Macarius the Great, *Homilies* 3.3–4, in *Spiritual Homilies*)

285. The true foundation of prayer is this: to be very vigilant over thoughts and to pray in much tranquility and peace . . . Man ought to labor to concentrate on his thoughts . . . He needs to collect them whenever they wander off in all directions, discerning natural thoughts from those that are evil. (St Macarius the Great, *Homilies* 6.3, in *Spiritual Homilies*)

286. "For where your treasure is, there also is your heart" (Mt 6.21). For the Lord knew that in this matter Satan gains the upper hand over the thoughts in order to turn them toward anxieties about material, earthly concerns.

For this reason God, in his concern for your soul, ordered you to renounce all this so that, even if you would be unwilling, you would still seek after heavenly riches and center your heart on God. For even if you should wish to go back to creatures, you would not find any tangible possessions around you. Whether you wish it or not, you are forced to raise your mind to heaven where you have put your whole treasure: "For where your treasure is, there also is your heart." (St Macarius the Great, *Homilies* 11.7, in *Spiritual Homilies*)

287. Go, therefore, to prayer. Examine your heart and mind. Desire to pour out your pure prayer to God. And see to it that there be nothing of hindrance preventing your prayer from being pure, nothing preventing your mind from being totally concentrated on the Lord, as the farmer concentrates on his farming, the married man on his wife, the merchant on his business. Let nothing hinder you from bending your knees in prayer, let not others distract your thoughts. (St Macarius the Great, *Homilies* 15.13, in Maloney, *Intoxicated with God: The Fifty Spiritual Homilies of Macarius*)

CHAPTER TEN

Holy Silence

> "It is good for a man that he bear the
> yoke in his youth. Let him sit alone
> in silence." (Lam 3.27, 28)

> "The silence of the soul is one of the
> mysteries of the coming age."
> (St Isaac the Syrian, in "The Four
> Books of St Isaac the Syrian, Bishop
> of Nineveh," 3, Arabic version)

I F WE CAST AN EXAMINING and comprehensive eye on our life, we will real-ize the amount of attraction we suffer from against our own will trying to conform to the way other people cling to the transient affairs of this world. It is certainly quite strange that although we can see the errors of other people clearly in their behavior, we never cease modifying our own behavior to con-form to these self-same errors. We might even go so far as to thrust ourselves into the clamorous drift of mankind as if struck by the same mania instead of trying to wrest ourselves from such a sweeping current. Not only so, but we try to make haste on our way and even invite others to share with us in our obscure stride toward an unknown predicament.

Perhaps you, dear reader, will see yourself in particular in these words. It makes no difference to me whether you are a monk, a priest, a preacher, or a layman, for I do not speak according to your outward form. My words are addressed to your naked self detached from all these transient forms: How much spiritual fruit have you borne as a branch in the vine?

. "Do not tell me, 'I have preached in your name, served your gospel, healed your sick,' lest you should bear the rest of the saying: 'Depart from me . . .' For you have already received your wages—honor, money, fame and good repute."

"Do not tell me, 'I have attended your church regularly, I have offered sac-rifices to you every day. Every evening and every morning have I raised incense to you.' For you might as well hear the chiding words: 'What to me is the multitude of your sacrifices? . . . incense is an abomination to me'" (Is 1.11, 13); "and for a pretense you make long prayers" (Mt 23.14; cf Lk 13.26ff).

All of these items just mentioned are not fruits. They are beautiful green leaves that are needed only for the time being but that will one day wither and leave us naked in the fall of our life. Your soul, my dear one, is the branch, and the fruit that the vinedresser seeks is the amount of growth your soul has achieved in grace, as well as your promotion in the faculties of the spiritual life. Pay attention then and look for your fruits, lest the strength of the vine in you and the sap you have exhausted should be fruitless. Your end would then be to be cut off and used for fuel.

If you wish to know whether you are fruitful or not, enter your chamber, shut the door behind you, and sit down in silence and prayer. Examine the depths of your soul. It is then that you will realize your nakedness and shame. You are not rich as you imagined before. You are poor, wretched, and naked. Your soul, the branch of your life, is void of any spiritual fruit. As for your works and ministration for which you have filled the air with shouting, they will appear to you as an unclean rag.

When you are completely alone with God, sitting in his presence in holy silence, you shall see your own image in the mirror of God. It is only then that you will discover how ugly you are! You will realize that you do not resemble him in any way.

But because of God's compassion upon you, he does not show you your shame and nakedness all at once, lest your soul be swallowed up in grief. He but unveils to you bit by bit pages of the lawsuits of your fornication, your haughtiness, your wrath, your rebellion, your theft, your calumny, your envy, and your jealousy. He shows you that they all stand against you still, but in suspension, sealed with the blood of Christ and waiting for an honest repentance and a holy covenant.

Man's discovery of his sins is a great blessing, for it is the only way that leads to healing. It is in silence that you shall plainly see your shortcomings and sins leading you to judgment. It is in silence that you shall find as well a chance to entreat God and weep, that your tears may wash away the filth of your deeds. You shall surely not depart from God's presence unless you shall have acquired every time new hyssop with which to wash yourself until you become whiter that snow.

But you should not reckon that a retreat merely consists in keeping yourself away from other people or that silence merely consists in entering your closed chamber. No. The inception of retreat springs from one's heart, and the source of silence is one's mind, not one's lips. He who has entered into solitude is he who has emptied his heart of everything: of joy as well as grief, of hope as well as despair, of love as well as hate. He has neglected every concern and every thought. He has abdicated everything. He is like one getting ready to enter his grave.

There is no share in silence and retreat for bodily activity. Solitude is a chance for the imprisoned soul to be released and go about its business. In the outset of practicing retreat, the flesh will be ill at ease and the mind will revolt, for the flesh and the mind will feel the darkness of the grave, where the soul will be still suffering in travail and discomfort while trying to break loose from the prison of the flesh and the darkness of its senses. One may thus encounter unease at the beginning of one's solitude, but this is the crucial point, which calls for faith and patience. It is not so difficult for the soul to endure such an experience, for it will soon feel that the light is at hand and that behind the darkness of the grave there lies the glory of the resurrection.

A retreat is likewise not a period of time that we spend in quietness away from people, returning afterward to our former ways of chatter, debates, silly arguments, laughter, politics, newspapers, slander, and gossip. Coming out of a retreat is a kind of resurrection from the grave in which the soul needs quietness, caution, silence, and distance from people as much as possible: "Do not hold me!" (Jn 20.17). But neither does it need pride or elation or contempt for others: "Handle me and see . . . and he ate before them" (Lk 24.39, 43). Whenever you are among people, keep your thoughts, senses, and emotions as pure as possible so that once you return to your solitude, it becomes easy for you to be unleashed into the presence of God without shame.

At the beginning of your practice of solitude, do not exhaust your senses trying to feel holy or attempting to see something divine, for in this way, you will wear out your mind and body in vain. God cannot be seen by flesh, nor can he be perceived by the senses. The only work you should do during your retreat is to cease from all work. Simply wait for God in silence and do not seek him in your fanciful thoughts or in his visible creation. All these attempts at effort will hamper the release of your soul and its abiding in God's presence.

If there is any work to be done by man in retreat, it is to ponder himself in much contrition and humility, in sorrow and anguish over the sins that have brought about the thick clouds, which have hidden his soul from God.

Such humble feelings may perhaps function in paving the way for the release of his soul.

When you become well trained in solitude, you will find precious occasions for practicing the presence of God and unveiling your soul before its Creator so as to repair every defect and every default in it. Thus will the branch abide in the vine and become qualified for bearing the fruit of the tree of life: "Love, joy, peace, patience, kindness, goodness, faithfulness, gentleness, self-control" (Gal 5.22, 23).

SAYINGS OF THE FATHERS ON HOLY SILENCE

288. Before all things we ought most carefully to observe the gospel precept, which tells us to enter into our chamber and shut the door and pray to our Father. This may be fulfilled by us as follows: We pray within our chamber when, removing our hearts inwardly from the din of all thoughts and anxieties, our prayers are disclosed in secret, in the closest intercourse to the Lord.

We pray with closed doors when with closed lips and complete silence we pray to him who searches not words but hearts. We pray in secret when with heart and fervent mind we disclose our petitions to God alone, so that no hostile powers are even able to discover the character of our petition. (Abba Isaac, *Conferences of John Cassian* 9.35)

289. The start of stillness is the rejection of all noisiness as something that will trouble the depths of the soul. The final point is when one has no longer a fear of noisy disturbance, when one is immune to it. He who does not go out in his intellect when he goes out (of his cell) is gentle, is wholly a house of love, rarely moved to speech. (St John Climacus, *Ladder of Divine Ascent* 27.4, 5, p 262)

290. An angel helps the [silent] solitary. (St John Climacus, *Ladder of Divine Ascent* 27.9, p 262)

291. The powers of heaven join in life and worship with the man who practices stillness in his soul. (St John Climacus, *Ladder of Divine Ascent* 27.10, p 262)

292. A small hair disturbs the eye. A minor concern interferes with stillness, for, after all, stillness means the expulsion of thoughts and the rejection of even reasonable cares. (St John Climacus, *Ladder of Divine Ascent* 27.52, p 269)

293. Intelligent silence is the mother of prayer. (St John Climacus, *Ladder of Divine Ascent* 11.3, p 158)

294. The man who recognizes his sins has taken control of his tongue, while the chatterer has yet to discover himself as he should.

The lover of silence draws close to God. He talks to him in secret and God enlightens him . . . "Better to fall from a height to the ground than to slip with the tongue" (Sir 20.18). (St John Climacus, *Ladder of Divine Ascent* 11.4, 5, 7, pp 158, 159)

295. Close the door of your cell to your body, the door of your tongue to talk, and the gate within to evil spirits. (St John Climacus, *Ladder of Divine Ascent* 27.19, p 263)

296. The ear of the solitary will hear wonders from God. (St John Climacus, *Ladder of Divine Ascent* 27.28, p 264)

297. The solitary runs away from everyone, but does so without hatred. (St John Climacus, *Ladder of Divine Ascent* 27.29)

298. In my prayer and office I never feel tired or exhausted, for I do not move according to my will. I only listen to the Holy Spirit who is within me. This fires me with love . . . and this is what is meant when it is said that the Holy Spirit prays within us in sighs too deep for words. (St John of Dalyatha, *Homily on the Gifts of the Spirit*, in "Spiritual Elder")

299. If your tongue is used to chattering, your heart will remain dim and foreign to the luminous intuitions of the Spirit. But if your mouth is silent, your heart will ever be aflame with the Spirit . . . Hush your tongue that your heart may speak, and hush your heart that God may speak. (St John of Dalyatha, *Homily on the Gifts of the Spirit*, in "Spiritual Elder")

300. A man who loves conversation with Christ, loves to be alone. (St Isaac the Syrian, *Homilies* 64, in *The Ascetical Homilies of Saint Isaac the Syrian*, p 316)

301. A private prayer said by man alone is better than a hundred prayers said with other people. (St Isaac the Syrian, in "The Four Books of St Isaac the Syrian, Bishop of Nineveh," 1.5, Arabic version)

302. If you love the truth, love silence. This will make you illumined, sun-like, in God: it will deliver you from the illusions of ignorance. (St Isaac the Syrian, *Homilies* 64, in *Ascetical Homilies,* p 307)

303. A silent mouth interprets God's mysteries, but the garrulous man is distant from his Creator. (St Isaac the Syrian, *Homilies* 15, in *Ascetical Homilies,* pp 84, 85)

304. Love silence, my Brother, for in it you have life for your soul. In silence you see yourself. Outside of silence you do not see except what is outside yourself. So long as you see others you will never see yourself. (St Isaac the Syrian, *Letter to a Brother on the Love of Solitude,* in "Four Books," 2.9, Arabic version)

305. Love uncouthness of speech joined with knowledge from inner experience more than to spill forth rivers of instruction from the keenness of your mind. (St Isaac the Syrian, *Homilies* 4, in *Ascetical Homilies,* p 32)

306. If you guard your tongue, my brother, God will give you the gift of compunction of heart so that you may see your soul, and thereby you will enter into spiritual joy. But if your tongue defeats you—believe me in what I say to you—you will never be able to escape from darkness. If you do not have a pure heart, at least have a pure mouth, as the blessed John said. (St Isaac the Syrian, *Homilies* 48, in *Ascetical Homilies,* p 236)

307. [Sorrow of mind is a precious gift before God; and the man who bears this gift as he ought is like the man who bears holiness in his members.] A man who unleashes his tongue against other men for good or for evil is unworthy of this grace. (St Isaac the Syrian, *Homilies* 51, in *Ascetical Homilies,* p 244)

308. If you wish to discern a man of God from other people, recognize him by his continual silence. (St Isaac the Syrian, in "Four Books," 4.1, Arabic version)

309. I beseech you to renounce your sensory will and keep silent. (St Antony the Great, *Letters* 8.3, in "The Letters," Arabic version)

310. Many times have I spoken and regretted it; but I have never regretted keeping silent. (St Arsenius 40, in Ward, *The Sayings of the Desert Fathers: The Alphabetical Collection*)

CHAPTER ELEVEN

Pray at All Times

> "[One] ought always to pray and not
> lose heart." (Lk 18.1)

I N ITS FINAL ANALYSIS, life consists only of two very simple, perpetual actions: the first is love, whose fountainhead is God; the second is worship, which flows from his creation: "God is love" (1 Jn 4.16); "I [am] prayer" (Ps 109.4). These two actions are perpetual and incessant, for God never ceases to love his creation, neither does his creation cease to worship him: "If these were silent, the very stones would cry out" (Lk 19.40). All the works of our life and its various activities will pass away and disappear after we shall have been convicted or vindicated for them. Nothing will remain except these two peculiar acts: God's love for us and our worship of him. These two shall never pass away even after this life is over. They shall last forevermore in the life to come. God shall never cease from loving us, neither shall we cease from adoring him. He finds his pleasure in loving us, "rejoicing in his inhabited world and delighting in the sons of men" (Prov 8.31), and we, likewise, find our pleasure in adoring him.

This adoration is a divine motive, which God has consigned to man's nature that he may delight in worshipping the source of his true happiness. We have often experienced this delight and thus know for sure that in prayer and worship lies eternal happiness. Is there any way then that may lead us into a life of perpetual worship and constant prayer? Is it possible to make God the center of our thoughts. Can we make him the pivot around which all our works and behavior revolve? Is it possible to live in God's presence from morning to evening and from evening to morning?

Certainly this is not an easy job. It needs much determination, perseverance, and extreme commitment on our part. However, we should not forget that in our determination, persistence, and commitment we only fulfill the ultimate aim and purpose of God. Neither should we forget that in fulfilling God's will we shall find succor, love, and guidance.

We may sum up the details of this practice as follows:

1. The Aim of Constant Prayer

—Perpetual existence in God's presence.

—Allowing God to share with us in all our works and thoughts. It is also a means of knowing his will.

—Abiding in happiness as a result of our proximity to God, the source of all happiness, and enjoying his love.

—Gaining a sublime knowledge of God in himself.

—Attaining a pleasant negligence of earthly life without regret.

2. Practical Guidelines for Attaining Constant Prayer

—Reminding ourselves always that God is present before us and that he sees and hears all that we do and say.

—Trying to speak to him from time to time in short utterances expressing our condition.

—Allowing God to have a share in our work by asking him to be present with us while we perform it. We should also deliver to him our report when the work is over. If the work is successful, we should thank him; if unsuccessful, we should apologize to him and trace the reason of our failure, for it might be due to our distance from him or forgetting to call upon his aid.

—Trying to discern the voice of God amidst our works. He often speaks to us from within ourselves. But due to our mindfulness of things other than him, we miss his judicious counsel.

—Calling upon God to consult him during critical moments, as on hearing disquieting news or when assailed by superiors or other people. In such hard times, God is our dearest and wisest friend.

—Turning to God when our heart begins to be frantic and our feelings excited. We should seek God's help when trying to calm these corruptive emotions that they may not find our heart a congenial climate for their growth. Jealousy, anger, slander, vengeance, and rendering evil for evil deprive us immediately of the grace of living in God's presence, for evil cannot sojourn with him.

—Trying as much as possible never to forget God. This is to be carried out by returning to him at once when we catch our thoughts wandering away from him.

—Never taking up a job or responding to any stimulus except after receiving the urge from God. But how can this urge be discerned? It is actually unveiled to us little by little in proportion to our fidelity in walking with God and to the rectitude of our aims in living with him.

3. The Main Principles for a Life of Constant Prayer

—Do you have faith in God? If you do, lay it down then as a basis for all your behavior. With it face everything that comes your way in this life—be it joy or grief. Do not allow your faith to change every day according to the vicissitudes of this life. Do not let success increase your faith in God; neither let failure, loss, or illness weaken or undermine it.

—Have you accepted to live with God? Put then all your trust in him at once. Never try to recant or regress in the least. Keep faithful to him even unto death.

—Surrender to God all your material and spiritual affairs, for he is certainly able to manage them all. Know that life with God is liable to everything—illness, hunger, and insult. Be not surprised if such harms befall you. If you hold out patiently, you shall see how all such matters turn at the end to your own favor.

—Love God with all your might. Do not allow the casual things that come your way to diminish your love for him. Rather, relish all suffering for his sake, for true love turns pain into pleasure.

—How blessed are those who are counted worthy of suffering for God's name! More blessed still are those who *long* to suffer for his name.

A Historical Account of Constant Prayer

Constant prayer is an ascesis on its own. It has its own qualities that directly affect the subconscious powers of the soul and particular brain centers. Constant prayer leads to a state of perpetual, spiritual sobriety and a permanent feeling of the presence of God. It also gives man absolute control over his thoughts and passions. For this reason, it is considered one of the most important and sublime spiritual actions through which man, if successful, may attain clear and sound results of first-rate spiritual magnificence.

This particular and peculiar ascesis is first heard of in the teachings of the early saints in Egypt. They are St Macarius the Great and St Isaac the disciple of St Antony. The lives of these saints covered the span from the beginning to the end of the fourth century. The sayings of the second were recorded by Cassian, the French traveler, before the end of the fourth century. We quote them at the head of "Sayings of the Fathers" later in this chapter.

From the sayings of these Fathers, we can clearly infer that this peculiar ascesis was paramount among the ascetic traditions they had received from the Fathers who preceded them. St Isaac, the disciple of St Antony, says in his discourse with Cassian:

> And as this was delivered to us by a few of those who were left of the oldest fathers, so it is only divulged by us to a very few and to those who are truly keen. (NPNF 11.405)

The effectiveness of this ascesis on the psychic and mental powers was known by the Fathers from the beginning. The aforementioned St Isaac says in this respect:

> For it embraces all the feelings which can be implanted in human nature, and it can be fitly and satisfactorily adapted to every condition and for all assaults. (NPNF 11.405)

The same saint reiterates the effectiveness of constant prayer on the mind:

> This is the formula that the mind should unceasingly cling to until, strengthened by the constant use of it and by continual meditation, it casts off and rejects the rich and full material of all manner of thoughts. (NPNF 11.407)

From the fourth century on, constant prayer spread in Egypt and, furthermore, occupied a major part of the ascetical theology of all the Eastern churches. We thus find it a focal point in the teachings of St Nilus of Sinai (died A.D. 430), then in the teachings of St John Climacus (A.D. 570–640), and later in those of St Hesychius of Jerusalem. This focus reached its sharpest point in the teachings of St Isaac the Syrian, bishop of Nineveh, at the end of the seventh century (A.D. 700).

These teachings retained their own peculiar, patristic quality without being classified under one unified discipline until the appearance of St Simeon the New Theologian (A.D. 1022) and afterward of St Gregory of Sinai. They invested this unified discipline with the shape of a special mystical method, giving it a Byzantine color. St Gregory of Sinai transmitted it to Mount Athos in Greece at the end of the thirteenth century. After him came his disciple Callistus, who became the patriarch of Constantinople and who made out of the method of constant prayer a fundamental Orthodox mystical discipline of the Byzantine rite in general. He collected all the sayings of the Fathers on this topic, classifying and interpreting them.

With the advent of Nilus of Sora at Mount Athos from Russia in the second half of the fifteenth century, a wide gate was opened admitting constant prayer among the Russians. It is through Nilus of Sora that the entire Eastern heritage with all its richness was transmitted to the Russian fathers. They zealously competed in applying it in all fidelity and precision. The method of constant prayer occupied henceforth a high position in the course of the ensuing generations. This becomes clear in the story of the *Way of the Pilgrim*.

But the method of constant prayer, having been moved from its original home in Egypt, lost much of its former simplicity. In its original form, it had allowed the praying person to live in the depth of its spiritual verve without paying attention to its method. It had enabled him to reap its fruits without exciting his ambition or spiritual greed. The point is that this method has shifted from its ascetical position as a humbling practice by itself to a mystical position, with programs, stipulations, technical and mechanical bases, degrees, objectives, results—all of which the praying person puts in mind before entering upon the practice. This has entangled the method of constant prayer in much complexity and artificiality. However, for constant prayer there still are its lovers and amateurs, and it still showers upon them its bountiful and profuse spiritual blessings. This writer acknowledges the blessings he has personally reaped from such prayer.

SAYINGS OF THE FATHERS ON CONSTANT PRAYER

311. I must give you the formula for contemplation. If you carefully keep this formula in front of you, and learn to recollect it all the time, you can use it to mount to the contemplation of high truth. Every monk who looks for continual recollection of God uses this formula for meditation, and with the object of driving every other sort of thought from his heart. You cannot keep the formula before you unless you are free from all bodily care.

The formula was given us by a few of the oldest fathers who remained. They did not communicate it except to a very few who were athirst for the true way. To maintain an unceasing recollection of God it is to be ever set before you.

The formula is: "O God, make speed to save me: O Lord, make haste to help me" (Ps 70.1).

This verse has rightly been selected from the whole Bible for this purpose. It fits every mood and temper of human nature, every temptation, every circumstance. It contains an invocation of God, a humble confession of faith, a reverent watchfulness, a meditation upon our frailty, a confidence in God's answer, an assurance of his ever-present support. The man who continually invokes God as his guardian is aware that he is always at hand.

The formula contains a fervent charity . . . The verse is an impregnable battlement, a shield and coat of mail that no spear can pierce . . .

Continuously and ceaselessly, in adversity that we may be delivered, in prosperity that we may be preserved but not puffed up, we ought to send up this prayer. Meditate on it, never stop turning it over within your breast. Whatever work or ministry or journey you are undertaking, go on praying it. While you are going to sleep, or eating, or in the last necessities of nature, think on it. It will be a saving formula in your heart, will guard you from the attacks of demons, will cleanse you from the stains of earthly life, lead you to contemplate the unseen things of heaven, and carry you up to the ineffable radiance of prayer which very few have experienced.

Sleep ought to catch you thinking about this verse, until you are so molded by its use that you pray it when asleep. When you wake it should be your first thought, it should force you from your bed to your knees, and thence send you out to your daily work, there to be always with you. You should think on it, in

Moses' words (Deut 6.7), at home or on a journey, going to bed or rising from bed. You should write it on the doors of your lips, the walls of your house, the sanctuary of your breast. Whether you kneel down to pray or whether you rise up from praying and turn to the needs of your daily life, this should be your prayer. (Abba Isaac, *Conferences of John Cassian* 10.10, in Chadwick, *Western Asceticism: Selected Translations of Christian Classics*, pp 239–243)

312. *Question:* What embraces all the labors of this work, that is to say, stillness, so that when a man has attained it, he can know that he has reached perfection in his manner of life?

Answer: When a man is deemed worthy of constant prayer. For when he reaches this, he has reached the pinnacle of all the virtues and has become a dwelling-place of the Holy Spirit. For unless a man has received in all certainty the grace of the Comforter, he will be unable to perform constant and unceasing prayer restfully. When the Spirit dwells in a man, as the Apostle says, he never ceases to pray, since the Spirit himself always prays [within him]. Then, whether he sleeps or wakes, prayer is never separated from his soul. If he eats, or drinks, or lies down, or does something, or even in deep slumber, the sweet fragrances and perfumes of prayer effortlessly exhale in his heart. (St Isaac the Syrian, *Homilies* 37, in *The Ascetical Homilies of Saint Isaac the Syrian,* p 182)

313. Then our Savior's prayer, wherein he prayed the Father for his disciples, will be truly fulfilled in us: "that the love wherein thou lovedst me may be in them, and they in us": and "that they all may be one in us." This unity will be when that perfect love of God, wherewith "he first loved us" (Jn 17.21–6; Jn 4.10) has passed into the affections of our own hearts. So his prayer will be fulfilled, and we believe that this prayer cannot fail in its effect.

Then God shall be all our love, all we desire and seek and follow, all we think, all our life and speech and breath. The unity which now is between Father and Son shall be poured into our feelings and our minds: and as he loves us with a pure, sincere, unbreakable charity we on our side shall be linked to him by a lasting affection that nothing can spoil. In that union, whatever we breathe or think or speak is God. So the end of his prayer is attained in us—"that they all may be one as we are one: I in them, and thou in me, that they also may be made perfect in one": and "Father, those who thou hast given me, I will that where I am, they may also be with me."

This should be the aim and purpose of the solitary: to seek to possess in some measure, even while mortal man, the first bridal gifts from the heavenly country and its glory. I repeat: this is the end of true goodness, that the mind may every day be lifted beyond the material sphere to the realm of spirit, until the whole life and every little stirring of the heart becomes one continuous prayer. (Abba Isaac, *Conferences of John Cassian* 10.7, in Chadwick, *Western Asceticism,* p 237)

314. This is truly a great blessing that we have received from experience: if anyone wishes to cleanse his heart he may call unceasingly upon the Lord Jesus, calling out against all mental adversaries. (St Hesychius of Jerusalem, in Moore, "Some Aspects of Orthodox Prayer," p 56)

315. Truly blessed is he who cries out to Him unceasingly in his heart, who is as mentally near to the prayer of Jesus as the touch of air on our bodies or a flame to a candle. The sun passing over the earth produces day; and the holy and adorable name of the Lord Jesus, unceasingly shining in the mind, gives birth to a countless number of sun-like thoughts. (St Hesychius, in Moore, "Orthodox Prayer," p 56)

316. A monk, whether he is eating, or drinking, or sitting, or traveling, or doing anything else, must constantly cry out: Lord Jesus Christ, Son of God, have mercy on me! that the name of the Lord Jesus, descending to the depths of the heart, may humble the snake nestling in the fields there, and save and vivify the soul. Therefore continue unceasingly with the name of the Lord Jesus, that your heart may embrace the Lord, and that the Lord may embrace your heart, and that these two may be one. (St John Chrysostom, in Moore, "Orthodox Prayer," p 56)

317. Do not separate your heart from God, but remain with Him, and always guard your heart with the remembrance of our Lord Jesus Christ, until the name of the Lord takes root in your heart and it thinks of nothing else—that Christ may be magnified in you. (St John Chrysostom, in Moore, "Orthodox Prayer," p 56)

318. The beginning of every action pleasing to God is calling with faith on the life-saving name of our Lord Jesus Christ . . . together with the peace and love which accompany this calling . . . for "God is love; and he that dwells in love dwells in God, and God in him" (1 Jn 4.16). These two, peace and love, not only make the prayer propitious, but are themselves reborn and shine forth from this prayer, like inseparable divine rays, increasing and coming to perfection. (Patriarch Callistus of Constantinople 8, *Writings from the Philokalia on Prayer of the Heart,* pp 169, 170)

CHAPTER TWELVE

Tears

> "She has wet my feet with her tears . . .
> Therefore I tell you, her sins, which
> are many, are forgiven, for she loved
> much." (Lk 7.44, 47)

I T IS HARD TO SPEAK OF TEARS. Are not tears a sign of the limitation of speech? When, in bewilderment, the tongue fails, the heart speaks, and the eyes utter tears.

But who can interpret this language? It is the totality of sentiments dissolved in a drop. It is a tongue that speaks in all languages. It is the language of a soul suffused with the most sincere feelings. It is the consolation of the oppressed, the country of the homeless, the father of the fatherless, and the comfort of the weary. It is the expiation of sins, the sign of regret, the covenant of redemption. It is the washing of the heart, the purifying of the members, the healing of sick souls. It is the language of the spirit, the prayer of the silent, the disdain of the world, the longing for heaven. It is the waiting for death.

Tears draw the scorn of the stonehearted, but they melt the merciful heart. But why should we care about the hearts of men? Tears have a higher honor; they enter into the presence of the Almighty and speak to him. "I have heard your prayer, I have seen your tears" (2 Kg 20.5). Although they fall on the ground as if worthless, God gathers them in his phial: "Put thou my tears into thy bottle" (Ps 56.8). They cannot move the stony hearted, but they shake the gates of heaven: "While I was speaking and praying, confessing my sin . . . and presenting my supplication before the Lord my God; while I was speaking in prayer, the man Gabriel . . . came to me in swift flight . . . and he said to me, 'O Daniel, I have now come to give you wisdom and understanding. At the beginning of your supplications a word went forth, and I have come to tell you'" (Dan 9.20, 21, 22, 23). Tears, which cannot change the stiffness of princes, can arouse God's compassion: "Turn your eyes from me; they overwhelm me" (Song 6.5).

How shall I describe you, O tears! How contemptible you are in the eyes of sophists! They make you a sign of the weakness and dissolution of human personality. But the words of the Lord are reason enough to boast: "Blessed are you that weep" (Lk 6.21).

St John Climacus tells us of his experience of tears: they are "the mother and daughter of prayer." This is true, for tears drive us to the quiet bedrooms of prayer. There, God entrusts us with their living springs, and we shed as many tears as sorrow asks of us. "O that my head were waters, and my eyes a fountain of tears, that I might weep day and night" (Jer 9.1).

Tears, the Mother of Prayer

We stand before God at the beginning of our spiritual life, and our souls, burdened with iniquity, encounter the sanctifying flame of God: "Our God is a consuming fire" (Heb 12.29). Our sins and impurities start to melt as mountains of snow melt before the heat of the burning sun, and our eyes are opened for the first time to pour a flood of penitential tears. The tears of repentance are nothing other than the snow of sins whose drifts have gathered over the heart. When the Sun of Righteousness rises, the snows melt and turn into the waters of purification and healing. With our tears we wash our bodies, stained by lust and sin, and then we may advance to prayer "lifting holy hands" (1 Tim 2.8), "with our hearts sprinkled clean from an evil conscience and our bodies washed with pure water" (Heb 10.22).

But the tears of repentance are not confined to a certain period of our life. They are our perpetual spring of healing for souls made sick by sin. We emerge from this spring to stand blameless before God in prayer: "Every night I flood my bed with tears; I drench my couch with my weeping" (Ps 6.6).

Tears, the Daughter of Prayer

Happy is the man who is sought by grace during the entreaties of his tearful and sorrowful prayer. He pours tears of pain and sorrow in bitterness; his eyes waste away in grief. But all at once, the light of Christ diffuses his heart and a mysterious elation overwhelms him. He smiles, and tears of joy pour forth like a torrent coming from the upper springs (Josh 15.19).

These joyful tears are one of the gifts of contrite prayer. Those who have tasted the pleasure of the tears of prayer importune heaven for the same blessing at all times. St Arsenius, the wonderful saint who shed tears until his eyelids wasted and his eyelashes fell, testifies to this truth. His tears remained his silent, perpetual chant until he left this world with his eyelids drenched in tears. "My tears have been my food day and night" (Ps 42.3); "For I . . . mingle tears with my drink" (Ps 102.9).

All can weep, but few can channel their tears into the phial of God: "Put thou my tears into thy bottle!" (Ps 56.8). For the tears that are shed away from God's phial count *against* you and not *for* you. They leave you with a corruptive melancholia, destitute of any spiritual comfort.

Your soul may often be troubled, your sentiments inflamed, and your eyes prone to shed tears. Examine your feelings lest the motive behind your tears be a trivial worldly one, which does not please God. If it be so, your tears will not be collected in God's precious phial, but be spilled on the soil of this world. They will raise thorns instead of wheat. Examine your tears, see that they are not aroused by a worldly, transient love, or an affection for an earthly homeland. Make sure that you do not weep to elicit the compassion of other people, or to complain of distress, illness, hunger, poverty, or persecution. In that case, your tears count against you, as a protest against God's just dispensation. Those who have become adept in the life of prayer know well how to channel their tears into God's presence. They shift their sentiments from the influence of people's love to the influence of God; from longing for an earthly, transient homeland to longing for heaven, the everlasting homeland with God. They no longer weep to elicit the compassion of men and women, they enter directly into the presence of the compassionate Father to shed their tears before him; they shed tears of contentment and thanksgiving, not tears of complaint.

If God entrusts you with the tears of consolation in your prayer, dear reader, take heed of the following cautions:

1. Let not tears distract you from their Giver. Otherwise you will become like a child who rejoices over sweets more than he rejoices over his father who brings him those sweets.

2. Do not think that the tears are granted to you on account of your worthiness or piety, or the tears will forsake you.

3. Tears do not distinguish you from others. They are for your encouragement; they are granted so that you may grow in the love of God, in submission
to his commandments, and in humility toward his children. The wise Father
is more compassionate in dealing with his weaker son than with his brothers,
so that this son may grow in obedience and love toward him and his brothers.

The Proper Rank of Tears in the Ascetical Theology of the Early Fathers

It may be claimed in haste that tears are a gift. But this judgment excludes
many kinds of tears that are not gifts. For the present, we can assert that tears
can be valuable and effective or dangerous and destructive. We can see this in
the teachings of St Isaac of Nitria (fourth century). He was a disciple of St
Antony who moved afterward to Nitria and stayed there after the death of his
master. The teaching of St Isaac, though very simple, is powerful and profound. We quote it here:

> **319.** *Abba Isaac:* Sometimes a compunction of grief overwhelms the
> soul, and the only way to express it is by a release of tears.
> *Germanus:* I have very little experience, but even I have experienced
> something of this compunction of spirit. Sometimes tears will rise
> when I remember my sins, and then I am visited by the Lord and
> refreshed by the unspeakable joy which you have described: and the
> joy, by its very power, has given me the assurance not to despair of for-
> giveness. I believe there is no loftier state of prayer than this. But the
> trouble is that it cannot be created when we choose. Sometimes, when
> I am struggling as hard as I can to excite a compunction of penitence,
> and I have decided to imagine my sins, I fail altogether in the effort: my
> eyes remain as dry as a flint, and I cannot squeeze a drop of moisture
> out of them. When I am granted tears, I am happy. But when I cannot
> call them at will, I am cast down.
> *Abba Isaac:* Not all varieties of weeping are evoked by the same feel-
> ing. There is a weeping because the heart is pricked by sin, as in the
> texts, "I have labored in my groanings, every night I will wash my bed;
> I will water my couch with my tears" (Ps 6.6); and "let tears run down
> like a torrent day and night; give thyself no rest, and let not the apple
> of thine eye cease" (Lam 2.18). There is a weeping which springs from

contemplating eternal good and longing for future light, and tears of joy and desire cannot help but break out; as the soul is athirst for the mighty living God, saying, "When shall I come to appear before the presence of God? My tears have been my meat day and night." And "Woe is me that my sojourning is prolonged"; "Too long has my soul been a sojourner" (Ps 42.3–4; 120.5, LXX; 143.2). There is a weeping which rises, not from the consciousness of mortal sin, but more from the fear of hell and the terrible judgment; and the soul makes its own the prophetic prayer: "Enter not into judgment with thy servant: for in thy sight shall no man living be justified." There is a weeping caused, not by self-examination, but by awareness of the sins of others and their impenitence. So Samuel is said to have wept for Saul; and the Lord in the Gospel and Jeremiah before him are described as weeping for the city of Jerusalem, "O that my head were water and mine eyes a fountain of tears! And I will weep day and night for the slain of the daughter of my people." And then there are the tears of Psalm 101: "I have eaten ashes for my bread and mingled my cup with weeping." This was not caused by the same feelings as those of the penitent in Psalm 6, but arose from the anxieties, poverty, and suffering of this life, the common lot of the righteous in the world. This is shown by the title as well as the text, for the title reads: "A prayer of the poor man, when he was in distress, and poured forth his prayer to God." It is clear that the psalm is placed in the mouth of one of those poor men of whom the Gospel speaks: "Blessed are the poor in spirit: for theirs is the kingdom of heaven" (Mt 5.3; cf Jer 9.1; Ps 102.9).

You can squeeze tears out of dry eyes and with a hard heart, but this is quite a different kind of weeping. I do not believe that this sort of weeping is altogether without profit, for the intention is good, especially in people who have not yet been able to reach perfect knowledge or to be thoroughly purified of past and present sin. But in people who have already progressed so far that they love goodness, this kind of weeping ought never to be extracted unnaturally. Even if it succeeds, it cannot rival spontaneous weeping as an occasion of elevated prayer. It is more likely, when the attempt fails, to depress the soul and drive it away from that intention towards heaven in which the prayerful and reverent mind ought to be stable. It will force the soul to relax its concentration and instead go feebly after a weeping which is forced and futile. (*Conferences of John Cassian* 9.27–30, in Chadwick, *Western Asceticism: Selected Translations of Christian Classics*, pp 227–29)

We can now sum up the main principles of Abba Isaac as follows:

1. Tears are a form of self-expression that accompanies the authentic motives of prayer. This kind of prayer springs from the depth of one's soul and appears all of a sudden. The soul is then overwhelmed with an exquisite happiness that can hardly be checked, a happiness that cannot be expressed before God except by spontaneous, copious tears.

2. There are diverse authentic motives for prayer, and there are also different kinds of tears. Every authentic motive for prayer is attended by a special feeling; each has an especially appropriate kind of tears.

3. There are five main motives for authentic prayer and, consequently, five kinds of authentic, fruitful tears:

— Tears of remorse for sin, which break the heart.

— Tears that come out of contemplating the benevolence of God and the glory that is prepared for us. This kind of tears is a fountainhead of joy and hope.

— Tears of terror. These come from the fear of hell and condemnation and have no affinity with the tears of a remorseful conscience.

— Tears shed over others, which are deeply depressing (they must be free from any judgment or rancor).

— Tears of tribulation shed by the poor people of God because of the tyranny of this world and its oppressors.

4. These five kinds of tears are linked together by two main traits. The first is that their motives are authentic, and therefore, the tears are also authentic. The second is that man never exerts any kind of effort, never forces himself to shed them, perpetuate them, or increase their flow. They are spontaneous tears, which essentially follow their authentic motives. They are never detached from these motives, nor do they ever precede them.

5. There exists another kind of tears that is not spontaneous, which man struggles to shed. This kind, although not authentic from the ascetical point of view, is acceptable since it is practiced by beginners who are not yet perfect in love. Their forced shedding of tears is stirred by a spotless motive of abnegation and self-rebuke. They force themselves to weep because their consciousness of sin has not yet reached its mature stage, where tears are shed spontaneously.

6. Last, the saint stresses the danger of a particular kind of tears, which he considers destructive to the soul. Because this kind is detached from the five previous motives, it can unloosen the ties that bind prayer together. Those are the tears that the person walking along the way of virtue tries to shed for the mere sake of shedding them. It is as if they were a gift to be hunted for, or an indispensable need, and he who sheds them is driven to a morbid sense of inferiority. Such tears are considered by St Isaac to be corruptive and sterile.

To comprehend, however, the value of tears and its authentic place in ascetical theology, we have to turn to another saint who is distinguished for his excellence in ascetic experience. This is St Isaac the Syrian, bishop of Nineveh. The experience of St Isaac the Syrian by itself does not follow any rationalistic scheme and contains no artificiality. It is inspired and led by grace. It is also identical in its originality and effectiveness with the experience of the early Fathers upon whom he drew with all fidelity—a fact that he admits in several places throughout his writings. What interests us in the teachings of St Isaac the Syrian is not the constructed method that contains his living experience but the living experience itself.

We present here a synopsis of the teachings of St Isaac the Syrian on tears, using his own words. This synopsis will suffice without a further listing of the sayings of the saint on this topic.

The Status of Tears in the Ascetic Life in General

In their ascetic context as a whole, tears draw a sharp line between life according to the flesh and life according to the spirit (things fleshly and things spiritual), that is, between the malady of sin (the life of the passions) and the healthiness of spirit (the life of purity). If man is not qualified for the gift of tears, this indicates that he still lives and works for the outer man. He has not yet begun to feel the hidden work of the inner man. He must forsake the things of this world; he must cross the bounds of flesh to enter the domain of the inner man. Once he takes this step, he is given this gift on the spot: the gift of tears. If he holds fast to this gift, so essential to the spiritual economy of man, and proceeds in the hidden life of the spirit, then these tears will hold him fast until he reaches the perfection of divine love.

So long as man progresses in his spiritual life, his lot of tears increases. They are constant; he drinks them in his cup and in his food. This constancy is a sure sign that his mind has left this world behind and has now begun to be sensible of the spiritual world.

But if the mind draws near again to this world, his tears begin to dry up and he loses their constancy. And once his mind becomes totally devoted to this world, he loses them altogether. This is a sign of regression into the tomb of sin (St Isaac the Syrian, in "The Four Books of St Isaac the Syrian, Bishop of Nineveh," 3.4, Arabic version).

Tears Take the Form of Successive Ascetical Stages

St Isaac the Syrian divides tears into two main kinds:

1. Tears shed at the remembrance of sins and the lapses of one's heart. These are painful tears. The head aches in their shedding. The result is that the flesh is affected, its passions cease and its lusts wither. It is as if tears burn man's sins and dry up his flesh. These are the tears of beginners. If man does not lose them by his sloth and negligence or by his ambition and pride, they remain his company. They will guide him until he becomes an adept, which is the rank in which man receives mercy (St Isaac the Syrian, in "The Four Books," 3.4, Arabic version).

2. God sometimes vouchsafes sudden spiritual illuminations to man, and the intensity of this new light prompts tears to flow, sincere and unforced. This is the second kind of tears, the joyful tears that make the flesh itself bloom with the flowering of the spirit after sin has withered away. They anoint the body as if with oil, and the joy of the heart changes the appearance of the whole man. These tears are the sharp line that divides the rank of fleshly men from that of spiritual men. In other words, they divide the ascetical works of the flesh from the spiritual works of the mind, that is, from contemplation. These joyful tears are therefore the sign of the fruitfulness of the inner man (St Isaac the Syrian, in "The Four Books," 3.4, Arabic version).

The Ascetical Value of Tears and from Whence They Spring

1. Weeping by itself is a partition that separates the soul from the maladies of sin (St Isaac the Syrian, in "The Four Books," 3.4, Arabic version). And so when man sheds tears, any inclination toward sin is hedged out. For the maladies of sin never press upon a weeping person.

2. If you ask what weeping springs from, and how it can be made to endure, I would answer: How can he who is full of wounds keep silent? How

can he remain patient without weeping? Is it possible for us to be afflicted with the sickness of sin and not weep? Does someone who has one of his relations lying dead before him need anyone to teach him how to weep? Your sins weigh on you; your soul is lying dead. It is worth more to you than the whole world. Do you ask me after all this, "How can I weep," and think that you are destitute of weeping (St Isaac the Syrian, in "The Four Books," 3.4, Arabic version)?

3. Calm yourself and learn how to keep silent. Be patient and endure the hardship of silence. It is only then that you feel the blame of your conscience and that weeping comes and cleaves to you (St Isaac the Syrian, in "The Four Books," 3.4, Arabic version).

4. Before anything else, we need always to keep God before our eyes and in our mind. He will surely then grant us the gift of tears (St Isaac the Syrian, in "The Four Books," 3.4, Arabic version).

5. If we win this gift, which is better than all other gifts, it will lead us to purity. This accounts for the Lord's saying, "Blessed are those who mourn for they shall be comforted" (Mt 5.4). We will then know what fruit tears bear (St Isaac the Syrian, in "The Four Books," 3.4, Arabic version).

6. If tears can thus move the mind of the weeping person from the sense and images of sin, how much more can they perform in those whose tears attend them day and night? Who, without weeping constantly himself, can ever know the amount of help gained by those who do so? By tears the gate of consolation was opened to all the saints. They entered into vision and marched in God's footsteps (St Isaac the Syrian, in "The Four Books," 3.4, Arabic version).

7. Tears are also the product of true, undistracted meditation. When the mind is given new light, the heart is moved and tears flow (St Isaac the Syrian, in "The Four Books," 2.9, Arabic version).

8. So long as man is inwardly nourished by the Spirit, tears will increase (St Isaac the Syrian, in "The Four Books," 3.11, Arabic version).

Tears Are Not a Necessity in the Ascetic Life

1. For beginners we say: Some are not qualified for constant weeping due to the feebleness of the body (either because of illness or because of a functional or congenital defect.) In this case, to curb the impulse of sin, there is a substitute for tears, especially in the case of casual, sinful passions. This substitute is

constant prayer and the emptying of the heart of its love for the world, for all worldly affairs. He should be intent on performing all his prayers. He should seek insight in reading spiritual books. Such a person can never be overwhelmed by the thoughts of sin or its maladies (St Isaac the Syrian, in "The Four Books," 3.4, Arabic version).

2. Concerning the end of the way: When you reach humility while laboring in silence, and when your soul nears its exodus from darkness, you shall have this sign: your heart will be set alight and will burn day and night, making the whole world look like ashes in your eyes. You shall then no longer desire to eat, neither shall you find food tasty. Your heart will be full enough with the new thoughts that will fill it. You shall then be granted a fountain of tears that will flood your eyes with a tranquil torrent. They will diffuse through all your works, whether they be prayer, meditation, ministry, or eating and drinking.

If this happens to you, be of good courage and know for sure that you have arrived at the other shore of the sea. Be heedful, work hard, that grace may abound day after day. If you have not yet seen this sign, know then that you have not yet ended your journey.

If your tears dry up afterward, this may be a sign that new and better changes will occur to you. But it may also be a sign of regression brought about by your pride or negligence. If it is for the better, this will be marked by increasing warmth. Tears will then cease and weeping will recede. For once the soul is entrusted with the warmth of the spirit, the contrition of weeping disappears, and joy and splendor are granted instead (St Isaac the Syrian, in "The Four Books," 3, Arabic version).

If the soul enters upon a phase of interior peace, that is, soundness of thoughts, the constancy of tears will withdraw from your eyes. Tears will not come afterward except in portion and in measure. This truth I have learned from a mouth that never lies. It is the outcome of no few works and struggles. It is also attested by the teachings of wise fathers and hard-working prelates of the church (St Isaac the Syrian, in "The Four Books," 3.11, Arabic version).

What Do Tears Signify?

1. Tears are a proof that the human soul has won divine mercy. It has been accepted by God through repentance and has now entered the phase of purity (St Isaac the Syrian, in "The Four Books," 2.9, Arabic version).

2. The quick realization that one has sinned is a gift from God bestowed on one's conscience. If man possesses himself of tears through this gift, especially during prayer, his prayer becomes a great oblation offered to the heavenly King. Man can thus raise his face before God and attain the forgiveness of his sins ("Homily on the Means Whereby a Man Can Acquire a Change of His Secret Intuitions Together with a Change of His External Discipline," in *The Ascetical Homilies of Saint Isaac the Syrian,* p 363).

3. There is a kind of tears that comes, in part, for the comfort of those who labor in the spirit before God. There is also another kind that never ceases day and night in which the eyes of man become like fountainheads. Such tears last for two years or more. They signify that man is sailing across the mystical gulf after which he is to enter into perfect peace. Permanent tears will afterward be withdrawn from him, and he will be comforted by God himself. He will experience an interior change similar to the peace that all will receive at the day of resurrection. It is a feeling that is hidden like a symbol.

SAYINGS OF THE FATHERS ON TEARS

320. Strive to enter the holy city, the Jerusalem, full of peace that is above all where Paradise is. You have no other way to become worthy of these amazing and blessed types, except that day and night you pour out tears according to him who says, "Each night wash I my bed and water my mattress with my tears" (Ps 6.6). For you are not ignorant that "those, who sow in tears shall reap in joy" (Ps 126.6).

For this reason the Prophet boldly declares: "Do not silence my tears" (Ps 39.13). And again: "Keep my tears before your sight as you have promised" (Ps 56.8). And: "My tears have been my bread day and night" (Ps 42.3). And in another psalm: "I have mingled my drink with weeping" (Ps 102.9). (St Macarius the Great, *Homilies* 25.7, in Maloney, *Intoxicated with God: The Fifty Spiritual Homilies of Macarius*)

321. For such a tear, that truly is shed out of much sorrow and anguish of heart in the knowledge of the truth and with the burning in the bowels, is food for the soul, supplied by the Heavenly Bread of which Mary pre-eminently partook as she sat at the feet of the Lord and wept, as the Savior himself testified. For he says: "Mary has chosen the better part which will not be taken from her" (Lk 10.42; 7.38).

O what precious pearls, those contained in the flowing of the blessed tears! O that immediate and prompt hearing! O what a strong and wise mind! O the intensity of the love of the Lord's Spirit that moves powerfully toward the spotless Bridegroom! O what a concentration of desire in the soul toward God the Word! O what intimate communion of the bride with the heavenly Bridegroom! (St Macarius the Great, *Homilies* 25.8, in *Spiritual Homilies*)

322. The tears that come after baptism are greater than baptism itself, though it may seem rash to say so. Baptism washes off those evils that were previously within us, whereas the sins committed after baptism are washed away by tears. The baptism received by us as children we have all defiled: we cleanse it anew with our tears. If God in his love for the human race had not given us tears, few indeed would be saved and they would be hard to find. (St John Climacus, *Ladder of Divine Ascent* 7.8, p 137)

323. He who has the gift of spiritual tears will be able to mourn anywhere. But if it is all outward show, there will be no end to his discussion of places and means. (St John Climacus, *Ladder of Divine Ascent* 7.14)

324. Hidden treasure is more secure than that which is exposed in the marketplace. Ponder this, and apply it to yourself. (St John Climacus, *Ladder of Divine Ascent* 7.15)

325. I have seen small teardrops shed like drops of blood, and I have seen floods of tears poured out with no trouble at all. So I judge toilers by their struggles, rather than their tears; and I suspect that God does so too. (St John Climacus, *Ladder of Divine Ascent* 7.26, pp 138, 139)

326. Theology and mourning do not go together, for the one dissipates the other. The difference between a theologian and a mourner is that the one sits on a professional chair while the other passes his days in rags on a dung heap. (St John Climacus, *Ladder of Divine Ascent* 7.27, p 139)

327. Those gifted with the heart's depth of mourning regard their lives as detestable, painful, and wearying; a cause for tears and suffering. They turn away from their body as from an enemy. (St John Climacus, *Ladder of Divine Ascent* 7.32, 31)

328. If your soul is still not perfectly pure, then be suspicious of your tears. (St John Climacus, *Ladder of Divine Ascent* 7.39, p 140)

329. There is no joy or pleasure to be had in prison, and genuine monks do not feast on earth. (St John Climacus, *Ladder of Divine Ascent* 7.41, 42)

330. The man wearing blessed, God-given mourning like a wedding garment gets to know the spiritual laughter of the soul. (St John Climacus, *Ladder of Divine Ascent* 7.44)

331. The man who takes pride in his tears and who secretly condemns those who do not weep is rather like the man who asks the king for a weapon against the enemy—and then uses it to commit suicide. (St John Climacus, *Ladder of Divine Ascent* 7.45, p 141)

332. God does not demand or desire that someone should mourn out of sorrow of heart; He wants him to rejoice in love for him with the laughter of the soul. Take away sin and then the sorrowful tears that flow from the eyes will be superfluous. Why look for a bandage when you are not cut? Adam did not weep before the fall, and there will be no tears after the resurrection when sin will be abolished, when pain, sorrow, and lamentation will have taken flight. (St John Climacus, *Ladder of Divine Ascent* 7.49, 50)

333. Silly men often take pride in their tears—hence some are not granted the gift of mourning. (St John Climacus, *Ladder of Divine Ascent* 7.52)

334. A widow: she has lost her husband, her only son is the single comfort remaining to her after the Lord. She is like a lapsed soul at the moment of death: the only comfort is the toil of fasting and of tears. (St John Climacus, *Ladder of Divine Ascent* 7.56, pp 142, 143)

335. Men have been moved to tears in cities and among crowds—I have seen it myself. This fact has given rise to the idea that great assemblies of people may actually do us no harm. Yet they may draw us back too close to the world; the evil spirits are working hard to bring this about. (St John Climacus, *Ladder of Divine Ascent* 7.77, p 145)

CHAPTER THIRTEEN

Fasting

"And when you fast, do not look dismal."
(Mt 6.16)

"That your fasting may not be seen by men
but by your Father who is in secret." (Mt
6.18)

"Do not labor for the food which perishes,
but for the food which endures to eternal
life." (Jn 6.27)

"My food is to do the will of him who sent
me, and to accomplish his work." (Jn 4.34)

"Woe to you that are full now, for you shall
hunger." (Lk 6.25)

F ASTING BY ITSELF IS NOT A VIRTUE. It is nothing at all. Without prayer, it becomes a bodily punishment that induces spiritual aridity and bad temper. The same is true of prayer; without fasting, it loses its power along with its fruits.

We may liken fasting to a burning coal and prayer to frankincense. Neither has value without the other, but together, the sweet savor of their incense fills the air.

Fasting calms the impulses of the flesh and quenches the fire of passion; it curbs the prattling of the tongue. Thus, it substantially prepares us for the work of prayer and the release of the spirit from slavery to the flesh. In this way, fasting allows the spirit to contemplate the truths of eternity and the age to come.[1]

---

[1] The author has treated the spiritual value of fasting in his book *The Communion of Love,* chapter 8: "The Deep Meaning of Fasting" (SVS Press, 1984), 109.

The following constitute spiritual meanings for fasting:

—Fasting is not a deprivation from certain kinds of food, but a voluntary abstinence from them.

—It does not humiliate the flesh, but refreshes the spirit.

—Nor does it fetter or imprison the senses; it releases them from all that hinders the contemplation of God.

—Fasting does not seek to repress the appetite for food. It renounces this appetite and, in renunciation, elevates it to relish the love of God.

—Fasting does not imply confinement or restriction, but aims at joy and magnanimity of heart.

SAYINGS OF THE FATHERS ON FASTING

336. The table of a man who continually perseveres in prayer is sweeter than the scent of musk and the fragrance of perfumes, and the lover of God yearns for this as for a priceless treasure.

Take for yourself the remedy of life from the table of those who fast, keep vigil, and labor in the Lord, and so raise up the dead man in your soul. For the Beloved reclines in their midst bestowing sanctification and he transforms the bitterness of their hardship into his ineffable sweetness. His spiritual and heavenly ministers overshadow both them and their holy foods. I know one of the brethren who has seen this with his own eyes. (St Isaac the Syrian, *Homilies* 15, in *The Ascetical Homilies of Saint Isaac the Syrian,* p 88)

337. There can be no knowledge of the mysteries of God on a full stomach. (St Isaac the Syrian, *Homilies* 4, in *Ascetical Homilies,* p 33)

338. Fasting, vigil . . . are God's holy pathway and the foundation of every virtue. (St Isaac the Syrian, *Homilies* 37, in *Ascetical Homilies,* p 171)

339. Fasting is the champion of every virtue, the beginning of the struggle, the crown of the abstinent, the beauty of virginity and sanctity, the resplendence of chastity, the commencement of the path of Christianity, the mother of prayer, the well-spring of sobriety and prudence, the teacher of stillness, and the precursor of all good works. (St Isaac the Syrian, *Homilies* 37, in *Ascetical Homilies*, p 171)

340. When a man begins to fast, he straightway yearns in his mind to enter into converse with God. (St Isaac the Syrian, *Homilies* 37, in *Ascetical Homilies*, p 171)

341. Fasting was the commandment that was given to our nature in the beginning to protect it with respect to the tasting of food, and in this point the progenitor of our substance fell. There, however, where the first defeat was suffered, the ascetic strugglers make their beginning in the fear of God as they start to keep his laws.

And the Savior also, when he manifested himself to the world in the Jordan, began at this point. For after his baptism the Spirit led him into the wilderness and he fasted for forty days and forty nights. Likewise all who set to follow in his footsteps make the beginning of their struggle upon this foundation. For this is a weapon forged by God, and who shall escape blame if he neglects it? And if the Lawgiver himself fasts, who among those who keep the law has no need of fasting? (St Isaac the Syrian, *Homilies* 37, in *Ascetical Homilies*, p 172)

342. What weapon is more powerful and gives more boldness to the heart in the time of battle against the spirits of wickedness, than hunger endured for Christ's sake? ... He who has armed himself with the weapon of fasting is afire with zeal at all times. (St Isaac the Syrian, *Homilies* 37, in *Ascetical Homilies*, p 172)

343. It is said concerning many of the martyrs, that when they foreknew, either by revelation or by information received from one of their friends, the day on which they were to receive the crown of martyrdom, they did not taste anything the preceding night, but from evening till morning they stood keeping vigil in prayer, glorifying God in psalms, hymns, and spiritual odes, and they looked forward to that hour with joy and exultation, waiting to meet the sword in their fast as ones prepared for the nuptials. (St Isaac the Syrian, *Homilies* 37, in *Ascetical Homilies*, pp 172, 173)

344. Therefore let us also be vigilant, we who are called to an unseen martyrdom so as to receive the crowns of sanctification. (St Isaac the Syrian, *Homilies* 37, in *Ascetical Homilies,* p 173)

345. When you sit at a well-laden table, remember death and remember judgment, and even then you will only manage to restrain yourself a little. (St John Climacus, *The Ladder of Divine Ascent* 14.34, p 169)

346. And when you drink, keep always in mind the vinegar and gall of your Lord. Then indeed you will either be temperate or sighing. (St John Climacus, *The Ladder of Divine Ascent* 14.34, p 169)

347. And so for nearly twenty years he continued training himself in solitude, never going forth, and seen but seldom by any. After this, when many were eager and wishful to imitate his discipline, and his acquaintances came and began to cast down and wrench off the door by force, Antony, as from a shrine, came forth initiated in the mysteries and filled with the Spirit of God. Then for the first time he was seen outside the fort by those who came to see him. And they, when they saw him, wondered at the sight, for he had the same habit of body as before, and was neither fat, like a man without exercise, nor lean from fasting and striving with the demons, but he was just the same as they had known him before his retirement. (St Athanasius, *Life of Antony* 14, NPNF, 2nd series, 4.200)

PART THREE

Impediments to Prayer

I MPEDIMENTS TO PRAYER EXIST both for those who are beginners and for those who are more advanced.

For beginners, such impediments result simply from an initial lack of familiarity with prayer (so that the mind is distracted by matters that appear to be more important than God), irregularity in prayer times, or a lack of understanding of the words of the prayers used, be they those of the Psalms or other parts of the Bible. The reader will find all these problems discussed in the various chapters of this book, for we have carefully dealt with each problem in its proper place.

In this part, we shall limit ourselves to dealing with the impediments that face those who have succeeded to some degree in the practice of prayer and the problems of those who are progressing in the life of prayer. However, we should inform the reader from the first that our prayers may often be impeded by physical weaknesses or by lack of physical strength, due to illnesses such as anemia in particular; lack of energy caused by mental exhaustion or stress; excessive fasting beyond one's ability; severe and chronic constipation; or overwork, whether physical or mental. All these problems need keen insight on the part of the individual and his director to diagnose them at once and prescribe the treatment. Otherwise, the condition of the soul will go from bad to worse, and there will be no way to avoid confusion. The lack of progress in prayer will then be imputed to negligence, sloth, coldness, sin, and so forth. If such causes are ascribed, despair will set in, for failure due to physical, mental, or psychological illness will be inevitable. However, the cause is actually what Christ explained to his disciples, who were weary and exhausted from lack of sleep and unable to watch and pray: "The spirit indeed is willing, but the flesh is weak" (Mt 26.41).

For those who are advancing in prayer, the basic factors that impede their progress may be attributed to three well-known and prominent experiences: (1) spiritual aridity, or dryness; (2) spiritual languor, or a lukewarm attitude; and (3) misdirection, or losing the sense of the purpose of prayer. We shall deal with the first two together, leaving the third to the end of this part.

There is a great difference between spiritual aridity and spiritual languor. Spiritual aridity is an experience that accompanies prayer. It does not hinder prayer, reading, or vigils, but it makes them bereft of any consolation, pleasure, or delight.

Spiritual languor, however, attacks spiritual activity itself. Prayer then stops and the ability to continue any spiritual practice is lost. Reading becomes difficult and vigil impossible. Exerting any effort, even in ordinary, simple services, becomes wearisome.

In times of spiritual aridity, we can easily pray and follow the meaning. Our mind is alert, our feelings attentive. We can study the word of God and concentrate on reading and writing. But through it all, we are destitute of any interior solace.

In times of spiritual languor, however, whenever we stand to pray or sit down to read, our mind is distracted and our heart becomes a stranger to us, and so the pursuit of prayer and spiritual activity becomes not only very difficult, but even beyond any hope of attainment.

CHAPTER FOURTEEN

Spiritual Aridity

> "O my God, I cry by day, but thou dost
> not answer; and by night, but find no
> rest . . . my strength is dried up like a
> potsherd, and my tongue cleaves to my
> jaws." (Ps 22.2, 15)

W HEN THE SOUL ENTERS INTO THE TRIAL of spiritual aridity, or dryness, for the first time, it becomes extremely dismayed. This is especially true if there was a disciplined devotion to worship in sincerity of heart. One begins to be troubled and to wonder why this has happened and to look for the faults that may be the cause.

But spiritual aridity is not a sign of any kind of failure in a healthy relationship with God. It is only an important phase that the soul has to undergo, which may be regarded as a kind of pruning to prepare the soul for a more advanced spiritual life, not contingent upon psychological incentives or subjective pleasures.

Spiritual aridity is a food that is somewhat hard to digest, but is very nourishing, so if we submit to this ordeal and bear it readily, attentively, and patiently; if we do not allow our spirits to flag from lack of consolation and incentive; and if we simply trust in the truthfulness of God's promises, we shall certainly be raised by this means to the stature of mature sons. We shall become worthy of discovering that exalted love that does not ask for its own pleasure or count on receiving, but is content with giving and sacrificing.

Close examination of spiritual aridity shows that it is by nature free from any kind of turbulence. Neither does it cause any distress to one's heart. Aridity only reigns over the spirit as far as feelings and sentiments are concerned. It never disturbs the peace or tranquility of the soul, but it is a peace without the warmth of affection and a tranquility without attraction or pleasure.

For this reason, it is only those whose souls are pampered who are disturbed by the trial of spiritual aridity, only those who live on comforts and incentives, only those whose godliness depends on receiving and whose growth relies on experiences.

The danger that threatens whoever passes through this phase of spiritual aridity is doubt. One may doubt the route itself and think that one's relationship with God has been severed and so stop praying. But, in fact, the nature of this experience, which is of spiritual aridity brought about by grace, allows for prayer to continue. Spiritual aridity does not take away the power to pray or to persist in prayer. It only deprives one of the fruit of solace one may have relied on in prayer. But if prayer ceases on the pretext of spiritual aridity or lack of comfort, the spiritual life begins to ebb, and then, needlessly, a dangerous, negative experience begins, namely, murmuring against God.

It is therefore wrong to be upset during the phase of aridity. It is also wrong to stop praying on the pretext of finding no pleasure in prayer, for aridity is a living part of the very nature of prayer. It is able, if we accept it with contentment and understanding, to raise us to the higher stage of pure prayer, which is not contingent on emotions, sentiments, or incentives of any kind.

Thus, whenever you feel that grace seems to have abandoned you, be content with its hidden action. Rely instead on the strength of the impetus previously gained from your life with God. This should be sufficient to take you through the early stages of this experience, and later on, your soul will find its rest in God without the need for incentives or any similar aid.

The traveler during this trial should also trust in the counsel of his director and follow his instructions carefully; they are of particularly great value especially at this stage. However, the best counsel at this time is to accept spiritual aridity as a call to humility and contentment. You should feel yourself the least among people and unworthy of comfort. Even if you consider spiritual aridity as a kind of chastisement, it is profitable for your soul (although aridity is not chastisement but pruning).

To stop to examine yourself and search for the reasons and causes that have brought about spiritual aridity is of no avail. Neither is it helpful to plan to get out of this trial by doubling one's vigils, prayers, or fasting. All such efforts are useless. Moreover, they push you beyond the plan of the economy of grace.

The best thing to do is to accept aridity as it is and persist in spiritual activity with calm and awareness. Allow yourself to exert every effort to keep on progressing at the speed of one who travels across the desert and is never deterred by the pleasures of the city he has left behind from striding across the arid wilderness until he reaches his destination.

Our best response to a spiritual trial is to accept it for its own sake and not for anything beyond it. Aridity is a spiritual trial in its own right. It is laid down as an intrinsic feature of the narrow way.

Spiritual trials in general are not undergone for the sake of attaining perfection, for this implies a sense of self-deification. Rather, we should submit to the sovereign purposes of God so that we may fulfill his will, for our obedience to God is the foundation of our life with him, and it is only this that leads us to perfection.

The Relationship between Aridity and the Will

We need to distinguish between the essence of the human soul and the qualities and responses that arise as a result of its activity.

The soul in its essence is one thing, and the emotion proceeding from it or affecting it is another. This also applies to thoughts and images, which may reveal the condition of the soul, but are neither the soul itself nor what represents it. Nothing can reveal the soul or represent it except free will. Therefore, man is neither held accountable nor condemned for his thoughts, images, or emotions. He is held accountable and is condemned only for what his will declares.

In spiritual aridity, we find that the faculties of the soul are no longer able to receive solace or transcendent spiritual incentives. Spiritual aridity thus remains an experience external to one's own will.

This is an extremely important fact, for it exempts man from an imagined responsibility. When comfort and interior pleasure cease with the experience of spiritual aridity, the conscience always tries to blame the self. It thus becomes clear that the relationship between the soul (or the will) and prayer can remain unimpaired in spite of aridity, for in its origin, aridity has nothing to do with the will, and so the activity of prayer can continue energetically despite the experience of aridity.

Prayer should continue without relying on the consolations and emotional incentives, which the soul used to receive through images, sentiments, and ideas. This is the major purpose of the experience of aridity. Grace introduces this experience for man's own good during his progression along the spiritual way. It aims at ridding him of all the attachments that bind the soul to feelings, human emotions, and mental images, for these hinder direct communication between the soul and God. The essence of the soul can never rest perfectly in God so long as emotional, imaginative, or mental activities intervene.

The moment prayer is unshackled from such attachments, it enters upon the phase of purity. Once man attains pure prayer, there is nothing in the world to separate him from God, for the essence of the soul will have been centered in God without an exterior agent. Then the soul can contemplate God in prayer without any hindrance and without any psychological stimulants, which may be liable to error.

Thus, it becomes clear that spiritual aridity is an experience that grace brings upon the soul so that it might grow in its direct vision of God. This is effected by blocking all the secondary outlets that distract spiritual vision, namely, consolations, pleasures, and incentives.

Aridity: A Chance for Evil Distractions

One of the dangers of the phase of aridity is the release of the senses, the mind, and the imagination to work in an area that is far from spiritual oversight. They may be captured by the enemy, who can cast them down from their original height and so indulge in evil thoughts and sinful images, which might never before have occurred to the mind. The reason is that grace feeds such faculties of the soul as imagination, thought, and emotion with spiritual solace, and the removal of that solace provides an opportunity for the enemy to parade his evil thoughts before these faculties.

It is thus possible that during the stage of spiritual aridity the mind may be involuntarily distracted by innumerable evil images, which may cause extreme humiliation to the soul. Here, we need to pay attention to the role played by the will. So long as the will is not content or in accord with these distractions and cannot even tolerate them and can express its disapproval, grief, and rejection of them to God in prayer, then prayer will always remain within the confines of purity, unpolluted by these mental disturbances and evil images. So, the responsibility for the purity of prayer falls first and foremost upon the will. The will can persist in rejecting these images and false ideas and can resolve to keep on struggling no matter how long the temptation may last. It is this that finally sets a limit for these images and ideas.

An evil thought might find its way into our mind. But as long as we do not endorse it or approve of it, God never holds us accountable for it. This is what we should believe with absolute confidence. However, we have to attest our objection by continual and unrelenting prayer. The will can hold fast to this objection. The determination of the inner man is able to resist. We can hold out without surrendering, and then every torture the enemy may inflict on our mind or conscience is at the end accounted to our credit as a pure sacrifice.

The prolongation of the period of temptation might cause habitual obsession of the mind with evil thoughts and false distractions, but this is not to be feared as long as the will remains alive, vigorous, and nourished by prayer. For in a single moment, the battle will end decisively when God comes down to embrace the soul after it has been stripped of its selfishness and dependence on emotion.

But why does God permit the enemy to torture the mind and conscience in a way so cruel that some saints have described it as hell? The answer is that our nature, which has been corrupted by sin, has become a target for evil. Our mind has been accustomed of its own free will to visualize evil. Even if this has happened only once, the enemy has gained the power to compel our mind to visualize evil in spite of itself. So, if God after that neglects us for a moment, that we might taste the bitterness of Satan's ruling power, he is by no means unjust. But, at the same time, he can never abandon us altogether. At the right moment, he intervenes and changes all our afflictions into instruments of power and salvation and glory. Our emotions, thoughts, and images are thus smelted in the trial of spiritual aridity, and we become ready at last for the stage of purity where we live in freedom in the presence of God.

CHAPTER FIFTEEN

Spiritual Languor

"For the enemy has pursued me; he has
crushed my life to the ground; he has
made me sit in darkness like those long
dead." (Ps 143.3)

IN TIMES OF SPIRITUAL ARIDITY, prayer does not stop. There is nothing to demand that it stop, since the entire soul is still inclined toward God and righteousness. It is not as if it has lost its power or will to strive or to pray, for spiritual aridity has no effect except the absence of the solace, pleasure, and loving encouragements that are the companions and fruits of prayer.

Spiritual languor, on the other hand, affects the will. Here, the attack is aimed even at our attempt to pray and to persevere in prayer. A man may stand to pray, but he finds neither words to say nor power to carry on. He may sit down to read, but the book in his hands turns, as St Isaac the Syrian says, "into lead." It may remain open for a whole day, while the mind fails to grasp a single line. The mind is distracted, unable to concentrate on or follow the meaning of the words passing before it. The will, which controls all activity, is impotent.

Although the desire to pray is present, the power and will to do so are absent. In the end, even the desire to pray may fade. Man becomes unable and unwilling to pray, adding to his suffering and sorrow. His problems seem entirely insolvable.

If man tries to plumb the depths of his soul, he finds himself at a loss, for its depths are beyond his reach. It is as if his spiritual footing has been lost, alienating him from the essence of his life. If he tries to examine his faith and secretly measure it in his heart, he finds that it has died, gone. If he knocks at the door of hope, if he clings to the promises of God he had once cherished and lived by, he finds in what he used to find hope has now turned to ice. Hope is stuck in the cold present and not willing to move beyond it.

The enemy seizes this opportunity, striking with all his firepower. He launches an offensive—to convince man of his failure, of the ruin of all his struggle and effort. The enemy tries to persuade man that his whole spiritual life was not true or real, that it was nothing but fanciful illusions and emotions. He clamps down on man's mind that he might once and for all deny the spiritual life.

Yet, amidst all these crushing inner battles, the soul somehow has an intuition that all these doubts are untrue and that something must exist on the other side of the darkness. It also feels that, in spite of itself, it is still bound to the God who has forsaken it. The soul continues to worship God without realizing or even wanting to! Deep within, far away from the mind's eye or discernment, the heart continues to pray—albeit it is a prayer that gives him no comfort or assurance.

When the enemy seeks to deal his fatal blow, trying to force the soul to renounce its faith and hope, he encounters no response. The soul may give in to the enemy in the battle of the mind in complete surrender and to the farthest limits of error. But it is absolutely impossible for the soul to take action, for at the point where imagination and thought turn into action, the will springs forth like a lion out of his den to terrify all the foxes of corruption.

Hence, behind spiritual languor there exists a relationship with God that, though inactive, is real and still very strong, stronger than all the whispers of the devil. Yet until the decisive moment of danger, this relationship sleeps. This relationship remains hidden from the soul. It is vain to try to convince a soul of its existence, that the soul might rely on this or reassure itself of its presence. For in this tribulation, the soul is called to stand alone.

The soul remains within the sphere of God's dominion. Although unaware, it is still making progress and on the right path. It is still led by an invisible hand and carried by an unfelt power. The tangible proof for all this is the extreme, constant grief of the soul over its fall from its former activity, zeal, and prominent effort into its present state.

The movement of faith was born one day within the heart of the pilgrim, now on the trek whose final destination is God. Faith was lit like a lamp with the light of God. It was kindled by love and zeal and has pushed the soul forward on its march. The pilgrim must not believe that this movement can be abruptly withdrawn from the depths of his heart, that he can be left in such sudden emptiness.

It cannot be assumed that a man will constantly see or feel the light or warmth of God. Yet both are constant and active, both in the light of this life as well as in its darkness, its coldness as well as its warmth, its happiness as well as its grief. The way of the spirit is not to be measured exclusively by periods of light, warmth, joy, or fruitful activity. Periods of impasse, of darkness engulfing the soul, of grief which oppresses the heart, periods of coldness paralyzing all spiritual emotion are inseparable parts of the narrow spiritual way. Such conditions seem adverse, painful, and deadly. What matters is how we face them. This is what determines our worthiness to proceed further, completing the blessed struggle until we receive our crowns.

Reasons for Spiritual Struggle

God does not randomly bring this tribulation upon man's soul. There are inescapable reasons requiring one to undergo such an experience. The soul's power of assessment in spiritual matters has to be adjusted, its path upward straightened, and its faith in the Invisible strengthened.

Spiritual Languor as a Discipline for the Ambitious Soul

When the ambitious soul becomes obsessed with its progress, it tries to double its speed. It goes beyond its ability to endure, beyond that which its foundations can stand. It also begins to ask for knowledge beyond its actual needs or its true capacity of vision. In spiritual presumption, it impertinently claims that this is out of faith. It barges into the realms of higher spiritual experience. It gazes into the light without the proper qualifications of insight, unsupported by work or experience. The simple result is that it comes to a sudden halt.

Logically, this deadlock might appear to be only natural, a result of an exhaustion in the reserves of spiritual energy or of a lack of balance between the available resources of faith and the premature trespassing upon such perilous heights. But the main reason is actually the intervention of God's mercy, compassion, and pity for the soul. He withdraws its ability to soar on the heights. Otherwise, it may be lifted beyond its ability in balance and endurance and fall and be shattered. Spiritual languor is the soul's life insurance, guaranteeing its protection from spiritual pride. If pursued one step further, such a path would bring about a plight like that which befell the builders of the Tower of Babel.

Languor is profitable for the soul, for it strips it completely of all ambition. It brings to an end excessive obsession with a false progress, which comes from the delusion of a will that magnifies its ego. Languor brings the soul back to the lowly steps appropriate for beginners. The soul is thus held back from climbing dangerous heights, for it now becomes obsessed with its own grief and sadness, the disgrace of its condition, and the loss of its proud hopes. It goes back again, groping its way again from the beginning in humiliation and humility. These are more of a guarantee for its salvation than performing signs and wonders or engaging in lofty meditations.

The sign that characterizes this kind of spiritual languor (discipline because of ambition) is the extreme grief and misery that take hold of the soul because of its present condition. This grief and misery are but a proof that the operation undertaken by God to maintain the soul's humility has been successful.

Spiritual Languor for Correcting Our Understanding of the Relationship that Binds Us to God

There is a danger when the soul is engrossed in its spiritual labor, its meticulous observance of prayer, or other spiritual practices. A feeling may surface that falsely links this activity and diligence to its relationship with God. The soul fancies that its own striving and faithfulness in prayer qualify it for the love of God and make it worthy of adoption by him. However, God does not desire to leave the soul straying along a false path that ultimately leads it away from deserving his love or living with him. He is thus obliged to deprive the soul of an energy and diligence that might bring about its ruin.

Previously God gave man such gifts as energy and ability in spiritual work as a pledge of his love and pleasure. But when God now withdraws from man such abilities, the soul loses the power and energy to perform any spiritual work. It is shocked at one astounding fact that it still rejects, namely, that God, in his fatherly love for us, is in no need of our prayers or works!

At first, man clings to the idea that the fatherhood of God must have been cut off by the failure to pray. God has surely forsaken and abandoned the soul because its works and fervor appear to be insufficient when measured next to his love. The soul tries in vain to rise from this downcast mood and grief to resume its fervor and activity, for the resolve to do so has blown away with the wind.

At last, the soul gradually begins to realize that the greatness of God should not be measured by the triviality of man. God's sublime fatherhood has condescended to adopt the sons of dust out of his compassion and grandeur and not as a reward for man's works or diligence. Our sonship to God is a truth that stems from God and not from us. This sonship continues regardless of our disability or sin, bearing witness to the goodness of God and his generosity.

Spiritual languor thus brings about in such people an essential change in their understanding of God. It alters their assessment of the spiritual relationship that binds the human soul to him. Man's idea of diligence and activity and of every spiritual work from now on is corrected. They are not the price to be paid for God's love and fatherhood, but only a response to them.

The symptoms of this kind of spiritual languor consist in the many bewildering questions that are asked every day throughout this trial. Has God forsaken me? Is it because of my sin? Have I provoked his fatherhood to anger by my sloth and laziness? Has he rejected me because my prayer is no longer acceptable to him?

The persons of the first kind, those afflicted with spiritual languor because of their ambition, suffer only from the cessation of prayer. As for those of the second kind, who are afflicted with languor because of their faulty idea of God's love and his fatherhood, they are dismayed not at the cessation of prayer but at losing their status as children of God, at losing his confidence and love. Inasmuch as their fear and anxiety increase, their affliction and dryness also increase. This goes on until truth is revealed to them at the end, strengthening beyond all expectations the bonds of love and kinship.

In fact, the mere existence of this fear most clearly testifies to the existence of faithful sincerity toward God. At the time, though, the soul is uncertain of this fact. It remains apprehensive until, despite everything it has gone through, it finally becomes certain of God's fatherhood and that that fatherhood supersedes everything else.

Spiritual Languor as a Means for Strengthening Faith in God beyond Tangible Things

Man may find great peace and happiness in God's complete provision for his physical needs. God may also watch over his emotional state with clear protection in all situations. Man can rest secure, for he is protected by the hand of God, watched over by him, and kept in his care. His confidence in God thus increases and his faith in him is strengthened because of obvious material evidence and tangible proof.

Then God suddenly cuts off all visible aid. As far as man can tell, God withholds all care and protection from him. One after another, tribulations begin to come upon man's soul. He becomes vulnerable to his enemies, a target for all who insult, ridicule, and resort to violence. This happens not only with visible enemies but also with the unseen, the inventor of every evil and all distress. Outer tribulations join those internal until man becomes astonished by the variety of the frequent blows dealt him. At first, he thinks that these difficulties are transient. The clouds will lift before long and life will once again return to its former peace and stability. But to the contrary, these tribulations grow in severity and variety until it dawns on him that the matter is beyond both his control and comprehension. He sits down in the dust, shattered, unable to make sense of the whole thing. What happened? Why did it happen? Where is all this leading?

Man then returns to himself that he may perhaps find a ray of hope to help him resume his former life. But he finds nothing save wreckage upon wreckage and a soul ripped to pieces, torn up by a thousand trials. It is not merely languor or aridity or a lack of comfort. It is a complete absence of a spiritual sense, for it is a sense built upon false estimations. With this absence comes hardship, grumbling, bewilderment, blasphemy, and the horror that dominates the soul in such a predicament. When the soul tries to repel the blasphemy springing from its depths, it finds no power to do so. When it tries to denounce the evil and filth that the devil hurls at the mind, it cannot but muse over them, driven like a captive of every iniquity and sin. The soul finally rests at the verge of despair.

Yet, what actually baffles the soul is neither its losses nor its failure nor its inability to pray or labor nor even its fear of God's abandonment. It is, rather, the feeling that the attitude that God has taken toward it is that of an adversary who finds pleasure in seeing it suffering, grieving, and being torn apart!

We find this tribulation in its most vehement form in the experience of Job the Righteous. What Job was most concerned about was neither the disastrous property losses he had suffered, the loss of his children, the sufferings of his body, nor the derision of everyone around him, even his own wife. Rather, Job fell under the illusion that resulted from the severity of his affliction—that God had turned against him in neglect and hostility, gloating over him!

Therefore I will not restrain my mouth; I will speak in the anguish of
my spirit; I will complain in the bitterness of my soul. Am I the sea, or
a sea monster, that thou settest a guard over me? When I say, "My bed
will comfort me, my couch will ease my complaint," then thou dost
scare me with dreams and terrify me with visions . . . I loathe my life;
I would not live for ever. Let me alone . . . till I swallow my spittle . . .
For the arrows of the Almighty are in me; my spirit drinks their poison; the terrors of God are arrayed against me . . . Why dost thou not
pardon my transgression? . . . For he crushes me with a tempest, and
multiplies my wounds without cause; he will not let me get my breath,
but fills me with bitterness . . . I loathe my life . . . I will speak in the
bitterness of my soul . . . Let me know why thou dost contend against
me. Does it seem good to thee to oppress . . . For I am filled with
disgrace and look upon my affliction . . . Thou dost hunt me like a
lion, and again work wonders against me . . . Let me alone . . . withdraw thy hand from me and let not dread of thee terrify me . . . Why
dost thou hide thy face, and count me as thy enemy? . . . I cry to thee
and thou dost not heed me. *Thou hast turned cruel to me!* [italics added]
Behold, I go forward, but he is not there; and backward, but I cannot
perceive him; on the left hand I seek him, but I cannot behold him; I
turn to the right hand, but I cannot see him. (Job 6.4; 7.11–20; 7.21; 9.17,
18; 10.1, 2, 15, 16, 20; 13.21, 24; 23.8; 30.20, 21)

It is with great sincerity that Job describes his feelings. Yet, he was mis-
taken in thinking that God had forsaken him, for in reality, God was not far
away from Job. Neither the losses he had suffered nor the hardships he had
undergone serve as proof of God's forsaking. Neither should the riches, care,
and protection that man receives from God be considered as an evidence
of God's pleasure. They should not be taken as a reason or springboard for
faith or hope.

None of the harm that befell Job managed to make him renounce his
integrity. Yet, as soon as he mistakenly felt that God had forsaken him and was
opposed to him, he lost the equilibrium of his faith. This is the cause of Job's
ordeal. The extent of it comes into focus at this point along with its awesome
mystery. It is through Job's tribulation that God intended to reveal to all
mankind that faith in him should withstand all manner of abandonment however dismaying, drastic, or painful it might seem to be. Faith transcends all

such feelings, and man believes confidently in the existence of God, his mercy, and his care, regardless of the trial.

This debilitating languor of the spirit is by far the direst tribulation of the soul, indeed the climax of its purging experience. It is similar only to death. Only under the wing of the Almighty's perfect providence can man withstand such a trial, for during this ordeal the soul in its grief, like Job, reaches the point in which it yearns for death:

> O that I might have my request, and that God would grant my desire; that it would please God to crush me, that he would let loose his hand and cut me off! ... What is my strength that I should wait? and what is my end, that I should be patient? Is my strength the strength of stones, or is my flesh bronze? ... Any resource is driven from me ... The night is long, and I am full of tossing till the dawn ... I regard not myself; I loathe my life ... My soul is weary of my life ... I hold my tongue, I shall give up the ghost. (Job 6.8, 9, 11–13; 7.4; 9.21; 10.1; 13.19)

During all these torments, the afflicted person is not totally deprived of the hope of God's mercy. He never stops looking up toward God, even on the verge of despair; rather, he waits for a great and wonderful salvation. Inasmuch as the tribulation presses hard, his soul becomes clearer and purer. The vision of the Almighty's majesty is unveiled, together with the intensity of his love and faithfulness toward the human soul. Previous sufferings seem to fall like scales from the eyes of the soul. It is here that the soul builds up its faith in God. It is not on the basis of blessings that pass away, on protection and visible care, nor on tangible evidence or reasonable proof, but on "the assurance of things hoped for, the conviction of things not seen" (Heb 11.1):

> But he knows the way that I take; when he has tried me, I shall come forth as gold. My foot has held fast to his steps; I have kept his way and have not turned aside. I have not departed from the commandment of his lips ... For I know that my Redeemer lives, and at last he will stand upon the earth; and after my skin has been destroyed, then without my flesh I shall see God [here is evidence of how Job's faith has moved from relying on things visible to things invisible] whom I shall see for myself, and my eyes shall behold, and not another ... As God lives, who has made my soul bitter; as long as my breath is in me, and the spirit of God

is in my nostrils, my lips will not speak falsehood, and my tongue will
not utter deceit . . . till I die I will not put away my integrity from me.
(Job 13.15, 16; 19.25–27; 23.10–12; 27.2–5)

In the same way, every soul that loves Christ will be, without exception,
vindicated at the end. No matter how bitter the spiritual experience, it still
knows its final share. It crawls forward, injured but looking toward Christ.
The soul, the forsaken beloved, calls to him who has bought her with his
blood, never once swerving from her trust in her Lover.

Trust may fade from view but is never lost. Faith may sometimes come to
a halt but never comes to an end. Feelings of love may sink out of sight, yet
they are still preserved in the depths of the soul to spring forth at the end of the
trial with an invincible power.

SAYINGS OF THE FATHERS ON ARIDITY AND LANGUOR IN PRAYER

348. Let us see, my beloved, whether in our soul at the time of prayer we possess divine vision into the verses of psalmody and prayer. For this is born of
true stillness. And let us not be troubled when we are found in darkness, especially if the cause of this is not in us. But reckon this as the work of God's providence for a reason that he alone knows.

At times our soul is suffocated and is, as it were, amid the waves; and
whether a man reads in the Scriptures, or performs his liturgy, or approaches
anything whatever, he receives darkness upon darkness. He leaves off [prayer]
and cannot even draw nigh to it. He is wholly unable to believe that a change
will occur and that he will be at peace. This hour is full of despair and fear;
hope in God and the consolation of faith are utterly extinguished from his soul,
and she is wholly and entirely filled with doubt and fear.

Those who have been tried by the mighty waves of this dark hour know
from experience the change that follows upon its completion. God does not
leave the soul in these things an entire day, for otherwise she would perish,
being estranged from the Christian hope; but he speedily provides her with an
"escape" (1 Cor 10.13). But even if the oppression of this darkness should be

prolonged, you should expect that a change to the better will proceed swiftly out of the midst of it.

I admonish and counsel you, O man, if you do not have the strength to master yourself and to fall upon your face in prayer, then wrap your head in your cloak and sleep until this hour of darkness pass from you, but do not leave your dwelling. This trial befalls those especially who desire to pass their life in the noetic discipline, and who throughout their journey seek the consolation of faith. For this reason their greatest pain and travail is the dark hour when their mind wavers with doubt. And blasphemy follows hard upon this. Sometimes a man is seized by doubts in the resurrection, and by other things whereof we have no need to speak. Many times we have experienced all these things, and we have written of this struggle for the comfort of many.

Those who pass their life in physical works are entirely free of these trials. They are assailed by another kind of despondency, one which is familiar to everyone, and which differs in its mode of action from the trials mentioned and others of similar kind. The healing of these latter troubles wells up from stillness itself. This is the man's consolation. But he will never receive the light of consolation from intercourse with men, and their converse will never heal him, but only briefly give him rest; thereafter these trials will rise up against him with great force. Of necessity he must have a guide who is enlightened and strengthened and has experience in these matters, so that by him he can be enlightened and strengthened at the time of his need, but not at all times.

Blessed is he who patiently endures these things within the doors [of his cell]! Afterward, as the Fathers say, he will attain to a magnificent and enduring dwelling. This struggle, however, does not cease immediately, nor in an hour; nor does grace come once and for all and dwell in the soul, but little by little of one and the other: sometimes trial, sometimes consolation. A man continues in these things until his departure. In this life we should not expect to receive perfect freedom from this struggle, nor to receive perfect consolation. For thus is God pleased to govern our life here: that those who journey in the way should be in the midst of these things. To him be glory unto the ages of ages. Amen. (St Isaac the Syrian, *Homilies* 50, in *The Ascetical Homilies of Saint Isaac the Syrian*, pp 241–42)

349. When it is God's pleasure to subject a man to even greater afflictions, he permits him to fall into the hands of faintheartedness. This begets in him a mighty force of despondency, wherein he feels his soul to be suffocated. This is a foretaste of Gehenna. From this there is unleashed upon him: the spirit of aberration (from which ten thousand trials gush forth); confusion; wrath; blasphemy; protestings and bewailings of one's lot; perverted thoughts; wanderings from place to place; and the like. And if you should ask what the cause of these things is, I answer that it is you yourself, for the reason that you have not taken pains to find the remedy for them. The remedy for them all is one, and therein, in its very hand, a man can find immediate consolation for his soul. And what is it? Humility of heart. Without this no man can destroy the barrier of these evils, nay rather, he will see them triumph over him.

Do not be angry with me that I tell you the truth. You have never sought out humility with your whole soul. But if you wish, enter into its realm, and you will see how it disperses your wickedness. For in proportion to your humility you are given patience in your woes; and in proportion to your consolation, your love of God increases; and in proportion to your love, your joy in the Holy Spirit is magnified [St Isaac here refers to the return of the soul to the state of humble contact with God without pride in righteousness]. Once men have truly become his sons, our tenderly compassionate Father does not take away their temptations from them when it is his pleasure to "make for them a way to escape" (1 Cor. 10.13), but instead he gives his sons patience in their trials. All these good things are given into the hand of their patience for the perfecting of their souls. May Christ God deem us worthy by his grace with a thankful heart to be patient in evils for his love's sake. Amen. (St Isaac the Syrian, *Homilies* 42, in *Ascetical Homilies,* pp 211–12)

350. God chastises with love, not for the sake of revenge—far be it!—but seeking to make whole his image. (St Isaac the Syrian, *Homilies* 48, in *Ascetical Homilies,* p 230)

351. Let no one think that the benefit one gains from the observance of prayers, or purity of mind, or joy of the heart, or comfort of tears, or discourse with God, is the only thing to be regarded as according to God's will. In my opinion, even the involuntary thoughts of blasphemy and vainglory, as well as the disgusting motions of fornication, which occur in spite of man's will— even if man is defeated but endures patiently without leaving his cell [here, leaving one's cell signifies renouncing one's struggle and abandoning the adherence to God alone], all of these are counted to him as a pure sacrifice and a spiritual work if he suffers on their account—provided he is not conceited.

[This is a clear indication to the trials of spiritual languor.] (St Isaac the Syrian, in "The Four Books of St Isaac the Syrian, Bishop of Nineveh," 1.5, 93–94, Arabic version)

352. If you suffer no lack in anything you need, your body is healthy and no adversaries threaten you, and yet you say that you can advance toward Christ in limpid purity, then know that your mind is sick and you are bereft of the taste of God's glory. [St Isaac here points out that tribulations mark a correct spiritual path.] (St Isaac the Syrian, *Homilies* 56, *in Ascetical Homilies,* p 277)

353. Brethren, let no one blaspheme against God or grumble at the time of tribulation. He should instead cast his burden on him who cares for his life and say: "O God, my hope and my supporter, manage my life according to your own will. The gall you choose for me is sweeter than the honeycomb I choose for myself" . . .

As for the devil of blasphemy, he incites the soul to blame God, to blaspheme against him; he stirs doubts concerning the divine mysteries and the Holy Virgin Mary. Man is given to think that his soul is the source of all these blasphemies. His bones dry up from distress, and he grieves bitterly over his soul.

Be not troubled, my brother, do not blame yourself. For your soul is not the speaker. She only hears what the devil says, and even this is against her will. And the proof of this is that when these blasphemies stop, the soul rejoices; she becomes enlightened and is confirmed in her faith.

This kind of blasphemy appears particularly during prayer, singing, and reading . . . One is bombarded by these thoughts, although his soul wants only to praise God. But these thoughts are not counted as blasphemy. For God distinguishes the praises of the loving soul from the blasphemies of the deceitful devil . . . In this trial, the soul almost undergoes the "great tribulation." Bitter in heart, yearning for death, the whole body turbid . . . The devil exerts his utmost pressure on the soul to make her give up and lose hope . . . but blessed is he who holds out in such a tribulation. Great indeed will be his reward! (John of Dalyatha, *Homilies on the Devils of Fornication and Blasphemy*, in "Spiritual Elder")

354. Moreover, what was written about Job is not lightly to be considered, just how Satan sought after him. For Satan was unable to do anything by himself

without permission ... Therefore, insofar as a person seeks God's help and is eager and fervent in grace, Satan desires him. And he says to the Lord: "Since you help him and come to his rescue, he serves you. But let go of him and hand him over to me. Surely he will curse you to your face." In a word, because a person is comforted, grace can withdraw, and he can be delivered up to temptations. The devil comes, bringing thousands of evils as temptations: despair, apostasy, and evil thoughts. He afflicts the soul so as to weaken and alienate it from the hope in God.

But the prudent person, beset by evils and in affliction, does not give up hope, but he holds on to what he holds and as much as the devil brings against him, he endures in the face of innumerable temptations, saying: "Even if I shall die, I shall not let him go." And then, if man endures faithfully to the end ... Then Satan is overcome by shame and has nothing further to say.

In the case of Job, if the devil had known that amidst temptations Job would remain faithful and would not be conquered, he would never certainly have desired him, out of fear of being humiliated. So also now in the case of those who bear afflictions and temptations, Satan is put to shame and is sorry because he has attained nothing.

Satan is never quieted, at peace and not at war. As long as a person lives in this world and is living in the flesh ... So also Christians, even if they are attacked in war by the enemy, still they turn to the Godhead as to their strength. They have put on the power from on high and the rest and have no concern about the war.

Even if war starts externally and Satan attacks, still they are fortified interiorly by the Lord's power and are not anxious about Satan ... So also Christians, granted they may be tempted exteriorly, nevertheless, interiorly they are filled with the Godhead and suffer no injury. If one has reached this degree, he has arrived at the perfect love of Christ and the fullness of the Godhead. But one who is not of this type still wages an interior war. For a certain hour he delights in prayer, but at another time he is bombarded by affliction and at war. This is what the Lord wishes.

Because such a person is still an infant, the Lord trains him in wars. And both things, like two personalities, spring up inside the same person: light and darkness; rest and affliction. Such persons pray in peace, but at another time they are found in distress.

Only if affliction and war beset you, you ought to resist and hate them. For the fact that war comes upon you is not your doing. To hate it, however, is up to you. And, then, the Lord, seeing your mind, that you are struggling and that you love him with your whole soul, drives death away from your soul in a very brief time. This is not difficult for him to do. And he receives you to his bosom and into his light.

In a flashing moment he snatches you from the jaws of darkness and immediately takes you into his kingdom. For to God in a flash all things are easily accomplished, if only you show love toward him. God needs the working of man, since the human soul is meant to have fellowship with the Godhead. (St Macarius the Great, *Homilies* 26.7, 8, 14, 15, 18, in Maloney, *Intoxicated with God: The Fifty Spiritual Homilies of Macarius*)

355. For tribulations, in fact, do not come with such violence except on those who have received the Holy Spirit. When they receive the Spirit, tribulations from the devil come upon them because the Spirit allows him to come upon them. The devil has no authority to try any of the believers severely unless he is given permission by the Holy Spirit.

When our Lord Jesus Christ took upon himself what belongs to us, he became an example to teach us the truth in every way. For when he was baptized, the Holy Spirit alighted on him in the form of a dove; and then the Holy Spirit led him out into the desert to be tempted by Satan. He tempted him by all sorts of temptations but did not prevail, as is written in the Gospel of Luke: "And when the devil had finished every temptation, he departed from him until an opportune time. And Jesus returned in the power of the Spirit into Galilee" (Lk 4.13,14). Such is the case with all who receive the Spirit and struggle and conquer temptations: the Spirit strengthens them and gives them great power in abundance, and protects them from all things.

My beloved sons, I wish you were near me to know my last tribulation, which resembles the last tribulation of Christ. For when he had carried out the plan and knew of his departure, he said, "My Father, if it be possible, let this cup pass from me; nevertheless, not as I will, but as thou wilt" (Mt 26.39). This was coupled with prayers and supplications. This was not due to failure, dread or disability, but for our own instruction, just as his first temptations were for our instruction . . .

The tribulation that befell me lately, my sons, was about to carry me down to hell itself. For the enemies of all good meant to throw me into it with their many wiles, and my labor, struggle, tribulation, and trouble were because of this. But I, poor as I am, give thanks and glory to my God whom I have served with all my heart from a young age till now, and I listen to him, because he did not forsake me, but supported and saved me. (St Antony the Great, *Letters* 19.5, 6, in "The Letters," Arabic version)

356. I will show you another work that can establish man firmly [on his way] from beginning to end. It is to love God with all his heart and intention and to worship him. God will then give him great strength and joy, and all the works of God will become to him as sweet as honeycomb. So will all labors of the body become light and sweet, along with his meditation, vigil and carrying the Lord's yoke.

However, on account of God's love for man, he unleashes upon him adversities so as not to be conceited, but stand firm in his struggle and proceed further in his growth. Instead of strength he feels languor and feebleness, instead of joy sadness, instead of sweetness bitterness. Many similar things befall him who loves God. Nevertheless, he is all the more strengthened in his struggle against them and eventually overcomes them. Once he does so, the Spirit of God stands by him in all things and strengthens him so as never to fear anything evil. (St Antony the Great, *Letters* 18.8, in "The Letters," Arabic version)

CHAPTER SIXTEEN

Loss of Purpose

> "What right have you to recite my
> statutes, or take my covenant on
> your lips? For you hate discipline,
> and you cast my words behind you."
> (Ps 50.16, 17)

P RAYER PETERS OUT BECAUSE we lose sight of sound motives. Sometimes our goals were never genuine in the first place.

Prayer is a spiritual work, and every spiritual work is prompted by motives and justified by its aims. Therefore, we must always question the validity of the reasons that press us to pray. We also have to probe the genuineness of the aim or goal we seek after in prayer. A sound motive guarantees that prayer will continue: a genuine aim keeps it fervent, revives its energy, and impresses it on our hearts.

If you ask me, "What is the sound motive that urges you to pray?" I would say, "It is the command that God so often repeats, urging us to pray: 'Pray . . . pray and do not lose heart . . . Watch and pray'" (Mt 6.6, 9; 26.41; Lk 18.1). God's command compels me to pray by its own force. So long as I cling with all my heart to such a commandment, in faithfulness and in the fear of the Lord, I will pray at all times. For within the commandment there is a latent driving force, namely grace.

Or, if you ask me, "What is the goal you are aiming at in prayer?" I would answer, "It is to satisfy my longing to live perpetually in God's presence"; or, "It is to offer myself as a sacrifice of love to God"; or, "It is to fulfill my dream of living with God a life of total submission and humility"; or, "It is to be able to surrender myself to him always so that I may be rescued from the grip of sin by his mercy and help."

As long as I set my sights on a special goal, which grace lays on my heart, the fervor of prayer will be revived and endure for all time, for the aim I set for myself, yearn for, and seek after is what makes prayer a pleasant task. It becomes a sacred means for fulfilling God's purpose.

Therefore, the reliance on motives alone without a clear vision of the aim in one's heart will strip prayer of its fervor. Gone will be the zeal that enables a person to pour himself out in truth. Equally, being satisfied with a certain aim—without having sound motives for it—is not enough to keep prayer going, for aims may change along the way or even cease altogether. In this case, motives would be the only thing that stirs someone to pray—a situation that may exist for a long time. So, whenever I lose sight of my aim in prayer, it should be sufficient for me to pray because it is a divine command.

However, incorrect aims and motives may surreptitiously creep into prayer. This may be due to man's ignorance of spiritual facts or to the lust of the human ego to glorify itself through spiritual achievements. The soul may be more attracted toward the world than toward God, or it may have more sympathy with the flesh than with spiritual manhood.

An example of an incorrect motive for prayer could be the acquisition of temporal goods and their enjoyment. The motive here would be earthly and not spiritual. Another motive might be success in projects, business, or problem situations, all in search of the praise of men. The motive here would be in the mind and for the world, not for God in the spirit. Another example would be to get rid of enemies in a spirit of hostility or retaliation. The motive here would be an evil one from Satan, not for the glory of God.

Such deviant motives are enough to stir up in a person false fervor and zeal in prayer to the extent of fasting with tears of contrition. However, all these motives are still false because they are fed by self-interest. Although prayer continues with fervor, it could not in this case have any integrity or be genuinely in accordance with God's will.

So, corrupted motives do not stop prayer, but they make it null and void. The loss of all incentives stops prayer altogether in time, even if the aims are sound, whereas when false motives intrude, prayer does not stop, but it becomes futile.

Proper Motives for Prayer

In order to clear the ground for the reader, we will try to assemble all the sound motives for prayer that occur in the Bible—that is, those that agree with God's will.

1. We pray because prayer is a divine commandment, which should be carried out without question, discussion, or delay.

2. We pray because prayer is the only means through which we may enter into God's presence. *Apart from prayer, we can never contact God.* Without prayer we lose our spiritual relationship with God, and our soul dies a spiritual death within us.

3. We pray because prayer is the means prescribed by God for enjoying his protection. In this way, we are saved from the peril of falling into the temptations of Satan. However, if we do fall, we may nonetheless hold out and conquer. Such temptations could then be transformed from a means of condemnation into a means of vindication. "Watch and pray that you may not enter into temptation" (Mt 26.41).

4. We pray because prayer is the only channel through which God will listen to our requests and look at them in the light of his mercy: "Have no anxiety about anything, but in everything by prayer and supplication with thanksgiving let your requests be made known to God" (Phil 4.6).

5. We pray because prayer is the hidden way for providing spiritual help to others who are under stress, in danger, or those who are suffering illness or delusion: "Pray for one another that you may be healed" (Jas 5.16).

6. We pray because prayer is the ministry of thanksgiving to God laid upon servant and son alike: "If then I am a father, where is my honor? And if I am a master, where is my fear" (Mal 1.6)?

7. We pray for our enemies who oppose us and seek to do us harm because it is our duty to do so.

But for all these seven divine motives, there are major clarifications, which cannot be ignored:

1. Since prayer is a divine commandment, it must be accompanied by obedience to the spirit of that commandment. It must be resolute and free from any delay.

2. Since prayer is the basic link that connects us to God, it must be done with awe and reverence and a sense of concern that takes priority over all other commitments. Otherwise this link will be broken.

3. Since prayer is a shield against temptation and a means of receiving power to overcome it, it must be accompanied by constant watchfulness and alertness.

4. Since prayer is a means of offering our requests to God, it must be accompanied with contrite supplication that God may raise us up when he comes to us.

5. Since prayer is a means of helping others, it must be characterized by compassion and self-sacrifice.

6. Since prayer is a divine ministry before God who is both a Master and a Father, it must be done with standing and prostration, true reverence, and all due honor.

7. Since prayer is a means for disarming hostility, it must include a spirit of forgiveness from a sincere heart and a clear conscience.

However, all these secret and interlinked actions are in their nature only varied aspects of the same power, namely grace. Grace dwells in a person's heart and directs it toward fulfilling God's commandments. Once man opens his heart to grace out of his own free will in deep longing, it is poured into his heart without measure.

In general, we find that these seven guidelines, which are put forward by the Bible as the correct motives for prayer, are in practice commandments. We are not free to pick and choose between them. We have to keep hold of all of them that they may be a permanent wellspring upon which we can draw to persevere in prayer. Once these motives are firmly established in a person's heart and faith, they become a divine power to overcome all obstacles that come across his path, even the threat of prayer petering out.

We might, for instance, say that if someone is faced with an essential material need, or with a situation of great danger, this could hamper his prayers, for it swallows up his whole life, invades all his thinking, and saps all his strength. The Bible intervenes here with its heavenly wisdom: "Have no anxiety about anything, but in everything by prayer and supplication with thanksgiving let your requests be made known to God" (Phil 4.6). Thus, the Bible manages to turn a major obstacle to prayer into a strong encouragement to pray.

But we should note that the incentive to pray for such needs—even if they are extremely pressing—is not an aim but only a motive for prayer. If I am obedient to the commandments of the gospel and to its wise heavenly counsel, when I pray for such pressing needs, I will not ask God to give me what I want. Instead, I will make these matters known to God so that he may do about them whatever he sees fit.

But the motives for prayer might go beyond the limits prescribed by God when he says, "Let your requests be made known to God." They might stray into the arena of personal wishes, where a person prays for what he is hankering after and sees would suit himself. In this case, prayer would lose its character as a divine work or commandment and so lose its power and effectiveness.

For instance, if a man is badly treated by enemies, we would say that he will inevitably lose his temper if he gives in to his instincts. These factors are enough to hamper his prayer and throw him headlong into sin both of heart and of mind. But Christ, in his divine wisdom, intervenes here to say, "Love your enemies and pray for those who persecute you" (Mt 5.44). Man can thus turn obstacles *to* prayer into motives *for* prayer. Once he forgives his enemies and begins to pray that God also may have mercy and forgive them, his prayer is greatly strengthened. It will raise him above all the emotions that disturb him, so that he may persevere in prayer without impediment.

Christ points out the framework of prayer for our enemies by saying, "So that you may be sons of your Father who is in heaven" (Mt 5.45). He transports the disciple from standing before his enemies to standing before God. He delivers the soul from the atmosphere of hatred, rancor, and vengeance in which it has been entrapped. He then brings the soul into the atmosphere of peace and serenity in God's loving care, notwithstanding all the wrongs or injustices it might have suffered, or may still be suffering, at the hands of its enemies. Therefore, the motive set by Christ in prayer for our enemies is that we be taken out of the transient sphere of animosity and hostility into the eternal sphere of God's presence and peace.

But in our ignorance, we might regard prayer for our enemies as a means of conquering them, of winning victory over them. This implies a dangerous trial for the soul in its relationship with God, for it may happen that God in his wisdom may allow their injustices and wrongs to remain. In this case, a man would have failed to attain the purpose he was aiming at in his prayer, namely, victory over his enemies. His soul will then collapse, and his prayer will cease. It will have swerved from its correct, God-given motive, which, in this case, would be "that you may be sons of your Father." The problem is that this kind of prayer has been misdirected to follow a personal end, namely, defeating enemies. In this case, the nature of prayer as a divine work limited by divine motives has been distorted. It has thus become devoid of any strength or effectiveness. It will therefore stumble and finally cease.

Therefore, in order for a man to guarantee that he perseveres in prayer and reaches the height of its strength and effectiveness, he must confine his motives to correct ones and never drift into following other aims he might set for himself.

The Proper Purpose

In order to make the way plain to man, we will try to shed light on the true purpose of prayer according to God's will.

God has set a purpose for the spiritual life of man on which all the divine commandments converge: the life of communion with God forever. This life begins the moment a man accepts the mystery of faith in Christ, the Savior and Redeemer, and is sealed with the seal of the Holy Spirit. His communion with God grows in strength from day to day through prayer, through which God reveals what he ought to do so that this communion may be complete.

This purpose is a genuine and God-given motivation for prayer—and even for all spiritual works in general. But it may not be revealed all at once to the heart of a person who is striving for salvation. Grace may be content with revealing only a small part of this purpose to avoid confusing the person in his struggle or endeavor. Grace goes hand in hand with man and progresses step by step with him along the way. Little by little it unveils to him reasons that suit his ability and help him in his struggle. Inasmuch as he progresses in his spiritual life, higher steps appropriate to his progress appear to him so as not to obstruct his growth. The ultimate purpose of the life of prayer and worship are the same, that is, a life of communion with God, or union with him in eternal life. But grace, however, divides this end into many grades.

The first grade unveiled by grace as a suitable aim for the beginner in his life of repentance is his longing to get rid of the bonds of sin along with the habits, images, and traces it may have left in his heart or mind. Here, grace transforms a man so that all his desires, all his hopes, thoughts, and efforts are focused on the expectation of being rescued from the bondage and authority of sin. The image of his sins and mistakes never leaves his mind. It sets him on fire and moves his heart to anguish about the past. His prayer then ignites into a blaze that never dies down day or night. The penitent never tires of shedding tears, pleading to be unshackled from the chains of sin. Grace also equips him with a power to search and examine his conscience to pull out all the hidden causes of sin by their roots.

In due course, grace will finish the inward cleansing and purification of man. Man's zeal for searching and examining his sins will then cease. But this is only in preparation for his promotion to a higher degree of prayer that befits his new condition. Man may mistakenly believe that grace has abandoned him because his fervor for lamenting his sins has forsaken him. He is now no longer able to continue remembering his mistakes and performing proper works of penance as he used to. But what has actually happened is that the aim of prayer that is set before him has been shifted without his realizing it. Instead of looking for his sins, the penitent is promoted to a higher degree that suits his soul in its present condition. He will then see, unexpectedly, a new aim pictured before his eyes. This aim will have begun to radiate a new kind of warmth and to have set prayer alight so that it is directed toward this new purpose. It is a desire for self-denial and humility and the rejection of all worldly pomp and glory. This is the beginning of the second grade of the real purpose of prayer.

In the same manner, man should remain responsive to grace as it stimulates his conscience and faithful to the guidance it gives to his soul. If he does so, he will embark on his promotion "from one degree of glory to another; for this comes from the Lord who is the Spirit" (2 Cor 3.18). This goes on until man reaches the end of all seeking and realizes the purpose of every prayer, that is, a life that is confident of its union with God.

The steps of grace upon which the purpose of prayer is graded are many. They can hardly be delineated or numbered. They start with relief from the yoke of sin and end up with the life of perfect communion with God. Their gradation also differs from one person to another. To one, the cross with its bitterness may be granted at the beginning of his life; to another, at its end. To the one, the joy of intimacy with God is given from the very first step; to the other, this joy is veiled for a long time. It is not within the reach of man, however holy or intimate with God, to prefer one step before the other in such a pursuit, which is so full of mysteries.

However, by way of example and not of categorical listing, grace usually sets before the elect, as they pursue this ultimate purpose, the following steps in their life of prayer:

1. A yearning for freedom from the bonds of sin in tears and regret: "Wash me and I shall be whiter than snow" (Ps 51.7).

2. A yearning for self-denial and humility, and a desire to be far away from positions of prominence and honor: "But I am a worm, and no man; scorned by men, and despised by the people" (Ps 22.6).

3. A yearning for full surrender of one's whole life to God and giving up one's private agenda once and for all.

4. A yearning for purity of heart, child-like simplicity, and actual reliance on the will of God alone.

5. A yearning for initiation into the depths of God's love, where union is accomplished without effort or the exertion of will.

But grace remains free to carry man wherever *it* likes and not wherever he likes. It may raise him to degrees he does not deserve or lower him to depths he may not expect. Grace may walk hand in hand with man among all these aims. Then, it may feel as if he were strolling in paradise, filled with joy, comfort, and happiness. He might think once in a while that he has reached the end, but in a moment, grace brings him back to earth with a bump! It is jealous for him, reining him in and pressing its demands until he fulfills all its requirements.

All the Fathers have taken pains to declare purity of heart as an aim always to be sought by man. This applies to life in general and to the time of prayer in particular. In all of the early Fathers, we read of the need for purity of the heart as a vital and fundamental aim. Abba Moses, a contemporary of St Antony, has dwelt profusely on the indispensability of such an aim. These two men declared that they had received this spiritual discipline from the Fathers who preceded them.

But throughout all these steps from the first to the last, grace infuses man's heart in a simple but all-consuming fashion. It spurs him to yearn for the genuine purpose of life as well as of prayer. This yearning consists in a fervent desire and extreme longing to offer one's soul as a sacrifice to God, whatever condition it may be in, whether in the lowly steps of beginners or in the highest steps of the advanced. This feeling pervades all the stages of grace that a person goes through along the way to fulfilling the twin goals of his life and prayer. It actually proves that he is called to attain this ultimate purpose, that is, union with God. It is also evidence that man's effort is sanctified and that his prayer is in its proper divine perspective.

The Importance of Purpose

The existence of an purpose for prayer is crucial. Without a genuine purpose, prayer can hardly be fervent or effective. This is especially true when we know that the purpose of prayer is related to the spiritual grade in which a person exists. The fervor generated by the soul's yearning for such a purpose, which grace reveals to the soul, uplifts the soul and promotes it from one grade to another.

A man who yearns to reach a spiritual goal little by little gets closer toward it with the help of grace. Such a person has a sense of commitment that fosters within his heart "celestial joy." It is well known that spiritual joy encourages the beginner's soul and validates prayer in his eyes. Joy nurtures the soul, as St Antony says:

> And so the soul, if it does not accept heavenly joy, cannot grow or rise upward; but the souls that accept this joy are those that can grow upwards. (*Letters* 13, in "The Letters," Arabic version)

However, a man may forget the goal of the spiritual life he lives in God. He can lose sight of the purpose of his prayer. This is a serious sign that his prayer is in danger of being confined to a narrow scope, namely, the concerns of the self. Prayer is thus destined to shrink and cease to progress or grow. This is so even though the motives remain sound. But what actually happens is that the soul's lack of aspiration for a living and genuine purpose for prayer is sufficient to infect the whole spiritual life, however long it takes. It can bring about the death of the motives that spur man on to pray.

In order to support this fact, we present an analogy, "The Hare and the Dogs," from the sayings of the Fathers.

> Abba Hilarion [founder of Palestinian monasticism] was asked, "How can it be right for a diligent brother not to be offended when he sees other monks returning to the world?" The old man said, "Let me tell you a story. Consider the hunting dogs which chase after hares; imagine one of these dogs sees a hare in the distance and immediately gives chase; the other dogs that are with him see this dog taking off and take off after him, even though they have not seen the hare. They will continue running with him, but only for a time; when at length the effort and struggle exhaust them, they give up the chase and turn

back. However the dog that saw the hare continues chasing it by himself. He does not allow the effort or the struggle to hinder him from completing his long course. He risks his life as he goes on, giving himself no rest. He does not allow the turning aside of the other dogs behind him to put him off. He goes on running until he has caught the hare he saw. He is careless both of the stumbling blocks in his path, whether stones or thorns, and of the wounds they have inflicted on him.

"So also the brother who wishes to follow after the love of Christ must fix his gaze upon the cross until he catches up with him that was crucified upon it, even though he sees everyone else has begun to turn back." (Budge, *The Paradise of the Holy Fathers*, 2.211)

In this story, the value of motives and purpose is clear. The motive that urged the first dog to chase the hare was its hunger and desire for the prey as well as its love for running and pursuit. As for its purpose, it was the living hare running before him, which embodied in the dog's mind a very delicious meal. We find that the purpose encourages desire and is commended by hunger. The dog never ceases to drool, in spite of the long chase, due to the pleasure visualized in his mind of the hare's flesh in his mouth. Thus, his speed increases in spite of his exertion and exhaustion, in spite of his wounds and the stumbling blocks.

As for the other dogs, we find that their motives in running come from their instinctive drives alone, that is, from their love of the chase and pursuit. In their case, we find that the purpose disappears completely. Although they cannot see the hare, they continue running, but their speed decreases according to their increasing exhaustion and fatigue, until these finally overcome the motive and destroy it. The dogs then stop running altogether.

In this realistic example, we can see that the purpose can maintain the full strength of the motive. We can also note the alliance of the purpose with the motive in defying hardships and adversities and overcoming obstacles. This is done in such a manner that exceeds natural ability under normal conditions. A lively and joyous sense of purpose expects no more and no less than what God has promised. Coupled with the grace of God given to the person who strives, it is enough to generate continually new abilities and potentials within a person. These enable him to overcome all manner of difficulties and obstacles and to make light of any loss or affliction, whatever it may be.

We can also discern the results that follow when a man loses his sense of purpose and how this saps his strength, making any effort or fatigue appear to be more than he can bear. After first bringing him down into a state of misery and boredom, it finishes by fixing him in despair, so bringing his progress to a halt. This happens to him even though his abilities are potentially the same as anybody else's: the conditions are the same throughout. What is it that actually distinguishes him who conquers in his struggle from him who fails? It is the sense of purpose of the one and the lack of vision of the other.

It may sometimes happen that false purposes violate man's spiritual life. Such purposes are figments of egotistical imagination. We cling to them for the ego-tistic rapture and false pleasure they create. They can be very similar to a gen-uine purpose in their ability to infuse fervor as we wrestle in prayer.

In the beginning, it may be hard to distinguish between someone who prays with a genuine intention, which is set before him according to God's pleasure and the guidance of grace, and another who prays with a false pur-pose, which he has invented for himself to gratify his ego. But after a while, the difference begins to appear and to increase with the passage of time. In the end, when you look for the seeker who used to wrestle in prayer for selfish, false goals, you find no trace of him. He is destined to give up the struggle for the false goal. Since it was concocted by his ego, it rapidly loses its savor or value. Or, it may turn out to be nothing but a mirage, which never really existed. In either case, after facing this fact, the soul withdraws into isolation and retreats from the spiritual battle altogether.

False purposes for prayer are quickly exhaustible. An example of this might be the desire to be commended, praised, or revered in people's eyes by prayer. When man realizes such purposes and gorges himself upon the pleasure they bring, he then discovers that they were honey mingled with poison. Inasmuch as he has found pleasure in them, he has become a victim to their poison.

An example of distant, false objectives for prayer may also be praying to become a saint or a wonderworker. For such a purpose, a man may compete and wrestle in prayer with all his might, only to discover that this purpose is nonexistent. Inasmuch as he believes that he has drawn closer to it, he finds that it has grown distant from him.

In general, false and counterfeit purposes fall into three kinds. (1) to pray to be glorified in men's eyes; (2) to pray to be vindicated in God's eyes; and (3) to pray to be justified in one's own eyes.

In order for man to make sure of his path and his prayer life, he should always examine the purpose for which he is striving. He should examine the origin of the fervor and zeal that mingle with his prayer. This should be done to avoid going astray after one of these false or delusive aims. Man should measure the purpose he eagerly seeks against the genuine purposes previously mentioned. Those are the reasons that conform with the will of God's grace. Comparing his purposes with them makes it very easy for him to discover the extent to which he may be led astray.

What actually happens is that as soon as man strays after any of those delusive aims, prayer begins to lose its focal point. It soon becomes devoid of any meaning, value, or power. Nothing remains except its outward observance, which man carries out meticulously to attain his false end. Such prayer remains attached to the false purpose on which it feeds to assume its consistency, shape, and fake ardor. Man's prayer then endures and gains strength and even pleasure and joy in proportion to the revenue it reaps from its selfish purpose, for it becomes a rewarding trade. As for its heavenly reward, it is lower than that of any honest trade, for any trade yields interest in proportion to the amount of capital a person expends of his own money or effort, and thus it becomes lawful.

But a person may have a genuine purpose and lose sight of it. He may have gone astray after a secondary, delusive aim without being aware of the deception for which he has fallen. In such a case, he should realize this from monitoring the intensity of fervor in his prayer and from his persistence in it. Sooner or later, he will inevitably lose his fervor and pleasure in it. His prayer, whether private or communal, will become a burden to him. He will feel that it is an unprofitable waste of time. Private prayer will increase his distraction and boredom. Communal prayer will increase his criticism of those who pray with him and even of prayer itself. Thus, he will emerge drenched in sin, claiming that the weakness of others and their misbehavior are the cause of his predicament. The real cause, however, is that his own soul has lost the spirit of prayer. It is not linked to any purpose that may strengthen it and focus it in God.

So, it becomes clear that the lack of a genuine purpose, which is in agreement with God's will and enjoys the provision of his grace, is enough to corrupt prayer and deprive it of its fervor. In the end, it is a heavy burden that the soul cannot bear, even wishing to be rid of it altogether. Such a person is like the lazy pupil who loses sight of the purpose of studying, so that his subjects seem burdensome, devoid of any meaning or value and not worth the effort that he must put in to learn from them.

SAYINGS OF THE FATHERS ON THE PURPOSE AND MOTIVES OF PRAYER

The conference of Abba Moses,[1] who dwelt in the region of Nitria (north of Kellia and Scete), as recorded by Cassian, on the importance of purpose in a monk's life.

357. All the arts and sciences, said he, have some goal or mark; and end or aim of their own, on which the diligent novice in each art has his eye, for which he endures all sorts of toils and dangers and losses, with cheerful equanimity.

The farmer, not shrinking from the scorching heat of the sun, nor flinching at the frost and cold, furrows the field unwearied. Again and again he brings the hard earth under his ploughshare, while he keeps before him his goal: by diligent labor to break up the soil, to clear it of its thorns and free it from its weeds. He believes that in no other way can he gain his ultimate end, which is to secure a good harvest and a large crop; and with this he can live free from care or enlarge his fortune. When his barn is full he does not hesitate to empty it and, with the same unwearied labor, commit the seed to the crumbling furrow. No thought to the empty stores of today; the harvest is coming.

Merchants, likewise, have no dread of the uncertainties and chances of the ocean, they fear no risks, while eager hope urges them forward to the goal: profit. And those who are fired with military ambition look forward to their aim of honor and power. They set at naught the danger and destruction in their wanderings, they are not crushed by present losses and wars. For they are eager to reach their end: the honors of their calling.

And our profession too has its own goal and end, for which we undergo all sorts of toils without fatigue, indeed in delight. On account of this, the want of food in fasting is no trial; the weariness of our vigils becomes a delight; reading and constant meditation on the scriptures does not pall upon us. All

---

[1] Abba Moses the Black, who lived near the Monastery of Baramous in the desert of Scete. From his second conference, chapter 2, it appears that he was, in his early years, contemporary with St Antony the Great.

the incessant toils, the self-denials, the privation of all things, the horrors of this vast desert have no terrors for us. It was doubtless for this that you yourselves despised the love of kinsfolk, and scorned your fatherland and the delights of this world, and passed through so many countries, in order that you might come to us, plain and simple folk as we are, living in this wretched state in the desert. Wherefore, said he, answer and tell me what is the goal, the end, which impels you to endure all these things so cheerfully. (St John Cassian, *Conferences* 1.2, *Abbot Moses*, NPNF, 2nd series, 2.295–96)

358. But what is our immediate object? We must have a mark, something that, by following constantly, will lead us to our end. What should this mark of ours be?

We frankly confessed our ignorance, and so he proceeded: The first thing, as I said, in all the arts and sciences is to have some goal; that is, a mark for the mind, a constant mental purpose. For unless a man keeps this before him, persistent in diligence, he will never succeed in arriving at his ultimate aim, the gain that he desires. As I said, the farmer who aspires to live free from care has his immediate object and goal: to keep his field clear from thorns and weeds while his crops are in the bud. He does not fancy that he can secure his own peace and prosperity unless he first devotes himself to that combination of work and hope by which he may realize his desire . . .

And so the end of our way of life is indeed the kingdom of God. But what is the (immediate) goal you must earnestly ask, for if it is not in the same way discovered by us, we shall exhaust ourselves, we shall strive to no purpose, because a man who is traveling in a wrong direction, has all the trouble and none of the good of his journey. And when we stood astonished at this remark, the old man proceeded: The end of our profession indeed, as I said, is the kingdom of God or the kingdom of heaven: but the immediate aim or goal, is purity of heart, without which no one can gain that end. (St John Cassian, *Conferences* 1.4, *Abbot Moses*, NPNF, 2nd series, 2.297 [paraphrased])

The Teachings of St Macarius the Great

St Macarius demonstrates the need to be clear about the motives that urge us as well as the goals to which we aspire. He also discusses the need for offering the whole soul as a sacrifice to God, so as to reach union with his Spirit.

359. But one cannot gain possession of his soul and the love of the heavenly Spirit unless he cuts himself off from all the things of this world and surrenders himself to the search for the love of Christ. His mind must be freed from all gross material concerns so that he may be entirely engaged in only one aim, namely, to direct all his affairs according to the commandments. In this way, his whole concern, his striving, his endeavor, and the preoccupation of his soul may be centered on the search for the transcendent Good; how the soul may be adorned with the gospel virtues and the heavenly Spirit; how it may become a participator in the purity and sanctification of Christ . . .

Let us, therefore, make ready ourselves that we may approach the Lord with fixed intent and indissoluble will. Let us love Christ passionately, that we may do his command. Let us "think upon his commandments so as to do them" (Ps 103.18). Let us separate ourselves completely from any attachment to the world and turn our souls completely to him alone.

Let us keep him alone before our eyes as our one concern and labor. Because of our creatureliness we give ourselves to divine obedience with less diligence, but let the mind not swerve from love of the Lord and from the ardent seeking of him. For if we strive with this perfect intention, keeping always straight on the path of justice and always being attentive to ourselves, we should indeed obtain the promise of his Spirit. Through grace we will be freed from the destructive power of the dark passions that attack the soul. And thus we may be considered worthy to enter into the eternal kingdom to enjoy Christ forever, glorifying the Father and the Son and the Holy Spirit unto ages of ages. Amen. (St Macarius the Great, *Homilies* 9.10–13, in Maloney, *Intoxicated with God: The Fifty Spiritual Homilies of Macarius*)

In another place, St Macarius the Great points out the importance of the purpose of prayer along with its effect and authority over the soul:

360. Persons, who love truth and God, who thoroughly wish to put on Christ with great hope and faith, do not need so much encouragement or correction from others. They never give up their longing for heaven and their love of the Lord, granted that from time to time they bear patiently a bit of a diminishment in that love [spiritual aridity]. But being completely attached to the cross of Christ, they daily perceive in themselves that they are spiritually progressing toward their spiritual Bridegroom.

Having been wounded by the desire for heaven and thirsting for the justice of virtues, they await the illumination of the Spirit with the greatest insatiable longing. And should they be considered worthy to receive through their faith knowledge of divine mysteries or are made participators of the happiness of heavenly grace, they, nevertheless, do not put their trust in themselves, regarding themselves as somebody. But the more they are considered worthy to receive spiritual gifts, the more diligently do they seek them with an insatiable desire. The more they perceive themselves advancing in spiritual perfection, the more do they hunger and thirst for a greater share of and increase in grace. And the richer they spiritually become, the poorer they consider themselves, as they burn up interiorly with an insatiable, spiritual yearning for the Heavenly Bridegroom, as scripture says: "They that eat Me shall still be hungry and they that drink Me shall thirst" (Sir 24.21). (St Macarius the Great, *Homilies* 10.1, in *Spiritual Homilies*)

Here, St Macarius indicates the effect of the lack of authentic motives and purpose on the soul:

361. However, there are other persons less dynamic and more sluggish who hardly aspire to obtain, while still on this earth, such gifts, namely, the sanctification of the heart, not partially but perfectly through perseverance and long suffering. They never have expected to receive the fullness of the Spirit-Comforter with full consciousness and certitude. They never have hoped to receive from the Spirit liberation from evil passions. (St Macarius the Great, *Homilies* 10.2, in *Spiritual Homilies*)

There are souls who make some progress along the way to the fullness of the Spirit. But then they slip; a complacent sense of self-sufficiency deceives them. Their growth in the Spirit stops, they are deprived of the blessings of prayer. St Macarius describes the case of such souls as follows:

362. Having received worthily the divine grace, they yielded to sin and gave themselves to cowardliness and indifference.

Such as these, having received the grace of the Spirit, enjoy the consolation of grace in peace and longing and spiritual sweetness. But they begin to rely on this fact and become puffed up. They live securely and forget the need for a broken heart and humility of spirit. They cease stretching out to attain the perfect measure of emptiness from passions. They fail to be filled with grace in all diligence and faith. But they felt secured and became complacent with their scanty consolation of grace. Such persons measured their progress by pride rather than a humble spirit. And so whatever gifts of grace had been given them were taken from them on account of their neglectful contempt and careless vainglory.

The person, however, who truly loves God and Christ, even though he may perform a thousand good works, considers himself as having done nothing because of his insatiable longing for the Lord. Even if he should tear down the body with fasts and vigils, he considers himself as though he had never even yet begun to develop virtues. Although various gifts of the Spirit or even revelations and heavenly mysteries may be given to him, he believes that he has acquired nothing because of his immense and insatiable love for the Lord.

But daily he perseveres in prayer with a hungering and a thirst in faith and love. He has an insatiable desire for the mysteries of grace and for every virtue. He is wounded with love for the heavenly Spirit, having a burning desire for the Heavenly Bridegroom through grace, which he always possesses within himself. This stirs him to desire perfectly to be regarded as worthy to enter into the mystical and awesome communion with him in the sanctification of the Spirit.

The face of the soul is unveiled and it gazes with fixed eyes upon the Heavenly Bridegroom, face-to-face, in a spiritual and ineffable light. Such a person mingles with him with full certitude of faith, becoming conformed to his death. He always hopes with the greatest desire to yearn to die for Christ. He certainly and completely believes that he will obtain liberation from his sins and dark passions through the Spirit. (St Macarius the Great, *Homilies* 10.2, 3, 4, in *Spiritual Homilies*)

St Macarius also reveals the danger of satisfying oneself with purity of motive alone without having spiritual aims for prayer; aims longed for, asked for, and sought after.

363. If anyone pushed to attain for himself only prayer, not having it, in order to receive the grace of prayer, but he does not strive earnestly for meekness and humility and charity and all the other commandments of the Lord, neither taking pains or struggling and battling to succeed in these as far as his choice and free will go, sometimes he may be given a grace of prayer with partially some degree of repose and pleasure from the Spirit according as he asks.

But he has the same traits he had before. He has no meekness because he did not seek it with effort and he did not prepare himself beforehand to become such. He has no humility since he did not ask for it and did not push himself to have it. He has no charity toward all men because he was not concerned with this and did not strive for it in his asking for the gift of prayer. And in doing his work, he has no faith nor trust in God, since he did not know himself that he appeared without it. And he did not take the pains to seek from the Lord for himself to have a firm faith and an authentic trust. (St Macarius the Great, *Homilies* 19.4, in *Spiritual Homilies*)

364. Whoever hammers a lump of iron, first decides what he is going to make of it, a scythe, a sword, or an axe. Even so we ought to make up our minds what kind of virtue we want to forge or we labor in vain [i.e., aimlessly]. (St Antony the Great 35, in Ward, *Sayings of the Desert Fathers*)

365. I never get tired of asking the Lord on your behalf, that you may know the grace that has been given you. For God, in his mercy, reminds every one of the means of the grace given to him. So never lose heart or be lazy, my children, in crying to the Lord night and day, that you may force the Father's benevolence to grant you aid from above. (St Antony the Great, *Letters* 5.1, in "The Letters," Arabic version)

366. I ask day and night from my Creator . . . that you may know your shame, for he who knows his shame is he who seeks the true glory, and he who knows his death has known his eternal life. (St Antony the Great, *Letters* 6.12, in "The Letters," Arabic version)

367. I, the miserable, wish to inform you as well that God has awoken my mind from the stupor of death by his grace, and I have acquired groaning and weeping as long as I live on this earth. For I ponder, "What shall we render to the Lord for all he has done for us?" (St Antony the Great, *Letters* 7.5, in "The Letters," Arabic version)

One of the teachings of St Isaac the Syrian is that union with Christ is a permanent goal of the spiritual life.

368. The beginning, the middle, and the end of this discipline is the following: the cutting off of all things through union with Christ. (St Isaac the Syrian, *Epistle to Abba Symeon*, in *The Ascetical Homilies of Saint Isaac the Syrian*, p 439)

Fruits of Prayer Life

> "But the fruit of the Spirit is love, joy,
> peace, patience, kindness, goodness,
> faithfulness, gentleness, self-control."
> (Gal 5.22)

> "But he who sows to the Spirit will
> from the Spirit reap eternal life."
> (Gal 6.8)

> "The spirit of wisdom and
> understanding, the spirit of counsel
> and might, the spirit of knowledge
> and the fear of the Lord." (Is 11.2)

I N THIS CHAPTER WE SHALL discuss the fruits of prayer life as they are manifested in physical or behavioral demeanor. We will concern ourselves with the spiritual attributes and virtues that the contemplative life may confer upon the individual. The contemplative life renews man. It presents him to human society as a new person of outstanding moral character who radiates holiness in the surrounding milieu. From such a person, the sweet scent of Christ is savored, while out of humility he feels unworthy to live among people.

Renewal of Senses

The contemplative undergoes a total change, which involves both his inward and outward lives together. His senses are most strikingly transplanted from a material into a spiritual existence. Formerly, the eye used to find its pleasure in created beauty, whether in beautiful natural scenes or graceful animals or birds or beautiful human faces. But now it turns most splendidly from these transient objects and their false, changing beauty to the Source and Creator of beauty. He is the true beauty, which shall never change or undergo a semblance of change. The eye henceforth finds its pleasure in him who transcends all beauty. It is now able to see God's beauty in everything. It thus moves from creature to Creator and from the vision of transient objects to that of unchangeable Truth.

So it is with hearing. The ear, which formerly used to cling to sensory sounds, is henceforth drawn to hear voices of praise, which the feeble sensory ear cannot catch. The spiritual ear can attain a very high sensitivity through which it may catch other melodies proceeding from eternity. These melodies are sweet and most tender. But they are also most powerful. They are able to break majestically through space and penetrate the din of this reveling world in order to reach the sensitive ear of the heart. They can thus lead the soul, enchanted by sweet melodies as such, to contemplate the joy of the age to come.

The lips and tongue tell of the glory of God and praise his living name. The sense of smell as well savors the purity of eternity. The sense of touch feels the presence of God. It can discern the periods when it enjoys his proximity from those when it is deprived of him.

> **369.** And if the mind conquers in this contest, then it prays in the Spirit and begins to expel from the body the passions of the soul which come to it from its own will . . . And the Spirit teaches the mind how to heal all the wounds of the soul and to rid itself of every one, those which are mingled in the members of the body . . . And for the eyes it sets a rule, that they may see rightly and purely . . . After that it sets a rule also for the ears, how they may hear in peace, and no more thirst or desire to hear ill speaking . . . but to hear about the mercy shown to the whole creation . . . Then again the Spirit teaches the tongue its own purity . . . and heals the motions of the hands . . . and instructs the mind in their purification, that it may labor with them in almsgiving and in prayer; and the word is fulfilled concerning them which says, "Let the lifting up of my hands be an evening sacrifice" (Ps 141.2) . . . and the belly to eat in moderation sufficient for the strength of the body, and in this way the saying of Paul is fulfilled, "Whether ye eat or drink, or whatever ye do, do all to the glory of God" (1 Cor 10.31) . . . and it gives the feet also their purification . . . that they should walk according to its will, going

and ministering in good works . . . And I think that when the whole body is purified and has received the fullness of the Spirit, it has received some portion of that spiritual body which it is to assume in the resurrection of the just. (St Antony the Great, *Letters* 1, in "The Letters of St Antony the Great," Manuscript 23)

370. We are often suddenly filled in these visitations with odors that go beyond the sweetness of human making, such that a mind which has been relaxed by this delightful sensation is seized with a certain spiritual ecstasy and forgets that it is dwelling in the flesh. (St John Cassian, *Conferences* 4.5, NPNF, 2nd series, 2.332 [paraphrased])

The saints often mention that during the visitation of divine grace, man becomes filled with the savor of a sweet, obscure fragrance. Such an experience, they say, transcends comprehension or analysis. The soul is transported by an overflowing pleasure to a state of amazement and forgets that it lives in this flesh.

As for this "sweetness," "fragrant savor," and other images, they are material figures of speech. They can by no means do justice to the reality of the spiritual gifts revealed to the senses of the soul once it reaches the spiritual order. How many times has the Holy Spirit tried to figure for us the beauty of heaven, the sweetness of intimacy with God, and the qualities of the heavenly Bridegroom! This has been done in material terms that we might perchance manage to grasp their actuality.

Says the Holy Spirit:

O taste and see that the Lord is good! (Ps. 34.8)

Your anointing oils are fragrant, your name is oil poured out; therefore the maidens love you . . . While the king was on his couch, my nard gave forth its fragrance . . . How much better is your love than wine, and the fragrance of your oils than any spice! Your lips distill nectar, my bride; honey and milk are under your tongue; the scent of your garments is like the scent of Lebanon . . . nard . . . with all trees of frankincense . . . with all chief spices . . . I am a rose of Sharon, a lily of the valleys . . . As an apple tree among the trees of the wood, so is my Beloved . . . and his fruit was sweet to my taste . . . The voice of my beloved! Behold, he comes, leaping upon the mountains, bounding over the hills ... I come to my garden, my sister, my bride, I gather my myrrh with my spice, I eat my honeycomb with my honey, I drink my wine with my milk ... His speech is most sweet, and he is altogether desirable. This is my beloved. (Song 1.1–10)

These metaphors and spiritual expressions look like riddles. Many Christians puzzle over them. But the Spirit by no means intends to present the word of God in the form of puzzles so long as it can be expressed plainly.

In these descriptions and metaphors, the Spirit portrays the beauty of the Bridegroom and that of the bride. He depicts all the mutual tender feelings of love and admiration they exchange. In portraying these sentiments, he employs the maximum potentials that our material senses provide for understanding. However, the import of all these figures will ever remain hidden from us so long as we tend to restrict them to their material limits. It is as if they were only accessible to our basic fleshly senses. But, if we wish to catch their real significance, we have to be first transported, together with our senses, thoughts, and imagery, from our transient, narrow materialism into the absolute sphere of eternity and the spiritual world. This being done, the true value of the soul and the qualities of the heavenly Bridegroom will be revealed to us through our inner senses. So also will the majesty of the Creator and the glories of heaven. It is then that we shall discover another meaning for beauty, for taste, for smell, for hearing, for touch. When we actually arrive at this point of spiritual perception, we will realize at once how little and childish our spirituality has been! How greatly our disability has caused us to fail in understanding the images used by the Spirit in describing God! "When I became a man, I gave up childish ways. For now we see in a mirror dimly, but then face to face" (1 Cor 13.11).

There is no way out of this physical confinement into the unbounded spiritual territories except by training ourselves for meditation and contemplation. Thereby we are elevated from one sphere of glory to another. Once we are able to visualize these realms and delve deep into their mysteries with the inner senses of our souls, we shall realize the true purport of their imagery. It is only then that we shall discover the real beauty of the spiritual life.

The Gifts of the Spirit

We read of the gifts of the Spirit. But, most sadly and despondently, we say they belong to a long-forgotten age. They have passed out of existence and disappeared.

This is not true. The gift is the power of the Church that attends her throughout the ages and up to the very end of all times. It is the sign and fruit of the Spirit that mark the work of God in his Church. However, it is our faith that is weak. There is a decline and negligence in the spirit of asceticism and worship, at least in worship that is free from inordinate desires, goal, or perverse inclinations. Due to the coldness that has crept in on the love that binds the group of the faithful together, the grace and power of the Spirit have become things to be marveled at. They are hard to find in this age of ours.

We are thus not unlike the people of Nazareth: "And he did not do many mighty works there, because of their unbelief" (Mt 13.58). The fault then is not with the Spirit but with ourselves. The promise is faithful and true: "And these signs will accompany those who believe; in my name they will cast out demons; they will speak in new tongues; they will pick up serpents, and if they drink any deadly thing, it will not hurt them; they will lay their hands on the sick, and they will recover" (Mk 16.17).

Neither is it the fault of time, for "Jesus Christ is the same yesterday and today and forever" (Heb 13.8). St Antony the Great says:

371. Everyone who cultivates himself with this cultivation, the Spirit is granted to him from generation to generation. (St Antony the Great, *Letters* 8.2, in "The Letters," Arabic version)

Everyone who trades in it acquires it as a gift from God, for God shows no partiality (Acts 10.34), but in all generations he grants this [divine power] to all who accomplish these works. (St Antony the Great, *Letters* 9.1, in "The Letters," Arabic version)

No generation ever lacked someone who reached this state of perfection, neither will the future generations lack them. (St Antony the Great, *Letters* 13.2, in "The Letters," Arabic version)

Likewise Christ ascertains: "And lo, I am with you always, to the close of the age" (Mt 28.20). The fault then is with ourselves and with our flimsy faith and aversion for spiritual matters: "Truly, truly I say to you, he who believes in me will also do the works that I do; and greater works than these will he do" (Jn 14.12).

There are gifts in the Church and there are also spiritual fruits, which are offered in return for endeavor in the way of righteousness. Owing to its strong faith, the Church does not draw a sharp line between the two. In clearer terms, it discerns an existing relationship between gifts, on the one hand, and endeavor or labor along the way of righteousness and sanctity, on the other. It is even inclined to believe that striving for grace leads to sanctification and acquisition of gifts. Such gifts are for the benefit of others and for strengthening the faith of the weak.

The saints in general have been the heirs of gifts ever since the earliest generations and up to the present day. They share those gifts in a mystical way with those upon whom the degrees of ecclesiastical authority are conferred. Such is the case if the latter live up to their ministry in sobriety and a life that befits their dignity. It is usually to these that visions, dreams, and prophecies are revealed. In this respect, the succession of apostolic benediction by the laying on of hands is of extreme importance. It holds and hands down the torch of fire that has descended on Pentecost.

The Coptic Church is distinguished for its boldness in petitioning spiritual gifts and fruits unhesitatingly for its children. There is, in fact, an old liturgy in the Coptic Church called the *Liturgy of Our Lord's Covenant,* which especially asks for spiritual gifts and their confirmation. In this liturgy, which Coptic priests celebrated until after the tenth century, the priest prays, "Lord, please uphold to the end those who have the gifts of revelation, aid those who have the gift of healing, and support those who have the gift of tongues."

St Antony the Great has an express view on this matter:

372. "If we are sons, then are we heirs; heirs of God, and joint heirs with the saints" (Rom 8.17).

My dear brethren and joint heirs with the saints, not foreign to you are all the virtues, but they are yours, if you are not under guilt from this fleshly life, but are manifest before God. For the Spirit enters not the soul of one whose heart is defiled, nor the body that sins; a holy power it is, removed from all deceit. (St Antony the Great, *Letters* 4, in "The Letters," Arabic version)

373. Seek this Spirit of fire with a righteous heart—and he will be given unto you. In this way Elijah the Tishbite, Elisha, and other prophets received him. He who tills himself thus (as I have described) is granted this Spirit forever and for ages of ages. Remain in prayer, seeking most arduously with your whole heart—and you will be given. For this Spirit resides in righteous hearts. And when he is received, he will reveal to you the highest mysteries. (St Antony the Great, *Letters* 8, in "The Letters," Arabic version)

The Fathers in general, however, warn against falling into pride whether before or after one attains any grace. They were always on guard against the delusion of the devils, who assume the form of angels of light. They do so to defraud those walking along the spiritual way and to mislead them in reaching the truth. The saintly fathers have written many warnings and offered guidance in this respect on the kinds of delusions and tricks of the devil. They have also prescribed the means to overcome and foil them, thus shedding light for those walking along the way of sanctity and righteousness.

374. The Lord does not manifestly show his power by some work and visible sign without need, lest the help we receive should be made ineffectual and turned to our injury. Thus does the Lord act when he provides for his saints . . . he leaves them to show forth a struggle and to labor in prayer in accord with their strength. But if they encounter something which is so difficult as to overcome the degree of their knowledge, and they grow weak and fall short of it, then he accomplishes it himself, according to the greatness of his dominion . . .

Consider what the holy and blessed Ammoun said to God when he had set out to receive the blessing of Saint Antony the Great and lost his way . . . He let him stray and showed him afterward the way clearly. Remember also Abba Macarius when he went to Scete bearing baskets. For he grew fatigued and weary, and he sat down because he could not walk any longer. But he did not ask from God that he do anything unto him by his power to give him comfort. Rather, he trusted himself to God, saying, "O God, Thou knowest that I have no more strength!"

Then at once, in a moment, he was taken up by divine power and placed there whither he wished to go. (St Isaac the Syrian, *Homilies* 60, in *The Ascetical Homilies of Saint Isaac the Syrian,* pp 291–93)

375. I have jotted down for you what you have asked from me for the growth and gradual progression of beginners and all who wish to ascend that spiritual ladder, at the top of which all the gifts lie ready, whether clairvoyance, revelation, prophecy, speaking in tongues or the tri-powerful gift of healing (that is, for body, soul, and spirit) and other gifts, which the Spirit has not allowed me to reveal on paper because of the faithlessness and lack of experience [of this generation]. (St John of Dalyatha, *Homily on the Preservation of the Outer and Inner Senses*, in "Spiritual Elder")

We thus find that the saints were not lacking in the endeavor to attain the fruits of grace. They were set on fire by St Paul's words: "Earnestly desire the higher gifts" (1 Cor 12.31). They also imitated the zeal of the apostles: "And now, Lord, look upon their threats, and grant to thy servants to speak thy word with all boldness, while thou stretchest out thy hand to heal, and signs and wonders are performed through the name of thy holy servant Jesus" (Acts 4.29–30).

Yet one of the express and definite principles of the Church is that gifts should not be the aim of our spiritual struggle. They should be, as St John Chrysostom says, a help for us to reach a better way: "But earnestly desire the higher gifts. And I will show you a still more excellent way . . . love . . . Love never ends; as for prophecies, they will pass away; as for tongues, they will cease; as for knowledge, it will pass away . . . when the perfect comes . . . Make love your aim, and earnestly desire the spiritual gifts." (1 Cor 12, 13, 14).

We have gained the right for purity and grace by being born in the baptismal font. It has therefore become an obligation to use this right in aiding us along the way to righteousness, holiness, and endeavor. With this, we train ourselves for receiving the flaming torch of the Spirit, which has been handed down to us ever since Pentecost:

376. I have prayed for you, that you too may be granted that great Spirit of fire, whom I have received. If you wish to receive him, so that he dwells in you, first offer physical labors and humility of heart and, lifting your thoughts to heaven day and night, seek this Spirit of fire with a righteous heart—and he will be given unto you. (St Antony the Great, *Letters* 8.1, in "The Letters," Arabic version)

There is a direct consequence of receiving the reviving torch of the Holy Spirit. The soul delves deep into, and interlocks with, the knowledge of spiritual matters. Wisdom is revealed that had hitherto been veiled by the darkness of bodily passions. The soul is then moved to join the band of spiritual beings. St Diodochus supports his definition of the soul that has reached this stage by describing it as "a soul of a sheer spiritual type." He means by this description that the soul not only contemplates spiritual things alone but also becomes the object of its own contemplation. It contemplates and speaks of things divine, not as if they were foreign to it but as things of its very nature.

377. The person, who has found the Lord, the true treasure, by seeking the Spirit, by faith and great patience, brings forth the fruits of the Spirit, as I said earlier. All righteousness and the commands of the Lord which the Spirit orders he does by himself, purely and perfectly and without blame. (St Macarius the Great, *Homilies* 18.3, in Maloney, *Intoxicated with God: The Fifty Spiritual Homilies of Macarius*)

SAYINGS OF THE FATHERS ON THE FRUITS OF PRAYER LIFE

Discretion and Knowledge of Mysteries

378. St Paul . . . prayed on behalf of his children that they might receive the knowledge of the greatness of such richness which he had known, which is true vision or discernment. There is nothing greater in the Christian faith than this. (St Antony the Great, *Letters* 11.1, in "The Letters," Arabic version)

379. Such are the saints, my beloved, in all generations. When they found this Spirit dwelling in them, they offered to God many thanks. For the Holy Spirit does not dwell except in the souls of such blessed people. He reveals to them great mysteries and grants them joy and comfort for their hearts in this world, and makes their night like day. (St Antony the Great, *Letters* 19.3, in "The Letters," Arabic version)

380. And, when man does not grieve the Spirit in any way but is in harmony with grace, keeping all the commandments, then he is regarded as worthy to receive freedom from all passions. He receives the full adoption of the Spirit: this is always a mystery. He receives spiritual riches and wisdom not of this world. (St Macarius the Great, *Homilies* 9.7, in *Spiritual Homilies*)

Zeal for Preaching Divine Things

381. Holy men soar aloft to the contemplation of things on high, bind the first-fruits of their spirit in the love of the heavenly country. But when they are weighed down by the load of human life and return to themselves, they declare to their brethren the heavenly goods they were able to contemplate, if only in a mirror.

They fire the minds of their brethren with the love of that inward brightness, which they are able neither to see as it is, nor to utter as they saw it; but while they speak their words pierce and set on fire the hearts of those that hear. (St Gregory the Great, *Homilies on Ezekiel* 1.5.13, in Butler, *Western Mysticism: The Teaching of SS Augustine, Gregory and Bernard on Contemplation and the Contemplative Life*)

Magnanimity of Heart

382. At that time you will ask not on your behalf only but on behalf of others as well. For everyone who accepts this Spirit should not only pray for himself but for others as well . . . As for me, my supplication is day and night that you should acquire the great pleasure of this Spirit accepted by all who are pure. (St Antony the Great, *Letters* 8.2, in "The Letters," Arabic version)

383. Sometimes they find themselves immersed in weeping and, lamenting over the human race and in pouring out prayers on behalf of the whole human race of Adam, they shed tears and are overwhelmed by grief because they are consumed by the love of the Spirit toward mankind. At another time they are so enflamed by the Spirit with such joy and love that, if it were possible, they could gather every human being into their very hearts, without distinguishing the bad and the good. (St Macarius the Great, *Homilies* 18.8, in *Spiritual Homilies*)

384. The consummation of the entire course consists in these three things: in repentance, in purity, and in perfection. What, succinctly, is purity? It is a heart that shows mercy to all created nature . . . And what is a merciful heart? It is the heart's burning for the sake of the entire creation, for men, for birds, for animals, and for every created thing; and by the recollection and the sight of them the eyes of a merciful man pour forth abundant tears. From the strong and vehement mercy which grips his heart and from the great compassion, his heart is humbled and he cannot bear to hear or to see any injury or the slightest sorrow in creation . . . For this reason he offers up tearful prayer continually. (St Isaac the Syrian, in *Ascetical Homilies,* in *The Ascetical Homilies of Saint Isaac the Syrian,* pp 344, 345)

Ease and Comfort

385. If God observes these good fruits in the soul, he accepts them as a choice sweet savor of incense. Together with his angels, he rejoices at all times with the soul, giving pleasure and guarding it in all its ways until it reaches the place of its rest. The devil is no longer able to overcome it, because he sees the higher Protector surrounding it . . . Acquire then for yourselves this power that the devils may fear you, that the labors you undergo may become lighter, and that divine things may become sweeter to you. For the taste of God's love is sweeter than honey. (St Antony the Great, *Letters* 9.1, in "The Letters," Arabic version)

386. In a similar way there is a day of light and the divine wind of the Holy Spirit, breathing through and refreshing souls who live in the day of the divine light. It passes through the whole nature of the soul, the thoughts and the entire substance of the soul and all the members of the body, as it recreates and refreshes them with a divine and ineffable tranquility. (St Macarius the Great, *Homilies* 2.4, in *Spiritual Homilies*)

387. Sometimes persons are guided by grace as persons who rejoice at a royal banquet. They are filled with joy and ineffable happiness. At other times they are like a spouse who enjoys conjugal union with her bridegroom in divine resting. At other times they are like incorporeal angels, they are so light and transcendent, even in the body. Sometimes they are as if they have become intoxicated with a strong drink. They delight in the Spirit, being inebriated, namely, by the intoxication of the divine and spiritual mysteries. (St Macarius the Great, *Homilies* 18.7, in *Spiritual Homilies*)

Love of God

"Because God's love has been poured into our hearts through the Holy Spirit which has been given to us." (Rom 5.5)

388. How much more those, whom the touch of the Divine Spirit of life has touched and whose heart divine love has pierced with a desire for Christ, the Heavenly King, have been captivated by his beauty and ineffable glory and by the incorruptible comeliness and incomprehensible riches of the true and eternal King, Christ! They are held captive by desire and longing for Him. (St Macarius the Great, *Homilies* 5.6)

389. They have tasted divine beauty and the life of heavenly immortality has dropped like dew onto their souls. Therefore, they ardently long for that love of the Heavenly King and they have him alone before their eyes in every desire. (St Macarius the Great, *Homilies* 5.6)

Meekness and Humility

390. The more that holy men advance in contemplation, the more they despise what they are, and know themselves to be nothing, or next to nothing. (St Gregory the Great, *Mor.* 35.3, in Butler, *Western Mysticism: The Teaching of SS Augustine, Gregory and Bernard on Contemplation and the Contemplative Life,* p 117)

391. Man becomes fearful of judging others and looks upon every other person as better than himself. And if he sees other people, be they adulterers or unrighteous, he considers them as better than himself—a fact that he truly feels in his hidden conscience and not something just claimed in his outward speech. This he does from a heart free from all impurities. He looks upon everything as good, for he looks and thinks with God's mind. (St Isaac the Syrian, in "The Four Books of St Isaac the Syrian, Bishop of Nineveh," 1.6, Arabic version)

392. *Question:* What is the sign that a man has attained to purity of heart? . . .

Answer: When he sees all men as good and none appears to him to be unclean and defiled. (St Isaac the Syrian, *Homilies* 37, in *Ascetical Homilies,* p 177)

Chastity

393. The prudent, however, when passions begin to rise up, do not obey them, but turn in anger against the evil desires and become enemies to their own selves . . .

They are not few, who are controlled by divine power, who may entertain certain thoughts when they see a young man with a woman, yet defile not their minds nor commit an interior sin . . . But there are others, in whom concupiscence is completely extinguished, dried up. Truly these are the ranks of the very great. (St Macarius the Great, *Homilies* 15.51, in *Spiritual Homilies*)

Fervent Worship

394. *A discourse between St Seraphim of Sarov and his disciple on acquiring the Holy Spirit:*

"My friend, we are both at this moment in the Spirit of God . . . Why will you not look at me?"

"I cannot look at you, Father—I replied—your eyes shine like lightning; your face has become more dazzling than the sun, and it hurts my eyes to look at you."

"Do not be afraid," said he, "at this very moment not you have become as bright as I have. You are also at present in the fullness of the Spirit of God; otherwise, you would not be able to see me as you do see me" . . .

"What do you feel?" asked Father Seraphim.

"An immeasurable well-being," I replied.

"But what sort of well-being? What exactly?"

"I feel," I replied, "such calm, such peace in my soul, that I can find no words to express it."

"My friend, it is the peace our Lord spoke of when he said to his disciples: 'My peace I give unto you,' the peace which the world cannot give; 'the peace which passeth all understanding.' What else do you feel?"

"Infinite joy in my heart."

Father Seraphim continued: "When the Spirit of God descends on a man, and envelops him in the fullness of his presence, the soul overflows with unspeakable joy, for the Holy Spirit fills everything he touches with joy . . . If the first-fruits of future joy have already filled your soul with such sweetness, with such happiness, what shall we say of the joy in the kingdom of heaven, which awaits all those who weep here on earth. You also, my friend, have wept during your earthly life, but see the joy which our Lord sends to console you here below. (Lossky, *The Mystical Theology of the Eastern Church,* pp 227–29)

A Happy End

395. There is a difference between those who are immersed in the affairs of this world and those engaged in *theoria* (or mystical contemplation). The ways of the former begin in jollity, glee, and pleasure but end in bitterness, gloom and darkness. On the other hand, those of the latter begin in bitterness, sadness and darkness but end in joy and happiness. He who has trodden both ways can appreciate the value of these words. (St Isaac the Syrian, *Homily on the Discernment of Different Degrees,* "The Four Books," 2.9, Arabic version)

Prayer: Access into the Father's Presence[1]

HOWEVER MUCH WE SAY ON PRAYER, it still remains in ultimate need of experience. In its reality, prayer is the experience of being in God's presence. Outside God's presence there is no prayer. The right to enter into God's presence, we have learned, was gained when Christ opened the way. It was consecrated on the day he was crucified and inaugurated the day he rose and ascended. He introduced a new and living way through his body, the temple curtain separating from man what belongs to God. It was torn open by God's hand. The tear proceeded from the top, which is God's dwelling, to the bottom, where we reside. Having previously been hidden in the Father, eternal life rushed into our being and appeared within us.

Therefore, if through his body we have a mystical ladder rising up to him, then it is by his blood that we have access to the heavenly holies. The Holy Spirit presents us to the Father, testifying that we are his sons. The Holy Spirit speaks in us and through us. He speaks words known well to those who have experienced him, hot and flaming words that set the whole body on fire. They make man forget his disability and insignificance, nearly lifting him off the ground. For the burden that weighed him down with sins and bound him to this earth disappears.

For this reason, we hear from the saints who experienced its power that prayer gives man wings to lift him up so he can fly. These wings are the elation felt at the proximity of Christ and the relief from the burden of a sinful conscience, which pesters our prayer.

---

[1]With the passing of about forty years since *Orthodox Prayer Life* was first published, the author has written this epilogue on the occasion of the seventh Arabic edition, published by St Macarius Monastery, Wadi El-Natroun, Egypt, 1995.

Once fervent prayer gets in touch with the Spirit, it immediately causes the one who prays to experience death to sin, resurrection in the Spirit, mystical ascension (though bound and limited as it is by time). Christ then gives us bold access to the Father, anointed by his blood. Grace totally engulfs us, completely covering our nakedness.

God allowed St Paul to experience the grace of being near him and seeing the very essence of that which is invisible. But what St Paul tells us about this access to the Father is not simply the excitement of the chosen apostle's unique experience. Rather, it is the inheritance of the only Son, having been generously given the children in good measure, pressed down, shaken together, running over. What had become St Paul's has become ours as well. He has given us his stamp and seal, which testifies to this fact from a faithful conscience. We are here supported by the testimony of the disciple whom Jesus loved: "And our fellowship is with the Father and with his Son Jesus Christ" (1 Jn 1.3). It is a fellowship of life and love in the warmth of prayer in the Spirit. It is the Spirit who covers us and swallows up a little of our darkness so we may feel, touch, and see what is invisible. This is what filled the apostle's heart with joy. So thoroughly taken by it, he was compelled to share it with us so we may take part in such a joy and fill up the measure of our inheritance in the Beloved.

—Matta El-Meskeen
October 28, 1995

Bibliography

Books and Articles

Blaiklock, E.M., trans. *The Confessions of Saint Augustine*. London: Hodder and Stoughton, 1983. [Excerpts from this book reproduced and used by permission of Hodder and Stoughton, Limited and William Neill-Hall Ltd.]

Budge, E. A. Wallis. *The Paradise of the Holy Fathers*. Seattle: St Nectarios Press, 1984.

Budge, E. A. Wallis, ed. *The Wit and Wisdom of the Christian Fathers of Egypt*. Oxford University Press, 1934.

Butler, Dom Cuthbert. *Western Mysticism: The Teaching of SS Augustine, Gregory and Bernard on Contemplation and the Contemplative Life*. 2d edition. London: Constable & Company Ltd., 1926.

Callistus, Patriarch of Constantinople, 8. *Writings from the* Philokalia *on Prayer of the Heart*. E. Kadloubovsky and G.E.H. Palmer, trans. London: Faber and Faber, 1992.

Chadwick, Owen, ed. *Western Asceticism: Selected Translations of Christian Classics*. Ichthus edition. Philadelphia, PA: The Westminster Press, 1958. [Excerpts from this book reproduced and used by permission of Westminster John Knox Press and SCM Press.]

Chitty, Derwas J., ed. *The Letters of St Antony the Great*. Oxford: SLG Press, 1975. [Excerpts from this book reproduced and used by permission of SLG Press.]

Climacus, St John. *The Ladder of Divine Ascent*. Trans. Norman Russell. The Classics of Western Spirituality. London: SPCK, 1982. [Excerpts from this book reproduced and used by permission of SPCK Publishing.]

Isaac the Syrian, St. *The Ascetical Homilies of Saint Isaac the Syrian*. Trans. Holy Transfiguration Monastery. Boston: 1984. [Excerpts from this book reproduced and used by permission of Holy Transfiguration Monastery.]

Lossky, Vladimir. *The Mystical Theology of the Eastern Church*. Cambridge: James Clarke & Co. Ltd., 1991.

Maloney, George, trans. *Intoxicated with God: The Fifty Spiritual Homilies of Macarius*. Denville, NJ: Dimension Books, 1978.

Migne, J.P. *Patrologiae cursus completus. Series graeca*. Paris, 1857–1936.

Quasten, J., and Burghardt, W.J., eds. *Ancient Christian Writers*. New York: Newman Press, 1982.

Roberts, A., and Donaldson, J., eds. *The Ante-Nicene Fathers*. Grand Rapids, MI: Eerdmans, 1973.

Schaff, Philip, and Wace, Henry, eds. *A Select Library of Nicene and Post-Nicene Fathers of the Christian Church*. First and Second Series. Reprint edition. 22 vols. Grand Rapids, MI: William B. Eerdmans Publishing Company, 1956.

Seraphim of Sarov, St. "The Exhortation of Our God-Bearing Father St Seraphim of Sarov the Miracle Worker." *Journal of the Moscow Patriarchate* 8 (1991).

Ward, Benedicta, SLG, trans. *The Sayings of the Desert Fathers: The Alphabetical Collection*. London & Oxford: Mowbrays, 1975. [Excerpts from this book reproduced and used by permission of SLG Press.]

Manuscripts and Unpublished Works

"The Four Books of St Isaac the Syrian, Bishop of Nineveh," copied from a manuscript in the possession of Fr Mina El-Baramousi (Pope Kyrollos VI, 1959–1971).

"The Homilies of the Spiritual Elder (John of Dalyatha)." Manuscript #19 Theology, Library of the Monastery of the Syrians, Wadi El-Natroun, Egypt.

"The Letters of St Antony the Great." Arabic version. Manuscript #23 Homilies, Library of the Monastery of St Macarius, Wadi El-Natroun Egypt.

Moore, Lazarus. "Some Aspects of Orthodox Prayer." 1945. Unpublished.

Abbreviations

ANF   *The Ante-Nicene Fathers*. Reprint edition. 10 vols. Grand Rapids: William B. Eerdmans Publishing Company, 1973.

NPNF   *A Select Library of Nicene and Post-Nicene Fathers of the Christian Church*. First and Second Series. Reprint edition. 22 vols. Grand Rapids: William B. Eerdmans Publishing Company, 1956.

PG   *Patrologiae cursus completus. Series graeca*. Paris, 1857–1936.